L. C. Hobson
from Father
Christmas 1902

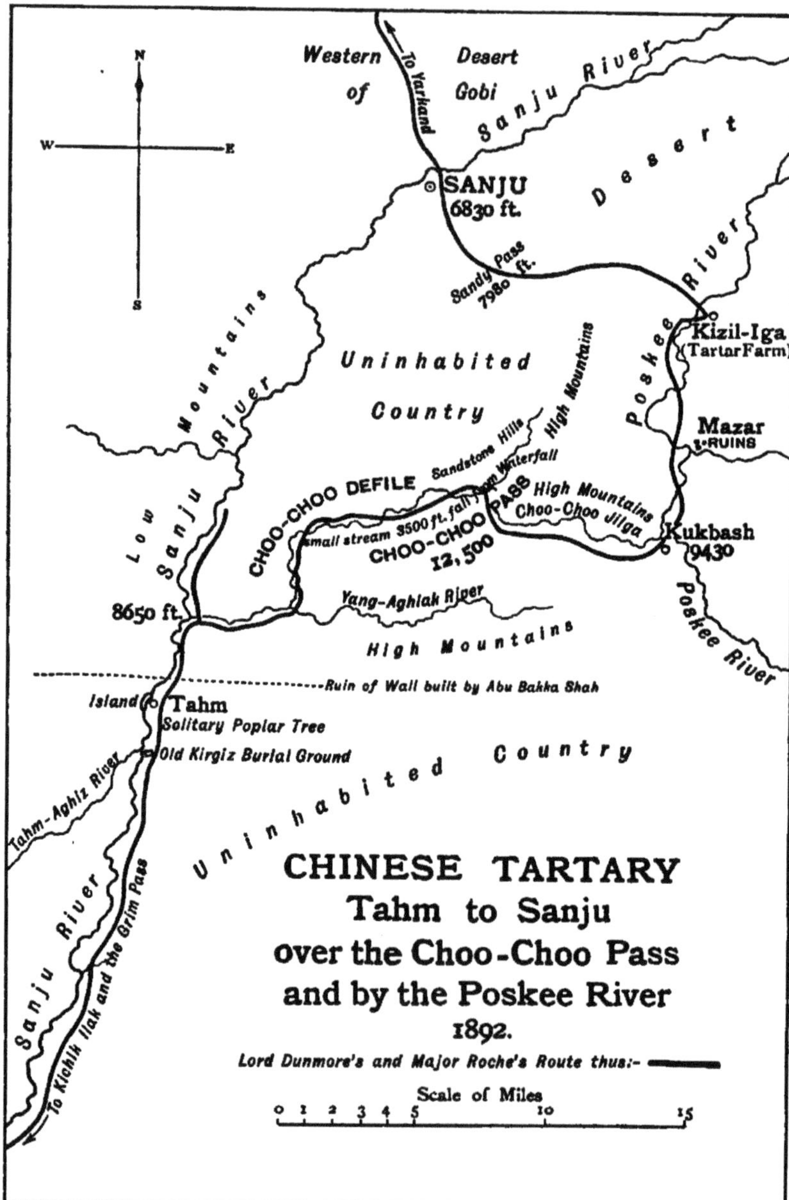

DRAWN BY LORD DUNMORE. [Frontispiece, Vol. II.

THE PAMPAS

[illegible]

[illegible]

[illegible]

[illegible]

LONDON:
JOHN MURRAY, ALBEMARLE STREET

THE PAMIRS;

BEING

A NARRATIVE OF A YEAR'S EXPEDITION ON HORSEBACK AND ON FOOT THROUGH KASHMIR, WESTERN TIBET, CHINESE TARTARY, AND RUSSIAN CENTRAL ASIA.

By THE EARL OF DUNMORE,
F.R.G.S.

SECOND EDITION.

WITH ILLUSTRATIONS CHIEFLY FROM THE AUTHOR'S SKETCHES AND MAPS.

IN TWO VOLS.—Vol. II.

LONDON:
JOHN MURRAY, ALBEMARLE STREET.
1894.

LONDON:
PRINTED BY WILLIAM CLOWES AND SONS, LIMITED,
STAMFORD STREET AND CHARING CROSS.

GLOSSARY.

AKOI	A Kirghiz felt tent	*Turki.*
ARGHOON	Half Ladaki, half Yarkandi.	
BABU	A clerk	*Urdu.*
BAGH	A garden	*Persian.*
BHEESTIE	A water-carrier	*Urdu.*
BOURAN	A blizzard	*Russian.*
BUNDERBUST	An arrangement	*Urdu.*
CARAVAN	Men and horses of an expedition.	
CHALMAH	White puggaree or turban	*Turki.*
CHAPAN	Quilted dressing-gown	*Turki.*
CHARPOY	Bedstead	*Urdu.*
CHERAI	A steep ascent	*Urdu.*
CHOKIDAR	Night watchman	*Urdu.*
CHOTA-HAZIRI	Little breakfast or early cup of tea	*Urdu*
CHUPPLIES	Kashmir sandals	*Kashmiri.*
COMPOUND	A garden or inclosure.	
DÂK	Post	*Urdu.*
DÂK BUNGALOW	Hotel or inn	*Urdu.*
DARIA	A river	*Persian.*
DEGCHI	A cooking-pot	*Urdu.*
DHOBEE	A washerman	*Urdu.*
DOSTER-KHAN	A present of fruit, &c.	*Turki.*
DURREE	A coarse rug for tent	*Urdu.*
DURZI	A tailor	*Urdu.*
EKKA	A country dog-cart	*Urdu.*
GHARRI	Four-wheeled trap, a cab	*Urdu.*
GHEE	Lard for cooking	*Urdu.*

GOMBAZ	A tomb	*Turki.*
GOOMPAH	A Buddhist monastery	*Tibetan.*
HALAT	A robe of honour	*Turki.*
JAMPAN	A palanquin carried by four men	*Urdu.*
JIGIT	A mounted messenger	*Turki.*
JILGA	A valley	*Turki.*
KHANSAMA	A cook	*Urdu.*
KHUD	A precipice	*Urdu.*
KIBITKA	A Kirghiz tent	*Russian.*
KILTA	Upright circular basket covered with leather	*Urdu.*
KITMURGAR	A waiter	*Urdu.*
KUL	A lake	*Turki.*
KURGAN	A fort	*Turki.*
LA	Pass	*Tibetan.*
LAMA	A Buddhist priest	*Tibetan.*
MAHDINE	The female of ibex, wild sheep, &c.	*Urdu.*
MAUND	80 lbs.	*Urdu.*
MEDRESSÉ	A college	*Sart.*
MULLAH	A priest	*Persian.*
MUNSHI	A secretary	*Persian.*
MUSSOCK	A water-skin	*Urdu.*
NULLAH	A valley	*Urdu.*
NUMDAH	A felt blanket	*Urdu*
PATHAN	An Afghan	*Pushtu.*
PERWANA	An Indian passport	*Urdu.*
PEYRAK	Ladaki women's head-dress	*Tibetan.*
POSHTIN	A fur-lined leather coat.	
PUGGARREE	A turban.	
PUSHTU	Pathan language.	
PUTTIES	Bandages wound round the leg	*Urdu.*
PUTTOO	Kashmir homespun	*Kashmiri.*
QOL	A valley	*Sarigoli.*
SEER	2 lbs.	*Urdu.*
SERAI	A public stable	*Turki.*
SHIKAR	Game	*Urdu.*
SOBRANIA	A club-house	*Russian.*
SYCE	A groom	*Arabic.*
TANGA	A coin worth 3½*d.*	*Turki.*

TARANTASS	Travelling carriage	*Russian.*
TCHAROOKS	Yarkandi boots	*Turki.*
TO LAY A DÂK OF PONIES	To arrange for ponies to be sent on to various stages	*Urdu.*
TONGA	A carriage on two wheels	*Urdu.*
TOPEE	A hat	*Urdu.*
TROIKA	Three horses abreast	*Russian.*
TURKI	Language spoken by the Kirghiz.	
URDU	Common language of Hindustan.	
VODKI	Russian brandy.	
YAK	Tibetan ox or cow, wild and tame	*Tibetan.*
YAK-DAN	A bullock trunk	*Urdu.*
YAMBU	A lump of silver worth 160 Rs.	*Chinese.*
ZEMINDAR	Farmer	*Urdu.*

CONTENTS OF VOLUME II.

CHAPTER XXV.

CHAPTER XXVI.

CHAPTER XXVII.

CHAPTER XXVIII.

CHAPTER XXIX.

CHAPTER XXX.

CHAPTER XXXI.

CHAPTER XXXII.

CHAPTER XXXIII.

CHAPTER XXXIV.

CHAPTER XXXV.

CHAPTER XXXVI.

LIST OF ILLUSTRATIONS TO VOL. II.

THE PAMIRS.

CHAPTER XXV.

Sariq-qoli Mode of Thrashing Corn—We meet an old Friend—Chahlung River—Old Fort at Cheile Gombaz—Tirak Pass—More news of the Russians—Our Caravan supposed to be an armed English Force—Difficulties in the Toilobolong Defile—A Severe Night—Yambulak Pass—A Kirghiz Host—Jan Mahammad—Arrival at Tashkurgan.

August 23rd.—The early morning was spent by Roche in pinning out his entomological specimens, as last night we had a great shikar, catching seventeen moths of different species, all of which were new additions to his collection. My time meanwhile was taken up in grooming my new horse Agha, giving him first a good washing in the river, which he stood like a lamb, being one of the nicest tempered horses I ever had anything to do with. When we did make a start we rode due south, following the course of the Kiaz river, picking our way as best we could through the rocky ground which borders it, down a very picturesque ravine walled in on each side by precipitous mountains, fully bearing out the sense of the name of Sariq-qol (yellow glen), as the colour of these hills is a creamy yellow; but the shadows are, notwithstanding, a delicate blue.

After riding for about an hour down the glen, we came upon a snug little farm of about eight acres, on which the people were thrashing their corn.

The *modus operandi* is as follows: The corn is laid down on the ground, and a large stick or pole is driven into the middle of it. To this pole are attached two cows and four donkeys harnessed abreast with ropes, a boy runs behind them urging them on to their best pace with voice and stick, and so they trot round and round, treading out the ears of corn as they go. Roche took an instantaneous photograph of this. A little further on we passed another small holding; there they were also thrashing, but the team this time consisted of four cows and six donkeys abreast.

All down the glen were small patches of cultivation, and very neat and tidy seemed the people—Sariqolis—(not Kirghiz) with their little mud houses. One farm at the junction of the Chahlung river with the Kiaz, called Kiaz Aghzay, especially struck me. It was larger than the average holding hereabouts, and the place was nicely timbered, and the fences were neatly kept; on one stubble field were a couple of mares and their foals, and there was a general air of comfort and a well-to-do look about the buildings, that one did not expect to see in such a wild ravine so many miles from any market, or village.

A man came out and offered us apricots, and, by the look of his cows, could have supplied us with plenty of milk as well, had we asked for it.

At this farm we altered our course from south to *west*, and, turning off at right angles, went *up* the Chahlung river, having just come *down* the Kiaz, a fall of 700 feet; these two, when joined, flowing due east as far as we could see. This was a geographical problem impossible for us to solve, for having come over the watershed of the Kizil Tagh range yesterday, at certainly not more than 10 miles from this point, this Chahlung river ought to have been running from east to west. This completely nonplussed us, and we cannot understand at all where we are. The maps we have are of no use, for all this part of the country is a blank. The range of mountains we crossed yesterday is not marked, nor are any of the rivers. I am endeavouring to make a rough map of the country, but without a sextant it is impossible to allocate the places correctly, or give more than a general idea of the watersheds, mountain ranges, and directions of the course of the rivers.

Near this farm I saw a very tidily built mosque, to which I suppose the neighbouring village people come to pray. I have noticed all through Eastern Turkestan that every village, however small, boasts its little mosque. They are certainly most unpretentious buildings, being simply a back and two side walls of mud, with a flat-topped roof; there is generally a wooden beam across the front which supports the roof, and a wooden upright in the middle of the open entrance which supports the beam, and makes the open front look much more like the entrance to a stable than to a house of prayer. Let us hope at any rate that it is used as the latter by the Faithful, because if they do not say their prayers inside these buildings they certainly never do outside. I have been accustomed, having lived many years amongst the Arabs, to see them worship regularly at the stated hours of prayer, no matter what they happened to be doing at the time; but these Central Asiatic Mahammadans never seem to say their prayers at all. Out of the thirty men we have with us twenty-one are Mussulmans, and nine are Buddhists, and I have never once since we started seen one of the former turn his face towards Mecca and prostrate himself according to the formula of his creed. Minimum Temperature, 60°. Altitude, 8520 feet.

August 24th.—We camped last night on the left bank of the Chahlung river. This west side of the watershed is as rich in springs of water as the east side is deficient; the consequence is that the latter is a howling wilderness of sand and rock, whereas the west side—although the physical configuration of the country is identical with the other—is well cultivated, by means of irrigation, with an unlimited supply of water. I left Roche busy pinning out more of his entomological specimens, and strolled up the valley of the Chahlung river with my gun, in search of game for the pot.

About a mile from the camp I came across a Kirghiz settlement, and discovered that here, right in the middle of the Sariq-qol district, which is under the jurisdiction of the Amban of Yarkand, a piece of country cuts in essentially Kirghiz, and as such is under the jurisdiction of the Amban of Yanghi Hissar, and it extends as far as Cheile Gombaz, two marches from here. It was very curious to see the Sariq-qolis on one side of the march in their peculiar dress, and less than 100 yards from their habitations the Kirghiz women, with their large white brimless linen hats, working amongst the cattle on their side of the march. I got a most excellent drink of milk from one of the latter, who, seeing me sitting on a stone by the river-side taking a rest, came out from one of the akois with a wooden bowl of that refreshing beverage. Close to where I was resting was a large bush of beautiful sweet-smelling lavender growing amongst the rocks.

About two miles further up the glen I came across a lot of horses, then I saw some Chinese soldiers walking about, and a little further on some mud houses, in front of which were two large blue and yellow silk flags, and some Lancers. The flags, which were the regimental colours, or rather the colours of the officer commanding, were stuck in the ground, furled, and in front of the largest of the huts. I had one Chinese interpreter with me as well as Ahmed Din, and we walked up to the colours and asked the sentry what officers were there, and he said it was the military Amban of Kargalik and his staff on their way to some fort.

So I walked in, and there was my old friend sitting on the mud floor with a cup of tea on one side of him and his everlasting pipe on the other. He jumped up, and seizing me by both hands pressed them to his breast and seemed genuinely glad to see me. We had a long talk, and on my asking him what was the latest news from the Pamirs, he declared that the Russians had retired from Aktash back to Murghabi. I felt so much inclined to ask whether this retrograde movement on the part of the Russians was owing to their having heard *he* was coming. It was just as well that I did not, because I had an opportunity of seeing afterwards that he was not blessed with the best of tempers. My horse, which my interpreter had been leading, was now brought by my orders up to the door, as I was for going on in case Roche passed me on the way (for this Chinese camp was a little off the track), and as I was about to mount, the Amban opened one of my holsters and pulled out my revolver, wishing to examine it. I took it, or rather snatched it, out of his hand, as it was loaded, and extracted the six cartridges, and then gave it him back to play with as much as he liked. But he was furious! It appears his feelings were deeply injured at my supposing that he, a great military commander, did not know how to handle a pistol. However, I explained, through the interpreter, that it was a very dangerous practice playing with loaded firearms, and that I never put a loaded weapon into anyone's hands for fear of an accident. But he would not be appeased, and when I met him again in the afternoon, with his colours flying and his escort and all his brave array riding up the valley to the permanent camp at Tashkerim, where he remains for the present, I reined in my horse to let him pass, and he looked straight to his front and never took the slightest notice of me at all.

After riding in a south-westerly direction up the same nullah all the afternoon, we suddenly turned off due west up a glen that widened out as we advanced. until it became quite a broad, cultivated valley, so rich in grain crop and so luxurious in grass that we could not find a place to pitch our camp for a long time. There was no track, and we rode through wheat, barley, oats, and grass nearly as high as our horses' heads, till at last we came to an early field that had been already harvested, and there we halted for the night.

The scenery is very beautiful and very wild, and these luxuriant fields of cereal crops and rich grasses seem quite out of keeping with their wild surroundings. In no country in the world, I should think, is the fertilising power of water so clearly brought home to one as it is here, for it literally turns a desolate wilderness into a happy valley of smiling corn-fields and rich grass meadows on which graze the sheep, goats, and cattle of a thrifty and contented people, primitive in their ways and habits, and too well-to-do to be vicious or dishonest. The one great safeguard against crime is that amongst the Sariq-qolis there is no coin current. All business—and it is very small—is done by barter; of grain they have enough for their own use and to spare. What is over is used to barter with their neighbours the Kirghiz, who grow little or no corn, but breed horses and cattle, and the Sariq-qoli farmer takes his corn to his Kirghiz neighbour on his back, and returns on a pony of his own. The same with his sheep. The Yarkandi trader arrives with hundreds of yards of town-made coarse cloth at about two or three annas the yard. He leaves his cloth in the glen for the housewife to put to purposes of her own, and for every thirty yards he gets a sheep. So, having started from Yarkand as a haberdasher, he returns under the guise of a sheep farmer. Minimum Temperature, 53°. Altitude, 8780 feet.

August 25th.—Rode up the Chahlung river all day through a broad and fertile valley until the afternoon, when it became much narrower and but sparsely cultivated. Towards evening we ascended to much higher ground, and got into a wilder country. The last we saw of cultivation was a large fertile basin surrounded by high yellow cliffs. Here was a Kirghiz encampment with camels, yaks, sheep, goats, donkeys, and horses scattered about feeding in picturesque groups; and the slanting rays of the setting sun gave a golden warmth to this pastoral scene. Several women came out of their Akois to take a look at the caravan as it passed, and many of our pony-men bartered the imitation mother-of-pearl buttons off their coats for tea, sugar, and drinks of curds and whey, these Kirghiz taking a great fancy to these said buttons. Galoum Rassoul came into camp buttonless, having cut all his off in exchange for tea and sugar.

Just about sunset we reached the foot of the mountain on which stands the Chinese fort of Cheile Gombaz. It is a ridiculous structure, built in an impossible situation, and as a place of defence is absolutely useless. No wonder the Chinese have abandoned it. I went up the hill opposite to make a sketch, for the scenery is magnificent. We are beginning to feel more at home now that we can see snow-clad mountains around us. We ascended 2250 feet in to-day's march, and are camped in the most lovely spot, at an altitude of 10,830 feet.

While we were searching for a camping-ground, we met an old Kirghiz just starting on a journey, and he insisted on returning to his little farm, two miles up the glen, to get us fresh milk from his cows, for he said, "You are my guests." The civility and hospitality of these good people is unbounded, and this old man, untutored and unlettered as he was, had an air of courtly grace about him, that would put many more civilised and better educated people to shame. Minimum Temperature, 42.°

August 26th.—Two men down with fever this morning, and several other minor complaints. We gave the fever patients a pony to ride between them, and the rest I said I would doctor when we arrived in camp this evening.

We crossed a very steep pass, called the Tirak Pass, 13,580 feet; ascending from our camp 2800 feet in three miles, which is a gradient of nearly one in five. It was a severe pull for the ponies, and as it was a hot day we all felt it. With the exception of the first two miles of the march I walked the whole way to-day, so as to get in good condition for the Pamirs. But if all accounts are true, we shall find more soldiers there than *Ovis Poli*.

As we were walking down the west side of the Tirak pass, we met a man from Tashkurgan on his way to Kizil Tagh to attend a marriage feast. He was full of news, saying that the greatest excitement prevailed amongst the Kirghiz on the Pamirs, in consequence of our advent on to the scene; our modest little caravan and equally modest and peaceable selves having been magnified into a large English force, commanded by a Lord Sahib, with other English officers, on the march to Tashkurgan and the Pamirs, to assist the Chinese and the Afghans in their endeavours to arrest the Russian advance. That was the first report.

The next rumour we heard was that a Kirghiz, named Kaurbom, had been sent from Surmatash on the Afghan-Pamir frontier by the Afghan military commander, to spy out what the Russians were about at Murghabi, and that on arriving there he turned traitor, and offered to lead the Russians up to the Afghan camp. This was done, the Russian party under the command of Colonel Grombchevsky marching up to Surmatash. A fight took place, and according to this man's report Colonel Grombchevsky and twelve of his men were killed, the Afghan loss being fifteen killed, and one officer and five men taken prisoners.* And last and not least among these "shaves," was one to the effect that 200 Kashmiri soldiers, under command of an English officer, had marched from Gilgit, and having crossed the Hindu Kush, were camped on the Taghdumbash Pamir. Mr. Macartney, moreover, was reported to have returned from Hunza, and was camped on the Taghdumbash Pamir, also awaiting our arrival.

Of course all these reports must be taken, as I said before, *cum grano*, and although some are more than absurdly extravagant, especially the rumour regarding ourselves, yet there may be some grain of truth in regard to the others. We are in utter ignorance of what has taken place anywhere, either in Asia or Europe, since

* This turned out to be absolutely incorrect

June 10th, which is the date of the last Indian newspaper we read in Leh, and for all we know to the contrary, Russia may be at war with Afghanistan. However, we may hear something at Tashkurgan if Jan Mahammad is there, and more still when we reach the Pamirs, if it is true that Mr. Macartney is in camp on the Tagh-dumbash Pamir.

After having been put in possession of all this valuable information by this Sariq-qoli, we sat down to digest his news and our midday meal at the same time. The very air is full of rumours of a more or less disquieting nature, and we have become so sceptical, that we shall believe only when we see. Every Kirghiz we meet has a tale to tell of the doings of the Russians on the Pamirs.

We travelled mostly south and west to-day, always following the course of some river or stream; thus we wound about a good deal. It was in a narrow defile at the foot of the Tirak pass, that we parted from our Sariq-qoli friend, and we followed for about two miles the course of the Tikka Sikrik river until we debouched into a broader valley, striking the Bramsal river at right angles, running south-east. We followed that for about four miles, until its junction with the Toilobolong, at a green spot called Pahst Robat, where we found more Kirghiz, who, needless to say, had more rumours to impart. We saw some youths galloping their horses about, and found they were practising for some horse-races and games, which are to take place in conjunction with a wedding feast next week. We turned sharp round to due west at the junction of the two rivers, and, going a short distance up the Toilobolong, halted for the night. It was with great difficulty we found a level spot on which to pitch the tents, and when all work was done, my patients came to be doctored. To one of the Panamik coolies, who had sprained his knee, I gave some Elliman's Embrocation, in one of our tin teacups, and thought I had made him understand he was to rub it on; but to my horror, and before I could stop him, he swallowed the lotion, and in a very short space of time was sprawling on his stomach, choking and spluttering; but, as soon as he recovered his breath, he got up and salaamed, saying it was very good. So, as he seemed quite pleased and none the worse, I did not enlighten him as to his mistake.

Roche has a touch of fever to-day, and Ahmed Din is also complaining. I was very much afraid at one time that we were going to have small-pox through the camp, but at present it has confined itself to the one coolie. I trust we shall not have it, as I have not the faintest notion how to treat it, beyond tying the patient's hands, so that he should not scratch his face. Minimum Temperature, 17°. Altitude, 14,580 feet.

August 27th.—This day's march was one of the most severe we have had since crossing the Himalayas.

We followed the river as usual, and, leaving all cultivation behind us, ascended a very steep and narrow gorge, crossing the Toilobolong seven times. The river being narrow and rapid, with here and there deep pools and very slippery stones, it made each crossing a work of some difficulty, especially as we had to find our own way, there being no track to show the fords, if indeed such things existed in this mountain torrent. In several places the rocks—which appeared as if they had been thrown about by some giant hand—presented such formidable barriers to our advance, that the ponies had to be unloaded and the baggage carried on the men's backs, and we had great difficulty in scrambling over these boulders, at the same time leading our horses, which tumbled and slithered about in the most alarming manner. This pass was, as Roche very aptly described it, a most bloodthirsty place, and after about three hours of this break-neck work we found ourselves on a sort of open table-land, at an altitude of 13,780 feet, or 4000 feet higher than at our camp this morning. In front of us rose great mountains covered with snow, and as we advanced the temperature fell fast, until at last the cold became severe. After about two hours' ride over this uninteresting table-land of coarse grass and granite boulders, we entered the hills again and into grand scenery, which reminded me very much of Scotland. It was a beautiful broad strath, through which the Toilobolong—now reduced to a mere mountain burn—ran brawling over its miniature falls, and between banks of grass of that peculiarly russet colour one sees so frequently in the deer forests of the west coast of Scotland. The hills that rose majestically on each side were covered with snow to about half-way down. They looked very grand, and their outline was wild and rugged to a degree. Just before sunset, which was a very angry one, the snow came on, and we had every indication that we were in for a rough night of it, as the wind blew strong from the north-east, driving the snow before it with pitiless force. So choosing the first convenient spot for a camp, we halted for the night, and then commenced that heartbreaking or rather finger-freezing work of pitching tents in a blinding snow-storm. Minimum Temperature, 15°. Altitude, 14,580 feet.

August 28th.—After a night of fearful cold, which told severely both on men and horses, especially on the former, I looked out of my tent at about 6.30 A.M., to find the whole country round deep in snow, and the thermometer standing at 17° of frost under the curtain of the tent. It had been blowing hard as well as snowing most of the night, and I had found it very difficult to keep at all warm. I tried every contrivance to keep the snow from drifting into my tent, and slept in my clothes, fur coat, fur boots, fur cap, and ended by wrapping my head in my Skye plaid. Roche was very bad with fever, and so was Ahmed Din, and all the men had got bad chills and more or less fever, owing to the sudden violent change of the temperature yesterday, from a broiling sun in the morning to being half frozen amongst perennial snows in the evening, especially as we were encamped under a glacier at an altitude of 14,500 feet, and many of them were sleeping out in the severe snow-storm all night, with no other covering but a blanket. Little wonder then that there were many cases of fever this morning.

At one moment I doubted the advisability of marching to-day; but, when I found we had actually burnt our last stick of firewood, and there was no fuel of any description to be found in the neighbourhood of the camp, I knew we had to proceed at all hazards. Roche was certainly most unfit to travel, especially in such extremely cold weather, and with the Yambulak pass to cross this morning; but to remain was to risk worse contingencies than to advance. About 8 A.M. the sun came out in all his glory, and the sky cleared, and by 10 A.M. the tents were dry enough to pack, and the men had a certain amount of caloric infused into their systems. So we made a start. We rode up the strath, passing hundreds of marmots sunning themselves at the mouth of their burrows; they were much larger than the ordinary marmot, and lighter in colour. We killed one to see what sort of skin it had, and found it a very beautiful soft fur, the animal itself being as large as an otter. About midday we came to the end of the strath and to the source of the Toilobolong river, which flows out of a lake surrounded on three sides by stupendous precipitous cliffs rising sheer up from the water, 2000 feet, with one huge glacier in the middle of them, which doubtless gives to the water the most beautiful emerald hue I ever saw. The altitude of this lake was 15,780 feet above the sea. Leaving the lake on our right, we found ourselves at the foot of the Yambulak pass (16,530 feet), which was not very formidable after what we had been accustomed to. It was barely 900 feet higher than the lake which bears the same name; but the *going* was very bad for the horses, being a mass of loose, slippery stones; the pass was very short and consequently very steep, and the stones kept rolling down, so that the horses could get no foothold. We all walked up, leading our steeds, except Roche, who was too ill to dismount. Curiously enough, he who had never felt any distress in breathing, when crossing much higher passes in the Himalayas, felt it to-day. The cold on the summit was intensified by a piercing wind blowing off the deep snow that lay on each hill-side bordering the pass, and I must confess I was more than thankful when I saw the whole caravan safe and sound on the Chichiklik plain, for not only was the pass a bad place for the baggage-ponies to cross, but we had so many men weak with fever that I was a little anxious in case of sick stragglers left on the pass by themselves, for every one has to look out for himself on these occasions. Again we had to undergo one of these violently rapid changes of temperature so trying to men even in the rudest of health. At 2 P.M. we were shivering amongst the snows of Yambulak, and at 3.30 P.M. we were sweltering under the burning sun of the Chichiklik plain, with the temperature at 96° in the sun's rays—a difference of 70° in that short space of time, and a difference of 81° between the heat of this plain and the cold of the camp in the early morning. It is that which causes so much fever amongst the men, who cannot regulate their clothing to suit the exigencies of these variable temperatures.

On emerging on to the plain we were met by half-a-dozen Kirghiz on horseback, who, seeing the caravan on the plain, had come to greet us from their encampment about five miles off. The chief man amongst them insisted on our coming to what he called his *place*—not his camp, which was too far out of our line of march, but a large sheep fank in the middle of the plain, in which he had spread some numdahs for us to sit upon, while he regaled us with milk and delicious thick cream. Built into the walls of this sheep fank were seven *Ovis Poli* heads, one with magnificent horns. He said they were the horns of old rams, which the wolves had killed last winter, and he used them as rings to tie the horses, camels, or cows to. During our midday meal, which we took to-day at 4 P.M., we saw about 500 yards from us a large, grey, hungry-looking wolf stealing across the plain; but he was too far out and the plain too level for us to attempt to stalk him. As it was now getting late, and we had still some way to go to get to our camping-ground, we parted from our Kirghiz host, who presented us on leaving with a very fine sheep, and crossed the south end of the plain, entering the hills again. We were forced to push on, as there was no good water nearer than the Kokmainuk pass, a very small affair (16,130 feet), which we crossed without any trouble whatsoever, barring the change of temperature again, for on the pass it was bitterly cold, and when the sun went down, which it did before we reached running water, we were riding at an elevation of over 16,000 feet, with a very cold wind blowing in our faces, and the thermometer considerably below freezing-point.

We had to ride some way down the pass before we found water, and then there was no wood for fuel. However, as there had been a Kirghiz camp in the neighbourhood some time ago, we collected the dried cakes of camel and cow's dung, with which we made some excellent fires, and after getting thoroughly warmed through, the whole camp turned in to seek that repose to which the men were fully entitled after the severe ordeal they had been through to-day. Minimum Temperature, 32°. Altitude, 14,630 feet.

August 29*th.*—The morning broke fine, clear and frosty, and, when I looked out from my tent, stillness reigned throughout the camp. The men were dead beat and all slumbering peacefully, and I was not sorry to have an excuse for turning in again and snatching another hour of rest and sleep. By 7 A.M. the camp was stirring, fires being lighted, kettles beginning to sing, and chupatties baked for the men's breakfasts. They all have their different messes; the Kashmir Shikaris by themselves, the Panamik coolies have their fire apart, the Ladaki pony-boys (so-called *boys* being mostly middle-aged men) in different groups by themselves, the two Chinese guides supplied by the courteous Amban of Yarkand, the Kirghiz, whom we have hired to show the Chinese guides the way, Ahmed Din's little establishment of his own, and our own mess. A heterogeneous mass of humanity, indeed, embracing eleven nationalities: Scotch, Irish, Punjabi, Sikh, Kashmiri, Balti, Ladaki, Tibetan, Turki, Chinese, and Kirghiz. And when they get round their fires of an evening, after the work of the day is done, and all begin chattering like a lot of monkeys, the Tower of Babel would not have been in it. We had serious thoughts of remaining where we were for the day, and thus giving the sick men a chance of recovery; but Roche and I at last determined it were better to push on to Tashkurgan, as our camp was in too cold and bleak a spot for the convalescence of fever patients. So orders were given accordingly. Our route was south-west down the south side of the Kokmainuk pass, which bore a striking resemblance to the Toilobolong defile, inasmuch as there was no sort of path, and we had to lead our horses down over impossible-looking places for nearly three hours, half the time actually in the stream, which was luckily very shallow. At length we debouched upon a large desert of sand and rock, without a vestige of verdure. This plain lay in the shape of a basin, with one small low range of sandy hills running through the centre, over the tops of which was to be seen more desert, up to the foot of a range of higher mountains running north and south. At the extreme northern end of this plain towered a huge snow-clad mountain standing out in solitary grandeur, and to the south we could see the hills above the valley of Tashkurgan. So turning our horses' heads due south we crossed the end of the desert, passing several heads of *Ovis Poli* lying on the ground, one large horn of which Roche picked up and measured, 69½ inches. Less savoury remains lay also in our path across this waste of sand, to wit, dead camels and an occasional carcase of a horse marking the track of the Chinese military transport; but of living animals we saw nothing, until after leaving the wilderness and entering a deep black gorge, when we came suddenly upon some confiding chikore, three of which I secured for the pot.

On emerging from this dark and forbidding-looking glen, which richly deserved its name of Karabulak (the black stream), a glorious bright and sunny picture burst upon our sight. In the foreground beneath us lay a large green plain, through which a broad river wound in sinuous coils like a silver serpent, and in the middle distance, the little village of Chusman, with its fields of golden corn, some already cut, all nearly ready for the sickle, flanked on each side by two old ruined forts. All round lay green meadows, on which the camels, horses, cows, sheep and donkeys, belonging to this picturesque little village, were grazing, and in the background the evening sun brought out in bold relief the white walls of the "stone fort" of Tashkurgan, behind which rose the dark purple hills of Sariq-qol, their snow-clad peaks tinged with a delicate pink, reflected from the dying rays of the setting sun. When we reached the plain we were met by Jan Mahammad, who, with several followers, had ridden out from Tashkurgan to meet us. He gave us a great deal of information regarding matters on the Pamirs, and as he is an agent of the British Government in India, stationed at Tashkurgan for the express purpose of keeping the said Government informed as to what goes on in the Pamirs, we had every reason to believe that what he told us is anyhow what he believes to be true himself.

The report about ourselves, he said, had been brought in by some Kirghiz, who had heard, etc., etc. It is true that an English officer is in command of 200

Indian and Kashmir troops, and is stationed at Lohb Jungal; but not on the Taghdumbash Pamir at all, which is Chinese Territory, but on the Hunza side of the Mintaka Pass, in the Hindu Kush. He also says, he has every reason to believe that the Afghan and Russian troops have come into collision, and that a Russian officer was killed, but he is not sure that it is Colonel Grombchevsky. The Celestials, with their proverbial phlegmatic nonchalance, are sitting still doing nothing, and more Chinese troops are expected to come and help them do the same. Mr. Macartney is at Hunza, or Gilgit, and not camped on the Taghdumbash Pamir. Also, it was not true that he, Jan Mahammad, had been the bearer of despatches between Gilgit and the Russian camp. All this information was given to us by him, as we rode over the plain that lay between us and Tashkurgan, where we arrived just after dark and took up our abode in two Kirghiz tents (Akois), which he had had prepared for us.

CHAPTER XXVI.

Sariq-qol—Description of and Geographical Features—People, Manners, Customs, Religion—March to the Pamirs—Snowed up—Chinese Fort at Ujad Bai—The Taghdumbash Pamir—Osman Beg—Arrival at Mintaka—Takta Mahammad and the Russians—First sight of *Ovis Poli*—Arrival at Kukturuk.

TASHKURGAN, means "stone fort," from the word تاش, Tash, "a stone," and قرغان, Kurgan, "a fort." Its ancient name is Varshidi. This is the metropolis of Sariq-qol, ساريق قول (Sirikol, as it is printed in the maps.)

The name is derived from Sariq, "yellow," and Qol, the Kirghiz name for a wide valley, as distinguished from Jilga, "a gorge." The name has been wrongly supposed to be that of a lake, after the manner of Issigh-Kúl, اسكده كول "Hot lake," which is formed with Kúl, lake, spelt with a different guttural, and pronounced with a different vowel. Sariq-qol is a mountainous district on the south-western frontier of the province of Kashgaria, and it certainly does not belie its appellation, as the hills in the northern and eastern part of the country, through which we have lately travelled, are of a creamy yellow. In the south, although retaining the same characteristic colouring, they are clothed with a certain amount of verdure, while the southern and western hills, which embrace the Taghdumbash Pamir, are famous for their excellent grazing, as well as for being the home of that rarest of wild animals, the *Ovis Poli*, the wild sheep first discovered by Marco Polo.

Sariq-qol is separated on the west from Wakhan and Badakshan by the Shindu, or Sariq-qol range of mountains, at the western base of which is the plain of Aktash (white stone). This is the boundary of the Sariq-qol country in that direction, and the commencement of the Wakhan district of the Pamirs, and is the original boundary between the possessions of the Amir of Afghanistan, and those now belonging to the Chinese Emperor.

Sariq-qol is composed principally of a mass of mountain ranges, wedged in between the Bolartagh range and the great Hindu Kush, at the junction of the latter with the Himalayas. It is separated from part of the great Pamirs on the north and west by the Tagharma range, and south and east from Kunjut (Hunza and Nagar), by the Mústagh, or Ice Mountains, a continuation of the Hindu Kush.

In the centre of this Sariq-qol country is a large valley, about forty to fifty miles long and five to six wide, running almost due north and south from Tashkurgan to Ujad Bai, through which flows from south to north a good-sized river, called by those Kirghiz who inhabit that district the Taghdumbash river; the Mintaka people call it after their district; and as it flows under the walls of the "Stone Fort," the people there call it the Tashkurgan river. There are also those that call it the Yarkand, simply because it joins that river near Armalik; and again there are others who call it the Sariq-qol river, because it is the largest of all the rivers in the district that bears that name.

Thus it goes by five different names, viz. the Taghdumbash, the Mintaka, the Tashkurgan, the Sariq-qol, and the Yarkand river.

The population of Sariq-qol numbers about 6000 souls, and is purely Aryan. They all belong to the Shia sect of Mahammadans, and there is a kind of religious freemasonry amongst them and the other tribes of Shia Mahammadans of Badakshan, Shighnan, Wakhan, Hunza, Chitral, and Gilgit, as an organised combination against the Sunni Mahammadans, which sect look down upon the Shias with profound contempt as heretics, and will not allow that they are true disciples of the Prophet.

The Sunni Mahammadans only recognise the three immediate successors of the Prophet, namely, Abubeker, Omar and Osman. The Shias, on the other hand, believe and declare that Ali was the direct and lawful heir, and consequently should have been the immediate successor of Mahammad.

In order to explain Ali's claims to the Khalifate, I must go back to the time of Abdul Mutallah, the son of Hashem, a wealthy merchant of Mecca, of the illustrious Arab tribe of Koreish.

Abdul Mutallah had six daughters and thirteen sons, of whom Abdullah was the favourite. Abdullah married Amina, and in the year A.D. 569 she gave birth to a son, whom Abdul Mutallah named Mahammad, meaning "praised," in consequence of a favourable omen attending his birth, his mother Amina having seen in a dream a ray of light proceeding from her body, which illuminated the Palaces of Bostra.

Mahammad, at the age of twenty-five, married the rich widow Khadija, in whose service he had been as a shepherd, and at the age of forty he assumed the title of Prophet, in consequence of a message he received from Jibrail (the angel Gabriel), who came down from heaven and assured him he was the chosen Prophet of God.

Mahammad and Khadija had four sons, who all died in their infancy, and he had no male offspring by any of his other fifteen wives, who were curiously enough all widows, with the exception of Ayesha, the youthful daughter of his friend (and afterwards successor) Abubeker; but by Khadija he had four daughters, the youngest of whom, and his favourite, Fatima, was married to her cousin Ali, son of Abu Taleb.

This is the Ali of the Shia sect of Mahammadans. In virtue of his being the son-in-law of the Prophet, besides being in his own right chief of the illustrious family of Hashem, and hereditary Prince of Mecca, he became the Prophet's confidential friend and adviser, and was held by him in the greatest respect and affection. The Shias assert that a short time before his death the Prophet expressed a wish to leave behind him some orders and instructions for the future guidance of the Faithful, but that Omar and his colleagues, divining his intention of appointing Ali as his successor in the Khalifate, removed all writing materials from within his reach.

After fourteen days' sickness of a fever, he died in A.D. 632, without having left any instructions to his followers, or appointing a successor in the Khalifate. The result was that his father-in-law, Abubeker, was elected to fill his place, and thus he became the head of the Muslim faith. But his election was not unanimous; there were many dissentients, notably the partizans of Ali, who declared that his rights had been most improperly overlooked.

Abubeker, notwithstanding, assumed the reins of government, but during his tenure of office the seeds of dissent were scattered broadcast, and soon party spirit ran high.

In the year A.D. 634 Abubeker died, and was succeeded by Omar, who was undoubtedly the ablest of the four successors of the Prophet. He was as much feared as he was respected. In private life he denied himself all luxuries. A stern judge, his love of justice was so great that he did not hesitate in awarding capital punishment to his own son, against whom a charge of adultery had been proved. It was during his reign that the Mahammadans carried their conquests from one end of the then known world to the other.

Omar was accused by the Shias of having treated the descendants of Mahammad very badly, and he especially angered the followers of Ali by depriving Fatima, Ali's wife, of a garden, on the grounds that it ought to be public property. On the death of Omar (who amongst other things compiled the Koran, which before was only in fragments), he was succeeded by Osman, who had been a sort of private secretary to Mahammad. Omar was assassinated in A.D. 644, and Osman only reigned for a short time, his career being also brought to an abrupt termination by the hand of an assassin.

The succession at last fell to the lot of Ali, who came to the Khalifate just when party spirit was running at its very highest, ample proof of which had been given by the deaths of the two former Khalifas, both of whom were murdered. This led to a civil war, in which Ali was for a long time engaged. It was all the more painful to him, inasmuch as the moving spirit of the opposite party was no less a person than Ayesha, the daughter of Abubeker, and widow of the Prophet. She was assisted by one Moavia, who claimed to be the successor of Osman.

At last, just when this civil war was brought to a peaceful termination, Ali himself was stabbed with a dagger while engaged in prayer.

His eldest son Hassan, who ought to have succeeded him, relinquished all claim to the Khalifate, not having any liking for the warfare and intrigue which appeared to him to be necessary concomitants of power and rule; so his brother Hussein was elected in his stead by the people of Kufa, to which place he, at their earnest solicitations, repaired, but he was attacked on the road by orders of Yezid, the son of Moavia, and he and all his followers were killed. Yezid had previously wanted Hussein to relinquish his claim to the Khalifate in favour of himself, which he refused to do. Hence his death.

The only survivors of this massacre were some female members of the family, and Hussein's one son.

From this period, the descendants of Ali never recovered from the blow they had received, and the Khalifate passed out of their hands; and although they were treated by successive rulers with the respect which was their due, yet they were always objects of suspicion, and looked upon in the light of possible agitators, ready at any moment to get up an insurrection against the ruling Power.

From the above it will be plainly seen that the course of succession to the Khalifate did not run smooth from the very outset, and the political rivalry, which made its appearance at the earlier stages, assumed later on the form of "envy, hatred, malice and all uncharitableness," which the two opposing factions, viz. Sunnis and the Shias, entertained towards each other.

In some places the Shias were in the ascendant, and in later years they set up kingdoms of their own, of which Persia notably presents an example. They hated, and still hate, their Sunni neighbours, the Turks, who in return, tried in every way to ruin them. The Sunnis spread their influence all over Turkestan India, and Africa, and although one occasionally comes across some Shias in these countries, they have practically no political importance. The present great stronghold of the Shias is Persia, where the people belong exclusively to that sect.

The Sariq-qolis say that they were originally Sunnis, but were converted to Shiaism about two hundred years ago, since which period they have steadfastly adhered to that faith. They differ in many respects from other Shias, being more liberal minded.

For instance, the great majority of this sect abuse Abubeker, Omar, and Osman, the first three successors of the Prophet, and will not hear their names mentioned in conjunction with the Khalifate, whereas, the Sariq-qoli Shias not only do not speak ill of these Khalifas, but, on the contrary, hold their memory in the greatest respect.

The Sariq-qolis say their prayers with the hands folded on the breast like the Sunnis, whereas all the other Shias pray with the arms hanging down at the side. There is another point of resemblance between the Sariq-qolis and the Sunnis, in their saying their prayers after any Mahammadan leader, and mixing with the Sunnis at prayer. The other Shias, on the contrary, never say their prayers after a leader unless he is a man of tried honesty and unimpeachable good moral character. The great and most striking difference between them is that the Sariq-qolis never practise the system of Motáa, or marriage for only a fixed period, such as a week, a month or a year. The Persians and other Shias look upon the system as perfectly lawful, and practise it extensively. The Sariq-qolis hold the marriage tie as very sacred, and believe that once married the couple are tied until death releases one or the other, then only are they free to enter into another marriage contract.

It has been said that Sariq-qolis take Ali for God, saying that he was the incarnation of God.

I tried very hard to find out whether or not they hold this creed, which borders on Buddhism; but these people are very sensitive about their religious tenets, very reticent on all subjects connected with their creed, and are generally the reverse of communicative on religious matters, especially to an Infidel. It may be true that some of the more ignorant entertain this belief, but the educated and enlightened Sariq-qoli laughs it to scorn. Their religion is based exactly on the same principles as that professed by the Wakhis, Shignanis, and Kunjutis. They all look upon His Highness Agha, Sahib of Bombay, as their spiritual leader, who in virtue of his being the offspring of the Prophet and himself a pious man, has alone the power of absolving his followers from their sins. Some of the Sariq-qolis who are his most ardent disciples go so far on the road towards Buddhism, as to believe that Ali takes birth in every successive Agha. The present Agha is a young man whose father, the late Agha, is said to have married the sister of Nasirud Din Shah Kajar. He seems to have got himself involved in some political intrigue in Persia, and had to fly for his life. When he left Persia, he went to Bombay, and settled down there. The Government of India treated him liberally and allowed him to be styled "Highness." All the Khojás of Bombay, and in other parts of India, are his zealous adherents, and he can count amongst other of his followers, the people of Gilgit, Hunza, Wakhan, Shignan and Sariq-qol. He also has a few in the Punjab in the persons of some low-class Hindus. The other Hindus will not mix with them, for it is said that a man of this class was once tested by the Agha as to his fidelity. He came to his house and sent for this man, who was one of his servants, and ordered him immediately to kill a cow (sacred animal) for a feast he was going to give. The man obeyed his orders, and of course became an outcast from that moment. The descendants of that man prepare bread for the Mahammadans, taking flour for their wages, which they make into bread and sell in the bazaar.

The influence of His Highness Agha Sahib over the above-mentioned tribes-men of Hunza and the Pamirs was such, that I have been credibly informed that the Gilgit authorities actually addressed the Government of India on the subject, proposing that the Bombay Government be moved to ask His Highness to use his influence with the Hunza people at the time of the troubles in that district.

To this Agha Sahib many votive offerings are made annually by the Sariq-qolis. If a man recovers from a bad illness, he immediately assigns a goat, a sheep, a yak or a camel to the Agha; on the occasion of a Sariq-qoli wedding, a similar offering of live stock is made. The Agha has agents in Sariq-qol for the purpose of collecting these said offerings, which are sold and the proceeds sent to His Highness in Bombay. These agents are generally "Sayads," the descendants of Ali, and I am told that a considerable sum of money is annually collected here in this way.

I heard an amusing story about the late Agha Sahib, needless to say not from a Shia, but from one of the Sunni Mahammadans, who ridicule the idea of Shias elevating the Agha to the level of a saint, or an Incarnation of Ali. The story ran as follows:—

His Khoja followers, who are mostly prosperous men

of business, used to pay fabulous sums to this Agha, in return for a chit addressed to the Angel Gabriel, asking him to pass the bearer into Paradise. These chits were of course only used when a death occurred in the families of these Khojas. The friends and relatives of the deceased used to place this chit in his coffin, and then bury him in the full belief that he would have a safe journey and certain entry into Paradise.

The passport bore the following address:—

اخویام جبریل (Akhwiam Jibrail.)

To my brother Gabriel.

Once however the tables were turned on the Agha. A very wealthy Khoja merchant died leaving a son who was an intelligent lad, and much wanting in faith in the Agha's supernatural powers. A request was made in the usual way by the relatives of the deceased merchant for one of these chits to place in the coffin, and the Agha consented to issue one on receipt of two lakhs of rupees (£20,000).

This ingenious youth, instead of placing the chit in the father's coffin, put it in his pocket, and about two months after the funeral went to the Agha with the chit in his hand, saying the Angel Gabriel had sent it him back, as he regretted very much he could not admit his father into Paradise. The lad in consequence demanded a restoration of the two lakhs, and the Agha, fearing an *exposé*, refunded the money without any remark. That is the Sunni story, which may be believed or discredited, according to the fancy of the reader.

* * * * * *

The Shias believe in twelve Imams or leaders, first, Hassan, son of Ali; second, Hussein, his brother; third, Zaimilabidin, son of Hussein; fourth, Jafar Sadik (the Trustful), son of Zaimilabidin; fifth, Mahammad Taki (the Pious), son of Jafar Sadik; sixth, Taki's son, Mahammad Naki; seventh, his son, Musa Kazim; eighth, his son, Musa Ali Raza; ninth, Mahammad Askri, son of the latter; the names of the tenth and eleventh I cannot remember; and twelfth, the Imam Mahdi, who is expected to arrive towards the end of the world, as the forerunner of the Christ. The impostor in the Soudan, who called himself "the Mahdi," who was originally a boat-builder at Dongola, had the effrontery to pose as this Imam Mahdi.

The Sariq-qolis believe that this chain of Imams, commencing from Hassan, son of Ali, has never been broken up to the present time; that the twelfth Imam, or Spiritual Leader, secreted himself from the persecution of the Sunnis, and eventually, when hard pressed by his enemies, fled to heaven, and will not return to earth until the end of the world, when he will appear as above stated. As for their Imam at the present date, a large section of the Sariq-qoli Shias are firmly convinced that he is the Agha in Bombay, although the majority of

Shias, other than the Sariq-qolis, totally ignore him in that capacity.

On contemplating the history of their Khalifas and Imams, the student of ancient history can only come to the conclusion that they were all singularly unfortunate in living in such troublous times, the Khalifa Abubeker and the Imam Zaimilabidin being the only two, out of fifteen, who were permitted to die in their beds. The other three Khalifas, Omar, Osman, and Ali, were all assassinated, and of the other ten Imams, Hassan was poisoned, Hussein murdered, Jafar Sadik, his son, his grandson, and great-grandson met with violent deaths by the dagger or the bowl, and the rest died from having molten lead poured into their ears.

* * * * *

The Sariq-qolis came originally from Shignan, which language they speak. They have no distinct tribal name, but call themselves Sariq-qolis, after the country in which they reside. The Kirghiz, who are not particularly partial to them in consequence of old tribal feuds, call them by the name of "Sart," and the Kashgaris have given them the appellation of "Tajik," which is the same as they apply to the nomads of Wakhan.

Their principal fixed abodes are Tashkurgan, Tisnaf, Chusman, Tagharma, Shindi, Bildir, Tughlanshar, Kozgun, Oochi, Maryang, Tong, Brangsal, Khusarab, Armalik, and Tar.

To the north of Tashkurgan stands out the great Tagharma Mountain, at the foot of which are the hot springs of "Sim Kung," in the healing properties of which the natives have most implicit faith, and make use of them accordingly. The climate of Sariq-qol is healthy and bracing, but very cold, and the winters are of long duration, and snow begins to fall on the low ground earlier than in other districts of the same elevation above the sea-level.*

There is plenty of good pasture in the district, but no hard-wood trees with the exception of willows, which grow on most of the river-banks. There is also plenty of cultivation, the people making the fullest use of the water for purposes of irrigation. They grow a great deal of wheat and barley, and occasionally I have come across fields of oats; and peas and beans are a favourite crop, as is also a species of pulse called *makh.* The only materials manufactured in the country are the felt numdahs, which are much thicker and stronger in texture and more durable than the ordinary Indian ones; and the "*galim,*" which answers to the homespun "*puttoo*" of Kashmir, is to be found in the course of being spun or woven in every homestead in Sariq-qol, it being used by the natives for clothing.

* This passage was written in my diary at a place in Sariq-qol, half-way between Tashkurgan and the Taghdumbash Pamir, on the 1st of September, 1892, on which day we were unable to proceed with our journey owing to the heavy snow-storm in the valley in which we were camped.

In former days the Sariq-qolis had rather a bad time of it, when they lived under a feudal system, as their chiefs ruled them with a rod of iron. One of their punishments was being sold to their neighbours, the Kirghiz, as slaves, from which bondage there was little hope of escape. In the tribal fights, which were constantly taking place between them and the Kirghiz, or the Kunjutis, many prisoners were sometimes taken on both sides, all of whom were made slaves of by their captors, whose property they became for life, unless exchanged for individuals, or bartered for stock, such as camels, horses, or sheep.

Twenty-five years ago slavery was a recognised institution in this country, and before the rule of the Amir Mahammad Yakub Khan lots of slaves, both boys and girls, as well as men, used to pass up to Badakshan for the Bokharan market; but that custom was put an end to by the Russians, when they became masters of the country. The said Amir of Kashgaria also greatly ameliorated the condition of the Sariq-qolis, when he practically abolished slavery in the country, and he instituted many innovations and improvements which tended to distract the thoughts of the people from tribal warfare and raiding their neighbours, and to turn them into the more wholesome channel of peaceable husbandry. His appointment of Toksabay Hussein Shah as Governor of Sariq-qol, in the place of Mahammad Arif, who cruelly oppressed the people, was a most politic act on his part, and gave the greatest satisfaction to the people. Under this new *régime* they were lightly ruled and fairly taxed through the Aksakals of the different villages, whose duties were to collect the "zakaht," or one in forty of the live-stock, together with the cereal tithes, and also to settle all disputes, and maintain law and order generally in their respective districts.

The morals of the villagers also came under the supervision of these Aksakals. Theft was punished by confiscation of cattle *pro rata*, according to the magnitude of the crime. Murder, though of very rare occurrence, was punished by the death of the culprit; and in cases of adultery, both parties were put to death.

But all this is changed under the present Chinese rule; the consequence being that the people, although not more addicted to vice than their neighbours, can give way to their amiable little weaknesses, undeterred by the fear of punishment; and their code of morality is certainly not at the present time of that high standard that obtained during the rule of the Amir, only a short twenty years ago.

Marriage amongst the Sariq-qolis is looked upon as a much more serious institution than by their neighbours of the Yarkand Province, for divorce is unknown, nor can a man marry a second wife during the lifetime of the first. A widow has to remain in mourning for one year, before she is allowed to console herself by taking another husband; but if, at the expiration of that period, she elects to remain in single blessedness, she leaves the house of her deceased husband's relatives and returns to her old home.

The Sariq-qoli women are not treated as mere machines, as they are in other Mahammadan countries, but are looked up to with respect by their husbands and children, and are entrusted with the entire household arrangements. Socially they are free to come and go as they please, without any restriction; and the use of the veil is practically unknown to them.

In the days of the Amir, for every wedding that took place the father of the bride had to pay a tax of two tillahs, and the bridegroom one, which went to augment the revenue; but the Chinese Government does not enforce that payment at the present day.

A young man who has pretentions to the hand of a young lady has to pay her father a certain sum in camels, cattle, and horses, according to his means, before he is allowed by the parents to be affianced. When these preliminaries have been adjusted to the satisfaction of both parties, the Mullah is called in, and in the presence of all the friends and relatives of both sides, the marriage ceremony takes place. A numdah, or carpet, is spread upon the ground, on which are seated the bride and bridegroom, side by side. In front of them stands the Mullah, and on one side is a large dish containing a roasted sheep, and on the other a plate of salt. After asking the question three times in Arabic, as to whether the bride will take the young man, and *vice versâ*, they each reply in Persian قبول کردم, Kubul Kardam, "I will," three times. The Mullah cuts up the sheep, and taking two slices of mutton says a prayer over each of them, and after dipping them in salt, puts one bit into the bride's mouth, and another into the bridegroom's. He then declares them to be man and wife, after which follow music, dancing and feastings, according to the social status or the means of the bride's father. If he is a well-to-do man, he entertains his guests for three whole days and nights, slaughtering sheep and oxen for the feast, while they pass the time in dancing, music, and revelry. At the end of the third day the wedding-guests disperse, and the bridegroom takes his wife to her new home.

September 1st.—We arrived here last night in the dark, and in pouring rain, having left Tashkurgan in the morning, and following up the course of the small river, our route lay over a stony plain, about five to six miles in breadth, on each side of which were high hills; those on the west side being singularly shaped, like sugar-loaves, very rocky and covered with snow from top to bottom; while on the eastern side they were devoid of any peculiar characteristic, sloping gradually down to the plain in grassy undulation, and free from snow, except on the high tops that had a fair sprinkling. We got far ahead of the caravan, as it was rather late in starting, and about 5 P.M. we began to look about us, in the hopes of finding grass for the ponies. About sunset a cold drizzle—half snow, half rain—came on, and yet there was no grass to be seen. At length, just as it was getting dark, we came upon some rough sort of pasture, and halted for the night. By this time it was sleeting hard and pitch dark, and we had no idea where the caravan was, and there was no wood with which to make a fire; so we sent our Kirghiz guide back to try and find Ramzan, and show him where we were.

In the meantime Roche and I sat huddled up together, trying to imagine we were getting shelter from a juniper bush three feet high. The ground was wet, and so were we, and bitterly cold into the bargain; our tobacco was also finished, and there we had to sit, wet through, and with a cold north-east wind blowing through us right into our bones. As we were ravenously hungry, we thought to pass the time by ordering imaginary dinners—Roche at the Naval and Military, I at the Guards' Club; so we shivered for two hours and then began to get drowsy. Suddenly we heard the shouts of the pony-boys, and soon the caravan appeared, to our great relief. After the tents were pitched on sopping wet ground, we got a fire to light with some difficulty, old Francatelli (as we call Rassoul) having luckily brought some wood with him, and by about 10.30 P.M. we got our dinner, viz. one tin of army rations and a cup of tea—rather different to the *recherché* dishes and '84 Pommery we had been ordering from behind the juniper bush. Of course this wetting brought on Roche's attack of fever again; and so I was not altogether sorry, on waking this morning, to find we were fairly snowed up, as it gave the men also a chance of recovering from their severe wetting. So the day was spent in taking quinine and drying clothes at a huge fire we were able to make in the afternoon, when the snowstorm ceased. Altitude, 11,380 feet. Minimum Temperature, 32°.

September 2nd.—Snowing again this morning; but, being determined to push on, we got off about 9 A.M., tents dripping wet. Route the same: up the valley—now less stony—by the side of the river, where I shot some ducks. Course still due south. Saw a magnificent eagle with white tail feathers. In the afternoon the weather cleared, and so as soon as the caravan came up to us we called a halt, as we had found a dry spot on which to camp; and there was just sun enough to dry our tents, and good grass for the ponies, and some rough brushwood for the camp fires. Altitude, 11,800 feet. Minimum Temperature, 32°.

September 3rd.—Being a nice sunny morning, we gave our tents the full benefit of it, and by 10 A.M. they were quite dry enough to be rolled up.

We rode for two miles in the same southerly

direction, following the river, as usual, until we came to the junction of the Kunjarab with what is now called the Taghdumbash river, as we have entered the Pamirs to-day. At the fork we altered our course to south-west, still following up the same river, only under a different name. The Kunjarab runs out of a huge nullah, called by the same name, and famous for *Ovis Poli*. Between the two rivers is a table-land or plateau, about 200 feet above them, over which we rode, so as to be able to see the lie of the country. This plateau, whose altitude we took, at 12,380 feet, extended to the south-east for some way over the Kunjarab river, making altogether a table-land of fully five miles in breadth, as far as we could judge. The country now began to get very wild and rugged, and everything was deep in snow in front of us. On descending from the table-land we came upon the Chinese Fort at Ujad Bai, where there were a few Akois, into one of which we were conducted by the Kirghiz head-man, and regaled with cream and the most excellent "slim cakes," hot off the gridiron. Here we met a Kirghiz from Mintaka, on his way to Tashkurgan, with a dâk for Jan Mahammad from Hunza, so thinking there might be something for us from Gilgit, we opened the parcel, but there was only the Mahammadan newspaper for Ahmed Din of the date of August 3rd. That we eagerly devoured, but found nothing in it at all, except some paragraphs about the Russian advance in the Pamirs, and what was going on in the Taghdumbash Pamir, every word of which, needless to say, was untrue, as we are on the very spot now, and can judge for ourselves. Everything else in the paper, being an Indian one, was simply local news of no possible interest to us.

We proceeded on our way, after thanking these good Kirghiz for their kind hospitality, for they presented us with five sheep, which, however, we insisted on paying for, and continued riding up the course of the river until we got into some very high and broken ground, full of large stones and bushes, which was simply full of hares. Visions of "jugged hare" not unnaturally floated through our greedy brains, and my gun was not long in coming out of its cover.

Roche had been most unlucky with his two hammerless guns; a pony stepped on one, carelessly left on the ground by one of the men, and smashed it to pieces, and the lock of the other having gone wrong, we found it absolutely impossible to mend it, although everything had been tried that our combined ingenuity could devise. Luckily his rifles are all right. We saw a large flock of wild geese flying westward, and one of our Kirghiz said he saw some ibex, but although we looked most intently through our telescopes, we failed to see anything of them.

We camped near a Kirghiz watch-tower, and while the tents were being pitched, I went for a stroll with my gun, and saw dozens of hares, but they were so wild I never fired a shot. Altitude, 12,600 feet. Minimum Temperature, 35°.

September 4th.—A most glorious morning, amidst glorious surroundings. The snow is decidedly melting, and although we are rising daily to a higher altitude. the cold is not increasing in proportion. As we are now nearing Mintaka, our river has changed its name again from the Taghdumbash to the Mintaka.

For the first few miles our course was south-west, and we had to ride over some very broken ground, extending on both sides of the stream to the foot of the hills, still covered with snow to their base. About midday we passed a nullah on our right leading to Aktash, about fifty miles distant. From here the stony nature of the ground changed to a beautiful broad grassy valley. We had to cross the river, which, owing to the melted snows, was very big, and as the water was well up to our saddles, we got very wet. We saw a Chinese patrol on the opposite side of the river, and seven horsemen ahead, coming towards us. When they got within 200 yards they all dismounted, and walked towards us, having previously tethered their horses. They turned out to be Osman Beg, chief of the Kirghiz of Mintaka, with a Tungani and three other followers, and Funtchuk and Sukkur Ali, the two men I had sent on in May, from Ladak. We had a long chat with Osman Beg, who spoke a little Persian and seemed a very superior man, with an intelligence much above the ordinary Kirghiz. On asking him for news from the Upper Pamirs, he corroborated the account we had heard about the fight which was reported to have taken place at Surmatash, between the Russians and Afghans, saying he had been told it officially by the Chinese Amban, adding that it was quite true Grombchevsky was killed in the fight, having met his death at the hand of the officer in command of the Afghan troops. If this is really so, there can be no shadow of doubt that war must have been declared between the two countries. It seems so curious to be on the spot, and yet to know nothing definite, people thousands of miles away knowing much more than we do, who have never seen a newspaper, except the one yesterday, for three months. He also told us that when the Russians came to Aktash, all the Kirghiz in Mintaka fled to the hills; but on hearing that an armed force under two English sahibs was marching on the Pamirs, from Yarkand, they came back again.

He also said that in consequence of my having sent the two men in advance with orders not to allow any sheep or cattle to be grazed in the Kukturuk nullahs, these simple-minded people had taken it into their heads that the Chinese Government had made over all that district of the Pamirs to the English, and that we were coming with an armed force to take possession.

Putting the extravagant absurdity of these rumours to one side altogether, the very fact of these Kirghiz returning to their homes only shows what extraordinary confidence they have in the English. Recent events which have taken place in the neighbouring districts of Hunza and Nagur have gone far to inspire this feeling of trust and safety. That Roche and myself were the accredited agents or envoys of the British Government, every one in Yarkand firmly believed, and when one of Roche's Kashmir servants received letters from home, Ahmed Din told me he saw that they were addressed to Nebra Sheik, shikari to Major Roche, English Ambassador to the King of Yarkand; and as rumours fly in this country like the wind, these reports gathered volume in their transit from Yarkand to Tashkurgan, until they reached the climax of our coming here with an armed force to take possession of this portion of the Pamirs in the name of the British Government. So when we marched into the Kirghiz encampment of Mintaka with only our caravan of sixty horses and thirty men, I am afraid these good people must have been slightly disappointed. They received us most hospitably and cordially notwithstanding.

One of the first things I did on arriving was to send for Takta Mahammad, the Kirghiz I had engaged on Mr. Lennard's recommendation, he having acted in the capacity of shikari to him and Mr. Beech when they were here last year, but he was not forthcoming; and at last Osman Beg said he had been obliged to arrest him, and he was now awaiting his trial before the Amban on his return from Hunza, for having gone to Aktash when the Russians made their demonstration there, and informed them that the sympathies of the Kirghiz were entirely with them, and that they were looking forward to the time when the Russians would turn the Chinese out and become masters of the country. We found two Akois ready for us, in which we took up our abode for the night, and we are to take them on with us to our permanent camp at Kukturuk, as well as a third which we shall use as a dining-room. What a luxury, after 129 days of living in a small tent, seven feet square, hardly high enough to stand upright in! When two of our coolies came into camp this evening carrying loads on their backs (they were Roche's photographic apparatus, too precious to trust to the tender mercies of a baggage pony), the Kirghiz were much concerned and asked whether it was for a punishment, and would not believe that our coolies had carried loads on their backs for upwards of 1000 miles. But to attempt to make a Kirghiz or a Sariq-qoli understand what 1000 miles mean is almost an impossibility, as they have absolutely no idea of distance or of time. As an instance of this, I asked Osman Beg on what day our dâk messenger from Yarkand had passed through Mintaka on his way to Gilgit. He proceeded to consult half-a-dozen of the men standing round him as to how many days ago it was, and after a conversation that lasted five minutes, he replied forty-six days ago!!

As a matter of fact, our messenger left Yarkand on August 8th, only twenty-seven days ago, and we are expecting him back every day from Gilgit with our dâk. Again, while at Tashkurgan, I asked Jan Mahammad if he knew this part of the Pamirs and he said he knew it well, so I inquired as to the length (in mileage) of the Kukturuk valley, and he replied two potais (five miles). Two days after I asked our Sariq-qoli on the march the same question, and he replied, "It is three times as long as from here to Tashkurgan." We were then twenty-two miles from Tashkurgan. So there were two men, who both knew the country well, and one said the valley was five miles long and the other sixty-six!!

They are perfectly hopeless, these people; the consequence is that in this unknown country we fail to know what to do or what to believe. Our plan hitherto has always been to have Ramzan in to speak to every night, on the subject of the morrow's march, and he tells us how many hours it is, roughly speaking, to the next water and grass, and we make our calculations accordingly, always allowing 2½ miles to every hour in a flattish country and 1½ miles in the hills, the hour of striking the tents the next morning being regulated by these calculations. But once off the regular caravan route, such as from Yarkand to Tashkurgan and on to the Pamirs, we are entirely at the mercy of a Kirghiz guide, the country being new to all of us; and he makes the most ridiculous mistakes, as for instance, August 21st, when, after riding two miles, we found ourselves at the end of a day's march and no other water for thirty miles. Another time we started at 4 A.M. prepared to march between thirty and forty miles and then not to get to water till dark, instead of which we arrived before noon and found the distance we had covered to be under twenty miles. We find all this is not improving to the temper, and if our different Chinese and Kirghiz guides could understand the Queen's English, they would hear many remarks distinctly unflattering to themselves. They also seem to have a passion for crossing rivers unnecessarily. Minimum Temperature, 25°. Altitude, 13,405 feet.

September 5th.—Left the cold snow-bound settlement of Mintaka for Kukturuk. Our last march I sincerely hope for many a day, as I am dead sick of having ridden and walked over 1000 miles at a foot's pace. Our route lay up a lovely strath, literally strewn with the skulls and horns of the *Ovis Poli*. We halted by the side of the Kukturuk stream, to take our midday meal, and saw some *Ovis Poli* feeding on the hill opposite, but on seeing our caravan they made off. About sunset we arrived at the place where Beech and Lennard had their camp for three weeks last year, but the locality did not suit us, for various reasons, so we just pitched our tents anywhere for the night, meaning to devote the morrow to selecting a convenient spot and laying out a permanent encampment. The scenery all round is lovely, and Scottish to a degree, exactly like that of a Highland deer forest. Minimum Temperature, 32°. Altitude, 15,050 feet.

CHAPTER XXVII.

We lay out our Permanent Camp—Extreme coldness of our New Home—First day after *Ovis Poli*—A Bear—Sleep out on the Hill—My first *Ovis Poli*—Roche's bad luck—Return to the Hill—Two more killed—A good Head—Lose a wounded one—Eagles hunting Hares—Wild Dogs—Mr. Macartney arrives from Hunza.

September 6th.—This day was spent by Roche and myself, first of all in choosing a site, and then in laying our camp. We found we could not improve upon the spot on which we had pitched our tents last night, as it was near water, dry, flat, and afforded good holding-ground for our tent-pegs. The permanent camp we laid out in a square of sixty yards each way. Our front faced due south and consisted of the dining Akoi in the centre, then our two Akois, one on each side, the three flanked by our two tents, Roche's on the left flank and mine on the right. Every measurement was most correctly taken, and a well-gravelled road was made running along the front of the camp, fifteen feet wide, and a ditch cut at each side. Round each tent and Akoi a trench was dug in case of wet weather, and every tent-peg was dressed in line on the front. In the centre of the square was the cooking tent and the kitchen fire-place, made of stones sunk into the ground. Behind this were the brushwood roots, neatly stacked for fuel, and two places for the men's fires, and out of sight was a large hole dug in the ground to contain kitchen refuse, to be cleaned out once a week. On the proper right of the cooking tent was Ahmed Din's tent, and in the rear, sixty yards from our tents and Akois, and exactly in a line with them, were the men's tents and the baggage tents (five of them), viz. two circular tents on the two flanks, and the other three between them. All sorts of rules were made and read out to the men, and by nightfall we were mostly unpacked and beginning to get settled in our new home.

On the sides of the camp were laid out the horse lines, thirty on each side, and a portion of grazing was given to our four yaks and our milk cows we brought from Mintaka, and to our flock of sheep; thus, after a hard day's work, we slept the first night in our permanent camp.

September 7th.—We begin to think our new home a very cold one, but I suppose we shall get accustomed to it and dress and live accordingly.

Understanding that there are two nullahs, one to the right of, and the other up the Kukturuk river, we tossed up last night, heads right nullah, tails left. Roche cried heads and the coin fell tails, so I take the left nullah for the first fortnight, and when we change Roche will take the right.

Therefore I started off this morning at daybreak to make a first acquaintance with my nullah, accompanied by a Kirghiz I took at Mintaka, who pretends he knows the country hereabouts.

I was not at all agreeably impressed with the look of the ground. A grassy valley for three miles, through which wound the Kukturuk river, high hills on each side, their tops covered with snow, and grass and stones from their base up to the snow-line, as open as the palm of one's hand—splendid ground indeed for the *Ovis Poli*, but impossible ground to stalk on. Further west up the glen the river dwindled to the size of a burn, rushing through a narrow ravine, the hills again of the same formation—grass and loose stones, steep bare open slopes, with hardly a rock to cover one. The whole ground was covered with skulls and horns, some of them very fine, but all in various stages of decay, a few of them ibex horns.

The thought that struck me after seeing this part of the ground was, that if it was all like this, it is very few *Ovis Poli* we shall get shots at. Why an animal considerably larger than a deer and utterly devoid of wool should be called a sheep, I do not understand. There is not one single point of resemblance between an *Ovis Poli* and a sheep, unless it is the horns, which are shaped like a black-faced ram's, but are from four to five feet long and enormously thick in proportion, and with two twists in them. The skin is like a deer's, not woolly

STALKING OVIS POLI.

like a sheep, and they stand as high as a twelve-hand pony. In fact, anything less like a sheep I never saw. After spying the ground carefully, I saw four rams on one of the hills on the south side, two of them with good heads. They were close up to the snow-line, and immediately they caught sight of us off they went up the snow, and over the top of the hill, out of sight. By this time I had reached a portion of the glen where a glacier had slipped down and blocked the way, deviating the course of the burn and making a big mess of things generally. On the side of the hill facing this glacier, but high up, I saw twelve more *Ovis Poli* feeding, and by the aid of my telescope I could see they were all males, although they were too far to be able to distinguish individual heads.

To approach this lot there was but one means, and that to make a big detour to get the wind, and then to come down upon them from above. This took two hours of hard climbing, which, at an altitude of 16,000 feet, I did not find conducive to free respiration. However, we arrived at the desired spot, only to find they had fed down on to more open ground, and were 500 yards from the nearest rock that could give me any cover, even supposing I could have reached that haven unobserved. So I left my Kashmir shikari, with orders not to take his eyes off them till my return, whilst I, accompanied by my Kirghiz, went a long way round to see if there was any friendly gully or even dip in the ground that would enable me to get near enough for a shot. As I lay gazing with hungry eyes at those beautiful heads I could not help saying to myself, "If

GROUP OF OVIS POLI.

[To face p. 59, Vol. II.

only I had Murdo* with me, I believe he would discover some way of stalking them." But, alas, there was no one but my Kashmir shikari, who was a fool, and my Kirghiz idiot! and so finding no possible means of approach, I made my way back to the place where I left the shikari, and by the time I arrived there not a beast was to be seen, a wild dog† having chased them all away. I then went about two miles further up the glen without seeing anything except a few mahdines.‡ I felt pretty sure when I started that I would not get a chance to-day, but I thought I might as well have a look at as much of the ground as I could spy before returning to camp, so as to have some sort of idea how to work it during the fortnight it was mine.

At last I found myself at the entrance of a large corrie, with fine feeding, the west side of it being abruptly cut off by a large glacier which stretched across from north to south. On the south side was another glacier, sloping right down to the bottom of this corrie, the ice actually reaching down to the grass, while facing it was a high rocky hill, forming the side of another small nullah, running into this sort of basin from the north.

* Murdo Macrae, Head Stalker to Mr. J. Platt in the Eishken Forest, and one of the best stalkers who ever went to the hill.

† There are several wild dogs as well as wolves that prey upon the *Ovis Poli* in the winter, when many a good ram gets caught in the deep snow by them.

‡ Mahdines, the Female of the Ibex; *Ovis Poli*; etc. (Hindustani).

It was now about 5 P.M., and suddenly, while watching the southern glacier, I observed first one speck come into view, moving over its glistening surface, then another, then three or four, and following these a string of about forty more grey specks, all moving in single file. I lay down with my glass fixed on this weird procession advancing slowly over the snow, until they came down to the grass, where they began to feed, for it was a herd of *Ovis Poli*, and I conjectured that they had come not only to feed but to sleep there. It was now high time to think of returning home, but I had already made up my mind of one thing, and that was that the only chance of getting one of these much-coveted animals was to catch them there at daylight, before they returned to their homes beyond that glacier; and the only way to do that was to sleep out on the hill, as the camp was miles too far away to shoot this part of the ground from, and this was evidently a favourite spot of theirs. So I left them and started to return home.

Just as I was passing the entrance to Roche's nullah I saw eight *Ovis Poli* feeding towards it, and suddenly as I was going over a small ridge, I found myself almost face to face with a large grey bear. Involuntarily I put my rifle up to fire, but remembering the eight *Ovis Poli*, I put the weapon down again and allowed Bruin to scuttle off, which he did in a most ungraceful manner. Had I fired, with the way the wind was blowing, not one of these *Ovis Poli* would have gone into Roche's nullah, but the shot would have put them away in the opposite direction, and I knew he was going out early next day. As it was I had the satisfaction of watching them feed well into his ground before I left, and was able to tell him when I got to camp that I knew of eight, anyhow, that he would find there in the morning, for these animals seldom move at night unless disturbed by a wild dog or wolf.

September 11*th.*—Returned last night, after three days and two nights spent on the hill, and although I have been rewarded by having killed my first *Ovis Poli*, still I was very glad to get back to my comparatively warm tent, as sleeping out in the snow, with the thermometer at only eight degrees above zero, at an altitude of 15,600 feet above the sea-level, was anything but warm. I started on the 8th and had a blank day, seeing very few *Ovis Poli*, and not even having a stalk; but just as night was falling I caught sight of two old rams, and marked them down into a gully, hoping they would sleep there, and determining to pay them an early visit before daybreak. So I stopped for the night, near a small burn under a rock, and made myself as comfortable as circumstances would permit.

I had brought with me two sticks and some rope and two waterproof sheets, with which I rigged up an impromptu tent. I placed the two sticks in the ground, seven feet apart, and stretched a rope across them, about four feet from the ground. I then guyed them with ropes attached to stones and threw one waterproof sheet over the rope and slept on the other one. For provisions I took two tins of army rations, two tins of hotch-potch, a packet of captain's biscuit and some cocoa. But, alas! I dared not light a fire in case the wind might change in the night, and these animals got my wind, or rather smoke; but I was determined to have a cup of hot cocoa before turning in, so, having a packet of candles with me, I cut one up into four small pieces, and making a little circular stove of stones, stuck my four candle-ends on a flat stone and placed my saucepan with the cocoa on the top and boiled it that way. The candles lasted just long enough to make my army rations *tepid* as well, and thus I dined, and after smoking a pipe, turned in all standing for the night, wrapping my head up in my Skye plaid. I woke at 4 A.M. with a beautiful moon shining, and rousing the Kirghiz, set off with him to see if we could find the two rams of the night before. We lay down within 200 yards of where we saw them last and waited for dawn. But, alas! when the sun rose their place was empty, so we went on until we were overtaken by a thick mist. The ground was white with snow, as there had been showers in the night. Once in the mist I saw three forms flit by me like ghosts, but they were out of sight before I could get my rifle up. We went up hill and down hill, trying to get out of this abominable fog, for three hours, by which time I had internal indications that I had had no breakfast, so I gave it up as a bad job and tried to find the way back to our bivouac, but that was not so easy, as the mist would not clear off. At last we made the river, and by that were guided to the spot, where we eventually arrived at 10 o'clock, having been five hours in the mist on empty stomachs. We soon made a fire and cooked some hotch-potch and some cocoa and had a good breakfast. At midday the mist cleared off and I sent the Kirghiz and the Kashmiri out to spy, while I lay down and had a sleep. At 2 P.M. they returned, having seen nothing. The *Ovis Poli*, like the Ibex and Markhor, are seldom to be seen in the middle of the day, as they go up among the rocks and hide themselves and sleep. So we moved up the valley to the two glaciers at the end of the nullah, and waited for evening. Again I saw the same procession winding down the glacier and at the same hour, when they scattered themselves about in the grassy basin, before described, and began feeding. I tried in vain to get near them, but the wind was wrong, and fearing to put them away, I left them alone and had to be content with a second blank day. However, I slept out again that night, right down below them in a ravine, but still dared not light a fire. After a cold frugal meal, I turned in about 8 o'clock P.M., and was woke at 2 A.M. by my impromptu roof coming down on the top of me.

The fact was it had been snowing all night and the weight of the snow had brought down my water-proof sheet, so there was no more sleep for me that night. It was bitterly cold, my beard and moustache being hard frozen, and my plaid and rezai were wet through with the snow. So I sat out in the snow and smoked and ruminated in the glorious moonlight, and my thoughts wandered homewards.

At 4 A.M. I woke my Kirghiz, and after scraping about in the snow to find my rifle case (I had not room to take it to bed with me, and so it was like every other thing, about three inches buried in snow), we sallied forth to try and circumvent these *Ovis Poli.* We arrived at the spot, where we hoped they had passed the night, just before daybreak, and in the clear moonlight, we could see their bodies against the snow. But as to getting near them, it was impossible; they were all lying about in the open and there was no place of concealment for me.

At last it struck me that if disturbed they would be sure to make for the glacier, as there was a regular beaten track over it that I had noticed the evening before through my stalking-glass. So I made my Kirghiz understand what my plan of action was going to be by signs and the few words of Turki I had picked up, and he fully understood, as the sequel will show.

I left him with orders to show himself after giving

me plenty of time to get near the glacier. There was not a breath of wind, all was as still as the grave and the moon was shining as bright as sunlight almost. I had to move as cautiously as possible, selecting every spot where to put my feet, as the rattle of a stone in that deathlike silence would have put the whole herd on the alert at once. Going a little way up the glacier, I posted myself behind a hummock of ice and waited to see how events would turn out. Presently I heard a rattle of stones, and shortly after four of the herd passed me. I only had my single-barrelled Henry 450 Express with me, as my 360 was of much too small a calibre for such big game, and my 577 was too unwieldy to carry. By this time the sun was struggling with the moon for the supremacy, and there was just light enough to see to shoot; so I let drive at the biggest of the four as they passed, about 120 yards off. But Shetland gloves are not conducive to accurate rifle shooting, especially when the hands inside them are half-frozen, and I saw with dismay that the shot had not told. So I loaded again, and before I had time to take off my gloves I saw that all four beasts were standing on the snow looking to see where the noise came from. I knew they would not remain there long, and as no others seemed to be following them, I thought I would risk a long shot, and putting up the 150-yards sight, I aimed at the biggest of the four, and to my delight saw him fall dead to the shot. I loaded again and waited for the rest of the herd, but my Kirghiz told me afterwards that at the first shot they all turned round and made off in the opposite direction. When we got up to the dead beast I was astonished at the size and weight of him. He weighed over twenty stone at least, as he lay, and was larger than a red-deer. His horns and head alone, I should say, were about fifty pounds, or even more. But as one cannot carry about weighing-machines in the Pamirs, it is purely guess work. We measured him afterwards to stand over twelve hands high.

After putting the carcase on a yak and sending it down to the permanent camp, I returned to my bivouac and had breakfast, after which I stalked my way home over the hills on the south side, where I saw five good rams. I followed them from 10 A.M. till 3 P.M., but never could get within shot of them; at last they disappeared over a glacier, where I declined to follow them, and so I returned to camp, where I was met by smiling faces, the caravan men having a good feast in view, as I had promised to give them every *Ovis Poli* I shot, not fancying the flesh of an old ram when I could get other mutton.

That evening, after dinner, Roche and I talked over the two days sport, when he had been most unlucky. To begin with, he was very much disappointed with his nullah, which he described as very small; secondly, with the exception of the eight *Ovis Poli* that I told him he would probably find on his ground, there was nothing else but mahdines. He had sent his Kashmiri shikari on ahead to spy the east side of the nullah, and consequently he (the shikari) had no idea of the presence of the eight animals shut out completely from his view, but as bad luck would have it, he crossed over to spy the other hills, and just as Roche was stalking the eight in a lovely easy piece of ground, and was feeling certain of a shot, down the hill came the ill-starred shikari in full view of the *Ovis Poli*, who made off just as Roche was getting within range of them, and that was the only chance he got in the two days. His description of his rage was most graphic; having nothing to lean against, he sat down on the ground to swear, and if all the hopes and wishes that he expressed for that shikari's future were to be fully realised, the man would do well to solicit instant cremation as the more pleasurable alternative.

Sunday, September 18th.—Permanent camp—Returned here yesterday afternoon, having been away all this last week, sleeping out on the hill again amongst the *Ovis Poli*.

The weather was very much against any chance of sport, as for three days out of the five it snowed heavily, and it was so thick and misty it was impossible to see further than a few yards in front of me. It was last Monday, I left the permanent camp to go up to my "forest," as I call it, Roche and I riding together part of the way on our yaks and separating at the entrance to his nullah. I did not reach my destination till 5 P.M., as this time I went as far as it was possible to go until stopped by the two glaciers. It was a coolish spot to choose to spend the inside of a week, as it snowed four nights out of five, and froze very hard into the bargain.

However, after hunting about for a quiet corner, where I could make a fire without fear of disturbing the "Guljias," as the Kirghiz call the *Ovis Poli*, I found a sheltered nook down in a ravine below one of the glaciers, and there I proceeded to make myself as snug as a man could at this time of year, amidst the perennial snows of the Pamirs, and with the thermometer only a few degrees above zero.

On Tuesday morning I was off before daylight, and as there was not a breath of wind and very little moon, I had to go to work very cautiously. So after proceeding a little way I lay down behind a rock, on the top of the low ridge overlooking the "green corrie," and waited for daylight. When the dawn broke, I observed two lots of *Ovis Poli*, one at the far end of the corrie and the other lot nearer, and as I thought in a fairly stalkable place. I proceeded to take stock of this nearest lot through my telescope, and found it consisted of nine rams, two of them old customers, one of which had a very fine pair of horns, so I turned my particular attention to this old gentleman, who went on feeding in the most unconcerned manner, little dreaming there lay within four hundred yards of him, a ruthless enemy thirsting for his blood. I began to look about me now for some way of approach, and turning to the right, crawled down the dry bed of a rivulet for about one hundred yards, when suddenly I heard the noise of stones being displaced to my right where there was a little bank. I peeped cautiously over the top, and there utterly unsuspicious of my presence, were two fine young rams with their backs turned to me, feeding within sixty yards of me. I hesitated whether to fire or not. This was as near a moral certainty as could be, but then it would be "good-bye" to the big head I was after; so I concluded to leave them in peace, and pursued my way after the lot which contained the old ram with the coveted pair of horns. After a long crawl I reached the spot which commanded the place where I judged they ought to have been, but to my consternation I found they had gone; in fact, I was just in time to see my old friend leading the rest at a trot about four hundred yards off, so with a muttered blessing (?) on the contrariness of things generally, and *Ovis Poli* in particular, I returned to wreak my vengeance upon the innocent heads of the two others, whose lives I had so recently spared. But they also had followed the example of the rest and were off. So I sat down and wished I had fired at them before, and repeated to myself the old proverb about the bird in the hand being worth two in the bush.

What had disturbed these animals I never could make out, but whatever it was it cleared the corrie of them in a very short time, and seeing there was nothing more to be done there that morning, I returned to my bivouac for the cup of cocoa and tinned meat which constituted my breakfast.

About midday I sent out the Kirghiz and the Kashmiri to spy, and at 3 P.M. they returned having seen the same lot back again in the "green corrie." So off I went in pursuit for the second time and soon came in sight of them, and getting my glass well on to them spent a most instructive quarter of an hour watching their every movement. Again I wondered to myself how on earth any rational being could ever have classified these animals amongst the sheep tribe, their habits, their looks, everything about them being totally unlike a sheep.

Fancy a sheep standing over twelve hands high and weighing from twenty to twenty-four stone *clean*, and with a skin like that of a deer. It is precious little woollen clothing we should wear if we had to depend upon this branch of the sheep tribe to furnish it off their backs.

Thus I lay and watched them with great interest, the more so as I knew that I was studying the habits of a tribe of wild animals least known to zoologists.

After having feasted my eyes on these curious animals, I set about to try and get within shot of them, but again the fates were against me, for just as I was approaching them, four other old rams came round the bend of the hill on my right, and walked slowly and majestically towards where I lay crouching flat behind a rock.

I was much in hopes these four would come down past my hiding-place within shot, as they seemed to be heading in my direction. But nothing of the sort. They lay down, they got up again as if suspecting the presence of an enemy, they stretched themselves, they fed a little, then they sniffed the air, in fact they were evidently uneasy; then one lay down again and another walked round, as if to make sure all was right, and finally they all laid down. This was too provoking, for I could not move to go after the others and these other beasts were much too far to risk a shot at.

Two long weary hours did they keep me there, lying in a most uncomfortably cramped position—for I dared not move for the life of me—till at last they all got up and walked slowly away, and eventually joining the others, marched off along with them to some more congenial spot to spend the night. Thus had I another blank day to add to my game book, but it only made me all the keener to get a shot at the possessor of that beautiful pair of horns which haunted me in my dreams that night.

After a night of perishing cold I awoke about 4 A.M., my beard and moustache all icicles, my fur cap frozen to my hair, and my hands and feet with no feeling in them. The only dressing I had to do was to pull off my fingerless fur gloves, and put on a pair of Shetland ones with fingers to them, and thus, with my faithful fool of a Kirghiz, made straight for the ridge overlooking that end of the green corrie, where we had last seen the herd the previous night. About an hour after daylight I perceived them up amongst the rocks above the corrie; they were very difficult to make out, as they were just the colour of the rocks, and they were in a place where it was utterly impossible to get near them. I managed by dint of crawling up a little dip in the ground, to get near enough to see with the glass that the big head was there safe enough, and there I left them, as I was resolved not to disturb them, but to leave them alone in the hopes they would shift their ground and feed down later in the day to better pasture. The one thing on which I was determined, was not to lose sight of them if possible, so with that view I left my Kirghiz with a telescope and made him understand he was to keep an eye on them until my return.

I went back to the bivouac place and got my Kashmir shikari, and after swallowing a hasty breakfast filled my pocket with biscuits, and started back with him to the place where I had left the Kirghiz.

We found all quiet just as I had left him, and we took it

in turns to watch the herd. When off duty I had a good sleep, and was awakened by the Kashmiri, who told me they had shifted their ground at last and had fed down into the hollow. I saw at once that if they would but remain there I would be able to stalk them easily.

By afternoon they seemed quite settled, many of them lying down, amongst others the ram with the good head. Evidently another small lot must have joined them, for I perceived a second very strong head which I had not noticed before, and in my greed I coveted both. I had only my single-barrelled Henry 450 Express with me, but it is such a beautifully accurate weapon, I always use it in preference to any other, and having shot with it constantly in various parts of the world for exactly twenty years (it was a present from the late Lord Lovat in 1872), I have more confidence in it than in either of the other double-barrelled Express rifles I have brought with me. So rifle in hand I made my stalk, which was a comparatively easy one, as the *Ovis Poli* were in the aforesaid hollow, some lying down and some standing amongst the rocks, and in a very short time I found myself within 100 yards of the nearest of them.

Curious and fantastic thoughts often come into one's head on the most solemn occasions, and on this one the thought that was uppermost in my mind was not, "which, if any, of this lot shall I kill, I wonder?" but, "what would so-and-so or so-and-so (thinking of one or two keen sportsmen) give now to be in my place?"

But business had to be attended to, and I turned my attention to it with a coolness that astonished myself when thinking it all over afterwards. Of course I need hardly say that the Big Head was one of the furthest off, and had three small beasts feeding in front of him, hiding his body completely from my view. I waited in vain to get him clear, those wretched small beasts seemed to be shielding him on purpose. While patiently waiting my chance, the second best ram came and stood most invitingly in front of me, giving me a broadside shot, that it was almost impossible to miss at about eighty-five to ninety yards. After my late experiences, this was not a chance to be lost; and the more I looked at his head, the more I liked it; so laying two spare cartridges down on the rock by my side, I fired and dropped him dead where he stood. I reloaded as quick as lightning, and was able to draw a bead on the big head before he got into his stride, for at the first shot the whole lot went off full gallop; and he was one of the last to get off. He was just breaking into a gallop when I fired at him, a broadside shot at about one hundred and fifty yards; and I nearly shouted with joy when I saw him roll right over like a rabbit. By this time my blood was up, and I never looked a second time to see whether he was all right, but ran like mad to cut off the rest. Reloading as I went,

I came up with them just as they were disappearing over the edge of the hollow. I had no time to pick and choose, but fired at the last ram, hitting him in the hind leg, breaking it at the stifle joint. He did not drop, but lagged behind the rest, stopping every now and again, and after following him for about twenty minutes, I gave him the *coup de grâce* through the heart, and finished him. So there I had three rams down, two of them extra good, which I thought a very creditable performance with a single-barrelled rifle. But, alas! pride is bound to have its fall, and after putting my knife into the throat of number three, I returned to gloat over my two beauties, when all I found of Big Head was a pool of blood—the animal had gone. I had made certain he was as dead as the first one, or I would not have run after the herd to try and get the third. But his off fore leg was hanging, as we saw him through the glass up the hill, and his shoulder was broken, and there was a hole in it you could put your fist in, and he was bleeding like a pig, so I gave my rifle to the Kashmiri, and told him to go up the hill and finish him, or if possible to turn him, and make him come down to better ground, as it would have been very difficult to get even a yak up where he was standing, with his tongue hanging out, poor beast. bleeding drop by drop to death. So while the shikari was carrying out these orders, I turned my attention to number one. He was indeed a beauty, with a magnificent pair of horns, enormously thick in span, being 18 inches, their length being 4 feet 10 inches. I took his dimensions with my tape, and being determined to find out the actual weight of one of these animals, I had brought up with me from the permanent camp the cook's weighing-machine, which goes up to 200 lbs. I could not weigh him where he lay, for two reasons, one was the weighing-machine was at the bivouac place, and the other was that the animal would have to be cut up and weighed in pieces. So the consequence was he did not get weighed until the next day, he thereby losing a great deal of weight; first, by being cut into three parts, and a lot of blood weight was lost; and secondly, his carcase was much shrivelled with being out on the hill all night, hard frozen. However, his bare carcase scaled as follows: Hind quarters, 113 lbs.; fore quarters and middle piece, 128½ lbs.; head and horns, 55½ lbs. Total, 297 lbs., or 21 stone 3 lbs. Making allowance for loss of blood from cutting up into three parts, and being out on the hill all night, we may fairly compute his weight clean at about 22 stone 3 lbs. His measurements were as follows: Height (measured as one would measure a pony), 12 hands 1½ inch; length from root of horns to root of tail, 65 inches; girth round the heart, 58½ inches.*

While I was taking these measurements, my shikari

* This Head is now hanging up on the staircase of the Marlborough Club, London.

was playing the fool up the hill with the wounded beast, and instead of turning it down to me, he was trying to finish it, for I heard the shot. It just struck me that he could not shoot with my rifle, being crooked stocked, and the result was that he missed it; and frightened by the noise, the poor animal made a supreme effort, probably his last, and went off higher up into the mist, where the shikari lost him. However, I made certain I would get his body the next day, and so we all returned to the bivouac. That night it snowed heavily, also all Thursday and Friday, so we could do nothing with regard to the wounded beast, who by this time was probably not only dead, but buried in 12 inches of snow.*

On Saturday it continued snowing and was most bitterly cold, so having been snowed up for three days, and not able to go out on the hill at all, and as we were all suffering more or less from the effects of the extreme cold, I made up my mind to return to the permanent camp, which I did.

September 19*th*.—The cold is becoming intense, the thermometer standing at 10° when I got up this morning, and having been down to 8° in the night. What it will be up in the "forest" near those glaciers tomorrow night, I tremble to think, but I must go up

* This *Ovis Poli* was found later on, and the skin of the head very little damaged, owing to the cold weather.

again and try and get another *Ovis Poli*, and also see if we can find the dead one. To-day I spent making myself a pair of gloves out of some Kashmir home-spun (*puttoo*), for my Shetland gloves are done for; having darned them so often, they are now nothing but a lot of holes sewn together, and my hands have suffered in consequence, being full of large cracks, especially on the tops of the fingers, which is most painful, and certainly not conducive to accurate rifle shooting. I have never suffered from cold so much as I have in these Pamirs, even in the Arctic regions, or during many Canadian winters, although the cold in those latter places is much more severe.

To-day all the coolies and pony-boys are employed in building a cooking kitchen and wash-house,* they carry stones up from the river, and while some are laying them, others are making a sort of mortar from the mud, mixed with water, and in the absence of lime it makes a most excellent substitute. Minimum Temperature, 8°.

September 24th.—Having left on the 20th for "the forest," I returned last night empty handed, having seen absolutely nothing. The weather was bitterly cold and the nights out were very trying, I spied the whole ground and never saw a beast. On the 22nd I

* It was owing to this that the report got about on the Pamirs that the English were building a *fort* on the Taghdumbash Pamir.

determined to cross the glacier at the end of the green corrie, over which I had twice seen the *Ovis Poli* come, imagining there must be some good ground on the other side of it. So I started before daybreak, and got on to the glacier about sunrise, and feeling my way each step with an alpenstock, arrived at the far side of it, after floundering about for three hours in the snow; and was bitterly disappointed to find nothing there but more glaciers, and a chaos of rocks and stony hills, with not a vestige of grass anywhere. So I returned to my bivouac, and the next day explored the hills on the north side, with the same result; so there was nothing for it but to return to the permanent camp, with the certain knowledge that every *Ovis Poli* had left my ground.

On returning I found Roche had been equally unsuccessful in his nullah, he also not having seen a beast.

There is no doubt we have come here at the wrong season of the year, the few other sportsmen who have ever shot here having come in the early spring, when the *Ovis Poli* are low down, being driven there by hunger, and the deep snow up in the mountains. On talking over our respective experiences on the hill during the last few days, Roche gave me an account of a very curious sight he had witnessed, which I very much regret not to have seen myself. It was no less than a hare hunt, by a couple of very large eagles.

There are a great number of mountain hares on these hills, and the ground where these eagles were hunting them was very open. It appears that when they made their swoop, the hare, which was running as hard as he could to get under some friendly stone, would stop dead short for a second, and then run backwards, when the eagle overshot his mark, and had to start all over again. Roche watched this for some time, and told me the hares always got the best of the eagles, who caught none of them.

September 30th.—We have had the thermometer as low as four degrees, and the cold is very severe. The only excitement we have had during the last few days has been the sight of a pack of Pamir wild dogs, who passed the other side of the river in full cry after some animal, which we could not see. I was writing in my akoi, when suddenly I heard the music of a pack of hounds in full cry. I rushed out to see what on earth it could be, and there sure enough, on the opposite side of the river, were eight of these wild dogs chasing something. We got our telescopes on to them and could see that they were dark coloured on the back, light in the belly, and had long bushy tails that curled over their backs. No wonder there are no *Ovis Poli* about if they have been hunting our nullahs!

* * * * * *

Mr. Macartney arrived here at the beginning of the

week from Hunza, where he had been to assist at the Installation of Mahammad Azim Khan, the new "Mir of Hunza." Two Chinese mandarins had also been sent from Kashgar, and they thought they were going to help at the ceremony conjointly with the British officers, in order to show that they had a say in the matter, as the Chinese consider they have a claim upon the Kunjuti country, but in this they were doomed to be disappointed, as Dr. Robertson, the political officer in charge at Gilgit, would not allow them to have any voice in the matter, but politely informed them that if they chose to be present at the installation as *guests* they would be welcome. With this they were fain to be content, but left Hunza and returned to their own country in high dudgeon. When Hunza and Nagar were independent states under the late Amir Suftur Ali Khan, they were then tributary to China.* Him we conquered in December 1891, in consequence of his turbulence and perpetual raiding of his neighbours, and also in consequence of the general unsatisfactory state of his country, which being on the borders of Kashmir, was a constant cause of worry and bloodshed; and the country is now under the same rule as Kashmir, to which it has been annexed.

Mr. Macartney was very anxious to explore the Kilik Pass in the Hindu Kush and take some observa-

* Suftur Ali Khan paid to the Chinese Government a small annual tribute of gold dust.

tions there, as it is one of the passes that might be utilised for getting into the Hunza country, thus avoiding the Mintaka, which is higher and more liable to be blocked with snow; so I accompanied him, and although there was plenty of snow on the summit of the pass, we crossed it and walked a little way down it, thereby crossing the Chinese frontier, and finding ourselves in British territory again. The view from this part of the Hindu Kush was very curious, very much shut in, as one sees nothing but countless snow peaks as far as the eye can reach. We came across a large herd of *Ovis Poli* on the move, but they were mostly mahdines, very few rams being amongst them, and those that were with them were young ones. In this part of the Pamirs the Chinese frontier runs along the top of the Hindu Kush, east and west, the water running south flowing into the Indus basin, and that running north into the great Tarim basin, in the plains of Turkestan. Thus the watershed makes the most natural boundary.

Amongst the many stories one hears in this country, pregnant with anecdotes more or less of an inaccurate character, is one concerning the Chinese and their frontier in this neighbourhood. When our little war was being waged against the Kunjutis at Gilgit and Nilt, last year, the Chinese, not knowing what the outcome might be in the matter of boundaries, sent secretly and at night, a newly-prepared boundary stone, on which was carved some Chinese characters, setting forth that this was the ancient Chinese frontier, etc., and dated it back several hundred years ago. This stone, together with an image of Buddha (to give an air of respectability, I suppose, as well as antiquity to the fraud), was buried at the top of the Mintaka Pass leading into the Hunza country, so that had there been any discussion between the British and Chinese about the Kunjuti boundary, the latter would have found this stone by accident, which proved conclusively, etc.

Last night some Kirghiz arrived in our camp and reported that 130 families had fled from Aktash and the neighbourhood, and were going to take up their abode with their flocks and herds in the valley between here and Mintaka. The reason for this very sudden immigration is that they declare that the Russians, who were left at Aktash to complete the demolition of the Chinese fort, had warned them that as they were living now in Russian territory, they would not only be liable to taxation, but also to conscription, a certain number of the men being liable to be enrolled for military service on the Pamirs.* The Russians having finished their work, retired upon their head-quarters at Murghabi. As soon as their backs were turned the Kirghiz struck their Akois, and driving all their stock with them, left

* This statement of the Kirghiz was denied by the Russian officer who demolished the Fort of Aktash.

Aktash, and, being joined by neighbouring encampments of these nomads, the whole 130 families arrived here and in the neighbourhood yesterday.

The Chinese declare that unless the Russians restore the fort they demolished they will make it a *casus belli.**

Two, therefore, of the reports we heard between Yarkand and Tashkurgan have proved to be true. 1. The Russians did march on Aktash, did demolish the fort, did turn the Chinese soldiers out of it. 2. The Afghans and Russians did have a fight at Surmatash, when several men were killed on each side, but Colonel Grombchevsky, although he was there, was not killed; on the contrary, he has been appointed Governor of Osh.

* * * * * *

I have had another hard day after *Ovis Poli.* I went and explored another nullah, where at the extreme end, just under a large glacier, were thirteen of them lying down. I got within about 600 yards of them, as the wind, for a wonder, was blowing *down* the nullah, instead of up; and as they were in an inaccessible place, I lay down behind a big stone and watched them through my telescope. They were all rams, nine big ones and four smaller ones. I thought they would come down in the evening to feed, and at about 5.30 they slowly rose to their feet and walked leisurely down to the grass. I

* Subsequent events have proved how much that declaration was worth.

had been waiting four hours for this and began to smell blood, especially as they fed up towards where I was lying. I remained motionless, feeling sure it was wiser to allow them to feed towards me, late as it was getting, and risk a shot in the dusk, than attempt to change my position with a view of getting nearer to them.

All of a sudden the wind dropped, and it became dead calm, and I trembled for what I feared might follow, viz. a change of wind.

After about ten minutes suspense I felt a cold air on the back of my neck and I knew it was all up.

The wind had changed and was blowing softly up the nullah, and the *Ovis Poli* stopped feeding, put their heads up and got my wind, and turning round made off at a trot and disappeared.

I had nothing left but to make the best of my way home in the dark, for there was no moon, and after about an hour's walking a thick snow-storm came on. It was very difficult work finding our way back to camp, as it was the first time we had ever been in that direction. Luckily Roche was in camp, and seeing what an awful night it was, he sent out men and our one lantern to look for us. They found us all right, and very glad I was to see the camp-fires below me, for it was a rough night to be out. The snow stopped about 11 P.M., and when I went to look at the thermometer it was at 2°.

CHAPTER XXVIII.

Roche's Sun-dial—After *Ovis Poli* again—A good Chance lost—Extreme Cold—More Wild Dogs—Bear and Ibex—Am checkmated by the Bear—Unpleasant Predicament on a Glacier.

October 1*st.*—Mr. Macartney left this morning for Tashkurgan and Kashgar, taking Ahmed Din and twenty of our ponies with him, as we are getting short of provisions for the men, and we shall require a month's extra provisions for men and horses when we start on our projected exploration of the middle and upper Pamirs. So Ahmed Din and the twenty ponies are to return in about three weeks with food. The cold is getting more severe every night, the thermometer having been as low as 2°. I expect it will soon be down below zero. Everything is hard frozen in our tents, on waking every morning, including ourselves. It seems impossible to keep warm, and we cannot make a fire inside our akois. Even our ink-bottles have to be put into boiling water every day to thaw them, as the ink freezes. But the greatest catastrophe that has overtaken us since we started, is the breaking of our much-cherished brown pottery teapot. Some tea leaves and a little water were left in it last night, and the leaves swelled and froze and burst the teapot.

Time is very difficult to calculate here. When Mr. Macartney came we found we were a day out. I came back from the forest, as I thought, for my Saturday till Monday, and found I came back for

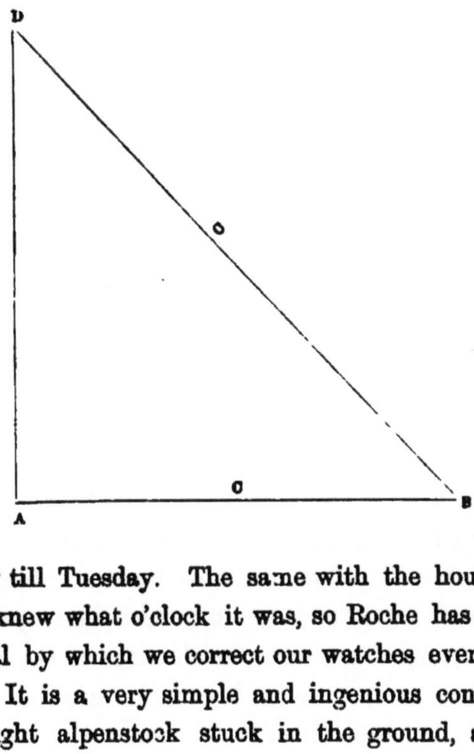

Sunday till Tuesday. The same with the hours. We never knew what o'clock it was, so Roche has made a sun-dial by which we correct our watches every day at noon. It is a very simple and ingenious contrivance. A straight alpenstock stuck in the ground, a weight attached to a string from the top to get it plumb. When the alpenstock is in a perfectly vertical position, place a compass on the ground, which has been previously levelled for the purpose, and get the exact due north. Draw a line from the foot of the alpenstock, A, due south to B; put in a small iron tent-peg at B, about six feet from the stick. Tie a string, C, round the foot of the stick and attach it taut to the tent-peg; lay the compass along it to see it is exactly stretched north and south, take a turn round the tent-peg and bring the string up to the top of the alpenstock, D, and attach it.

When the shadow of the upper string, C, falls upon the lower string, C, and exactly covers it, then it is as near twelve o'clock noon as it is possible to make it without a sextant.

So now we have got the day of the week right, and the day of the month, and the proper time also, which is an advantage.

October 2nd.—This morning I started early for the hill, as there had been a good deal of snow during the night, and I thought it might have brought some of the *Ovis Poli* down. After about two hours climbing I saw eight small rams, and leaving them alone proceeded further up, till I got over the shoulder of the big hill behind the camp. Here I saw six good rams and proceeded to stalk them. As usual they were in a very open place, and I could not get within a quarter of a mile of them. I waited for them to move, which they did after about half an hour, going over a high ridge. I followed them, and, reaching the top of the ridge, peered very cautiously over, expecting to find them below me, but they were nowhere to be seen.

And now occurred one of those terrible incidents which a man regrets all his life.

Most of the ground below me was visible from where I lay up on the ridge, with the exception of a small piece which was hidden by a projecting rock on my right. As it was snowing hard and nothing in sight, I gave up my rifle—which up to this time I had been carrying myself—to the shikari to put in the cover to keep dry, and was just about to go on, when it struck me it would be more business-like to "make all the ground good" before me, and with that object I told my man to go and peep cautiously over that projecting rock on the right, which he proceeded to do, *taking my rifle with him*, which fact I did not notice at the moment. The six good rams *were* there after all, and the idiot must have shown his head, for he put them off and they came clattering up towards me whom they did not see, and passed just underneath me, about seventy yards off, and there was I without a rifle! Of course the shikari ran up to me as hard as he could, but by the time he had put the rifle into my hands the rams were 150 yards off, and going straight away from me; but, meaning to try a shot, I put my fingers in my mouth and gave a shrill Highland shepherd's whistle, which made them stop for a minute and turn round to see from whence proceeded the noise. I took a steady aim with the 200-yards sight up, at the only one that offered a broadside shot, and holding just on the top of his back, fired. I heard the dull thud of the bullet as it struck him, and my shikari, who had his glass on him when I fired, saw the shot strike him right through the belly, but it was not in a vital spot and off he went with the rest. We followed him for four hours, tracking him in the snow by his blood, and we saw him five different times, but never could get on terms with him. At last, after tracking him over two glaciers, he took us up over the top of one of the highest mountains in the range, when it came on a heavy snow-storm. That effectually put an end to the proceedings, for in half an hour's time every mark of blood and his own hoof tracks were obliterated by the fresh snow, and so I had to leave him.* It was most unfortunate, but it is a lesson I shall not easily forget, never to be parted from my rifle. Had the man been properly cautious, I might have got a standing shot at them at seventy yards from the rock. So I returned home very cold and very cross, and found the camp deep in snow. Roche's man had been up his nullah to spy and saw nothing, except two wild dogs, so they are still hunting that ground.

* A Kirghiz found him afterwards in the snow and brought him in to camp, the skin of his face uninjured owing to the cold.

October 3rd.—Last night the thermometer went down to zero, but as there was no wind in the night, we did not feel it so very cold in our akois. We have both given up sleeping in our tents on account of the cold, and have moved our beds into the akois. I don't know which is coldest.

To-day I went out to the nullah nearest Mintaka, and found twelve *Ovis Poli*, as usual in a perfectly inaccessible place, and after careful investigation came to the conclusion there were none of them worth shooting, being all small heads but one, and he was barely good enough. However as there was nothing else in the nullah, I thought I would try and get above them, and so get a shot. So after a long climb I got on to a rock above them and fired at the biggest, thinking he was about 200 yards off. I missed him and off they went. I went down to look at the place where he had been lying in the snow and I saw the mark of my bullet more than a foot short. When I looked up at the place from which I fired I saw that I had miscalculated the distance when I reckoned it 200 yards, which is easy enough to do anywhere, when shooting immediately down beneath one, but here in this rarefied air it is very difficult to judge distance, everything looks so close, and in this case I was the best part of sixty yards out in my calculation.

October 4th.—Three degrees below zero was the reading of the thermometer this morning. As I wanted to find out how cold it really was in my akoi, I took a cup of water and covered it up and wrapped a puggaree round it, and placing it on a box near my bed, put a stalking cap over the whole thing. This morning the water was frozen right down to the bottom of the cup.

I left camp early for Roche's nullah, as he is now working Kukturuk and the green corrie beat, my fortnight having been up on the 23rd ultimo, and I am on his old ground. On arriving at the mouth of the nullah, which runs north and south, I found a strong south wind blowing right up it, so of course I dared not enter, as every animal in it (if there were any) would have got my wind in no time.

So I determined to see if it was not possible to get round the back of the hills that formed its eastern side, and so arrive at the head of the nullah, and work south against the wind.

With that object in view, I made my way up a broad glen with an easy gradient, until after two hours' hard walking through deep snow, I came to a palpable horizon, over which I thought we should have a nice gradual descent, and find ourselves at the head of the nullah. Instead of this, we came to a dead-lock. It appeared we had been walking over a large glacier all the time, and the snow horizon was the top of it. It reached right across from one hill to the other, and what I had fondly hoped would be a nice easy descent, turned out to be a sheer precipice of ice and snow about 700 feet down. From an artistic point of view, it was certainly very fine and grand, but from a sporting point of view it was a decided nuisance, as it meant turning back and retracing our steps and having to give up the whole thing as a bad job.

On reaching the south end of the nullah again, there came on a very heavy snow-storm, which lasted about an hour, after which it cleared up, and the wind veered round to the north, which enabled us to enter and spy the glen. The first animal which came within the field of my telescope was a large grey bear, walking about by the side of the burn, and a little further up to his left was a herd of ibex, two of which had very good heads. Their coats were very much darker in colour than the Kashmir ibex. By this time it was beginning to get late, and I saw that I had not much time to spare, if I was to get a shot before sunset; but this was rather an *embarras de richesse*, and I had to make up my mind which of the two to stalk. I settled to go for the ibex and leave the bear to his own devices.

No sooner had I started than down came another heavy thick snow-storm, of which I took advantage to improve my position in regard to the ibex. When the shower cleared off I found I had rather overshot the mark, and was in full view of these animals, but the bear was nowhere to be seen. I therefore lay down behind a rock waiting in the hopes they would move down towards me as they were feeding. The place in which I lay hidden was on the slope of the hill, a perfect chaos of huge boulders which had evidently been hurled about by some convulsion of Nature. It was a frightfully rough place to move over and the snow made it worse. While patiently lying there and watching the ibex below, I suddenly felt a tug at my foot, the shikari pointing to something straight in front of us. There on the skyline of the slope, which was not more than eighty yards off, was a large grey shaggy mass swaying from side to side and coming straight towards my place of concealment. This was the old bear who had left the burn and was coming slowly along the hill-side, threading his way through the rocks until he was quite close to me. When he was about twenty yards from me I began to think it was time to stop his nearer approach, but I had to be very careful how I fired, as a single-barrelled small bore rifle is not exactly the weapon to select to meet a big bear of that sort with, especially at such close quarters. Had he given me a broadside chance I would have fired long before, but he was so hidden by the rocks I never saw more than his head and upper part of his chest, for he was coming dead straight on to me. To have hit him in the head would most probably have killed him, but then it would have shattered his skull, which was the only part of him I wanted to keep.

To fire at what I could see of his chest would have been useless, as it is not a vital part, and I might have had a wounded bear on the top of me almost before I had time to reload.

So I waited for him, knowing that if he came on any further he must pass to the right or left of me, and thus give me a chance of putting a bullet into his heart, I also knew that even if he got our wind and made off, I would get a chance of seeing more than his head and neck as he turned. He remained motionless facing me for about a minute, then he waddled forward again and was hid from my sight. Thinking he was behind one of the rocks and still coming towards me, I remained with rifle at full cock, ready for any emergency; but after two minutes had elapsed and he never re-appeared, I thought as he would not come to me I would go to him, and I crept up to where I had seen him last; but imagine my dismay, when I found that just halfway between us there was a little sort of dry water-course, about four feet deep, into which he had stepped, and he was trotting up the hill 300 yards off, in this sort of ditch, and was out of my sight before I could get my rifle up. Whether he had got my wind, or whether it was his usual way home, I know not, but anyhow he completely checkmated me. Had I gone ten yards further in the snow-storm I should have been just on the edge of this miserable ditch, and I think the bear's skull would probably have been amongst my other "Trophies of the chase." As it was, I could only regret I did not put a bullet through his head when he stood so immediately in front of me, only twenty yards off.

By the time this little episode was over, it was too dark to think of the ibex, so I went home not in the best of tempers, where I found Röche just returned, and suffering from the same complaint. We have been here a month to-day, during which time he has had two shots, and I have killed three, wounded two* and missed one *Ovis Poli*.

October 6*th*.—Yesterday I was out in the north-east nullah and only saw two *Ovis Poli*. One had a very fair head and the other a moderate one. The wind as usual was blowing up the nullah and so I dared not venture far in. It is too vexatious the way this wind continues blowing from the south. It appears to me that it never blows from any other quarter; anyhow, we have had thirty-one consecutive days of south wind, the result being that as the only two nullahs worth anything here for game run due north and south and open south, we can never go into them without putting every animal out of them, as they get our wind at once. To go round and get to the head of these nullahs is also impossible, as there are nothing but impassable glaciers all round them. I nearly came to serious grief on one of them to-day trying to get to the head of the north-east nullah.

* These two were got afterwards.

HOME OF THE OVIS POLI. [To face p. 97, Vol. II.

Yesterday I lay and watched the two rams till evening, but they never shifted their position at all, so I was determined to try and get to the north side of them to-day. The wind was as usual blowing from the south, when I started from the camp early this morning to explore the back of the hills on the west side of the nullah, with a view of getting round to the head of it. For the first two hours all went well until we (my shikari and I) got up above the perennial snow-line and then our hard work began. We plodded on for some time up to our knees in snow, until at last we saw on our right the hills we recognised as overshadowing the north end of the nullah. In front of us and below us was a large smooth-looking glacier, which sloped down to the right at a not very steep incline. Over this glacier was the only way into the nullah, and after examining it through our telescopes we resolved to make the attempt.

We had some little difficulty in getting down on to it, but, when fairly on the top of it, which was nearly flat, we found the snow was considerably above our knees. We laboured on feeling every step in front of us with our alpenstocks until we gained the edge of the slope. Here unfortunately the snow was only about six inches deep and very soft, and underneath was glare ice. If we had had axes we could have cut little footholds, but having none we were obliged to try and make the descent as best we could without. We strapped ourselves together and jamming the sharp iron ends of our alpenstocks into the ice, began our rather perilous journey. We had not gone many yards before both my feet slipped from under me and I fell sideways, my weight dragging the shikari down with me.

I have done a good deal of tobogganing in Canada, but I don't think I was ever shot down an incline at the rate I was to-day, down the face of that glacier. I had no time to think about what there was at the bottom. I only remember the feeling of flying through a blinding white mass, and then one of suffocation. Our headlong career was mercifully checked by our falling into a small crevasse, luckily only about five feet deep, and full of fresh soft snow, and as we had brought down a lot of snow with us and that and the shikari were lying on the top of me, I was fairly buried and half suffocated. The shikari soon pulled me out and then I was able to breathe again, after which we surveyed our position, which was not a particularly pleasant one. To begin with, both our alpenstocks were gone, so we had nothing left but our hands and feet to depend upon. We easily got out of the hole, as the left side of it was, as it were, open to the slope of the glacier, which down here was much narrower and we could see rocks and stones peeping out of the snow on the left, and if we could but gain them we should be all right. So off we started again, this time independently, and by dint of picking out frozen patches of snow we managed to crawl on our hands and knees to the side, and never was I so glad as when I grasped hold of the first rock and, scratching away the snow, found we were on earth again and not on ice.

When we eventually got to the bottom of the hill and looked up at the glacier, we saw what might have been our fate had we not been providentially caught in that friendly crevasse.

I did not care to look up at it twice.

The head of the nullah being now reached, we thought we should have a chance of approaching the two rams of last night, as we could go up wind to them. But, alas! after carefully spying the whole ground we found the nullah was empty, and we had risked our necks for nothing! It was the old story—those wild dogs again—we could see their tracks all over the place, and when eventually I got back to camp, I found Roche had had a good stalk interrupted by these brutes, and one of his shikaris saw forty-four *Ovis Poli* flying for dear life, with a pack of these wild dogs after them in full cry. They have completely spoilt our sport here; ever since we came have these dogs been hunting all the nullahs in the neighbourhood. The whole place is full of them and consequently there is not a head of game to be seen.

October 7th.—Went out to see if I could come upon the bear again, or fall in with the ibex. After a long walk I suddenly saw fourteen ibex high up, galloping as hard as they could. They were being hunted by these detestable dogs. Nebra, Roche's shikari, came in to camp this evening having seen three of the wild dogs within twenty yards of him, he says they snarled at him and then made off. It was a great pity he had not had a gun or rifle with him.

It is no earthly use remaining on here, for every animal has been scared away. Roche is going to put part of a dead sheep down in his nullah and lie in wait for the dogs, and I have made up my mind to go to Aktash and see what the Russians have been doing to the Chinese fort there, as it is impossible to believe all these Kirghiz tell one.

CHAPTER XXIX.

Leave for Atkash—Hare-hunting on Horseback with a Pistol—A surprise—Kirghiz Feats of Horsemanship—Refugees from Aktash—The Pa-ik Pass—The Plain of Aktash—A Scene of Desolation—Burial-ground—Aktash Fort demolished by the Russians—Chinese Demands—Return to Permanent Camp—Bad News from India.

October 9th.—Yesterday was spent in making preparations for my journey. We had to catch some of the ponies and shoe them, as they are all running loose and unshod on the hills. The weather is a bit warmer now, the thermometer has not been below zero for three days. I got off by about 9 o'clock this morning, taking only five men with me including Ramzan. Ahmed Din being away at Tashkurgan, I am without my interpreter, so I shall have to do as best I can without him, as Ramzan and I can only speak to each other in Hindustani. We rode till 6 P.M. down the Mintaka river and camped on its banks, on a grassy spot, a long way past the Kirghiz encampment, which has now been moved further up the river. We crossed a plain covered with hares in the morning, and I amused myself chasing them on Agha, who stands fire very well, for I kept firing my revolver at them. I had lots of shots within twenty yards, but I never managed to hit one, although they certainly looked easy enough, especially when they were sitting. A good shot with a pistol would have killed a score there. The difference of temperature between this place and our Permanent camp is simply marvellous. I dined in my tent to-night without cap or Poshtin, and up in the camp we dined in our akoi, muffled up in fur coats, fur boots and caps, and even then could not keep warm. Still we are not twenty-five miles apart. I verily believe that camp of ours is the coldest spot in Central Asia.

October 10*th.*—Osman Beg, chief of the Kirghiz of Mintaka, came in to my camp early this morning to pay his respects and to accompany me part of the way on the march. He knew I was going to Aktash, for I had sent a man on two days ago to Mintaka to order a Kirghiz, to be ready on my arrival, to show me the way across the mountains.

Osman, who rode with me down the Mintaka river, had prepared a surprise for me, but had not warned me of what was coming, so I really was rather taken aback, when all of a sudden, on coming on to a plain, I saw what I thought was a body of cavalry advancing in line at the charge. These 120 horsemen came straight on with shouts, yells and cries, then pulled up short just in front of us. These were the Kirghiz, who had fled from the Russians last week at Aktash, and I had to remain for at least an hour and witness some exhibitions of horsemanship and feats of various sorts performed by these men.

Their principal game—if thus it may be called—consisted in one man galloping off with a sheep-skin stuffed to represent a live sheep, and all the others trying to catch him, which they invariably did, and then some very rough horse-play took place, many of the men being pulled off their horses in the struggle. After some time of this game, I proposed to Osman Beg that they should have a half-mile race with only boys up. So ten boys, varying from eight to twelve years old, were put up, and a starter sent down with them to a suppository half-mile post on the plain; and uncommonly well these urchins rode, a little fellow about nine years old winning on a chestnut. He rode so well that I gave him a rupee, at which he was delighted. Nothing would satisfy these hospitable people but I must come to their encampment to be entertained by them. So, accompanied by this escort, I rode to their camp and was made to dismount and go in to the chief's akoi and have a bowl of tea, which I accordingly did. There was a large encampment of them, and they had 2000 sheep at least, and hundreds of yaks and camels grazing. I went into several of their akois and remarked what I had noticed before in all the Kirghiz camps I have been in, viz. any amount of old women and children, the latter being invariably boys, but they don't seem to have any girls at all. After remaining half an hour with these good people I remounted my horse, and having obtained a good guide started for Aktash, which I hope to reach to-morrow, or the day after, camping to-night at the foot of the Pa-ik pass. After riding for about two hours in an easterly direction, we suddenly turned up a small nullah and headed due north. We continued up this gorge for about five miles, and then debouched on to a broad valley, with grass on each side of the stream. We followed the river till sunset, then halted for the night. There was not a living thing to be seen in the shape of game, with the exception of a small silver fox that got up close under my horse's feet, but there were several relics of ibex and *Ovis Poli* in the valley.

October 11*th*.—This morning I made an early start, as none of us knew anything concerning this Pa-ik pass that we have to cross to-day, except our Kirghiz guide, out of whom it is perfectly hopeless to try and get any information. All he has vouchsafed to us at present, is that Aktash is "just on the other side of the pass." How much, or how little the word *just* represents in his computation of distance remains for us to find out by practical experience. We rode for two hours up the valley of the Pa-ik river, which takes its name from the pass, although it rises a long way to the westward of it, in fact, when we turned off from the river and breasted the hill which leads up to the pass, I could trace the windings of the little stream like a silver thread for miles up the broad valley. We took exactly an hour and fifteen minutes from the time we left the river, until we reached the top of the pass. It was in no way a formidable one, although at the beginning it threatened to be, as the commencement of the ascent was very abrupt and rocky. The summit, 16,370 feet, was deep in snow. Our horses being out of condition after six weeks on the grass, suffered a good deal going up, and as I was in better condition than Agha, I walked up when I saw how distressed he was. The descent on the northern side was very easy, being a gentle incline, also deep in snow. Here I found another stream that has its source on this north side of the pass; it is also called the Pa-ik, and this we followed for some miles, until it became quite a respectable sized river. Its course was through a broad valley, gradually changing from north to north-west, and eventually due west. This valley was at a very high elevation, 14,900 feet; in fact, we descended considerably less than 1000 feet from the summit of the pass, and that was so gradual, it was wellnigh imperceptible. But it was easy to see how high this valley was, because we were riding on a level with the snow-line, and the hills on each side of us appeared small, though deep in snow. The country was much more open than in the Eastern Taghdumbash Pamir, and it certainly was not nearly so cold. The sun was now getting low, and on consulting my watch I saw we had but one hour's more daylight, so again I interrogated the Kirghiz guide as to the position of Aktash. Stretching out his arm, he pointed with his whip to some blue hazy hills in the distance, and then giving a sweep with his hand to the right, gave me to understand that Aktash was situated somewhere round those hills. There was no question about reaching it to-night, the only doubt in my mind was whether we should get there to-morrow. And this is what he was pleased to call "just on the other side of the pass," which was a good eighteen miles behind us, and, by the look of it, Aktash was as many miles off in front of us. However, I am so accustomed to this sort of thing, that I thought no more about it, but set to work to find a comfortable place to camp in.

October 12th.—Got up very early, and telling Ramzan to follow as soon as possible, I mounted Agha, and armed with my sketching materials, rode off in the direction of Aktash, accompanied by the Kirghiz. After a little while we came to the summit of a long ridge, which reached nearly across the valley, from the top of which we had a magnificent panoramic view.

At my feet lay the great plain of Aktash. On my left were the northern and western spurs of the

Taghdumbash Pamir, which terminate somewhere near Bozai Gombaz, the place where Captain Younghusband was taken prisoner last year by the Russians.

In front of me was the range of mountains, known as the "Little Pamir range," behind which lies the lake discovered first by Wood, and now known to geographers as the Victoria lake, the Kirghiz name for which is Gaz Kul. Over the tops of the little Pamirs could be seen, in the clear morning light, the snowy peaks of the "Great Pamir range," while to my right the grand light-coloured cliff, which gives the name to the locality, stood boldly out into the plain like a headland does into the sea.

That was the Ak-Tash, or White Rock. Winding through the plain could be seen the river Ak-su, or White-water, which has its source in the Chakmaktin lake, at the foot of the Little Pamir range, and which after passing the Aktash Headland, flows in a northerly direction, until it passes the 38th parallel of latitude, when it takes a bend to the north-west and joins the Murghab, and the waters of these two rivers then flow due west for about 140 miles, under the name of the Murghab river, until they join the Oxus at a place called Kala Wamar. As I rode down from this elevated plateau on to the plain below, I passed many a spot where the Kirghiz encampments had so lately stood. It was a piteous scene of desolation, and one could not but feel sorry for these poor people being forced to fly from the country which had known them so long. At one place where the marks on the ground showed that there had been several akois, was a poor half-starved dog, who had evidently been left behind by some oversight—the only living thing besides ourselves in this wide ocean of magnificent desolation. He was a large grey sort of wolf-hound, who looked askance at us, not knowing whether he had to deal with friend or foe. We tried to make friends with him, as I wanted to take him away with me, but he rejected all overtures, and finally took to his heels and was lost to sight on the plain. Close to the right bank of the river was the Kirghiz burial-ground, called Ak-Pid Gombaz; the best of the tombs were dome-shaped, and although built of mud, were not lacking in rude architectural merit. There was a strong resemblance between those tombs and those of the Arab Sheiks one sees in Egypt and Syria.

Leaving this last resting-place of these nomads on my left, I rode onwards down the riverside for about three miles, until I reached the spot I had come to see, viz.: the Fort of Aktash, or as much of it as was left. It was a total ruin, for the Russians had literally not left one stone standing upon another. This fort had evidently been more pretentious than the majority of Chinese forts that I have seen in this country, inasmuch as it had been built of stone, and not of mud.

It was situated at the foot of a long spur of sand and gravel that ran out of a gully, in a large cleft of the Big Rock of Aktash itself. Round it was a ditch, but so full of débris, that I could not judge of its depth. I looked, and wondered what the outcome of this high-handed act of the Russians would be, for the Chinese say they will insist upon the Russians building it up again for them. It is not for me to prophesy, but in my humble opinion that fort will remain in ruins for some time to come.

Having made one or two sketches, I turned Agha's head southwards and rode back to rejoin my little caravan, and selecting a grassy spot, under the shadow of the hills which border the east side of the plain, pitched my tent for the night, by the side of a small river called the Khanjola, which joins the Pa-ik just below my camp, the waters of both flowing into the Ak-su.

October 13*th.*—As I intended to re-cross the Pa-ik pass to-day and so do two marches in one, I started very early, and, retracing my steps over the same ground, arrived very late at the foot of the pass, having been retarded by the snow which fell last night. It was therefore dark when we reached the summit, but the snow lighted it up for us, so that we had no difficulty in the ascent. But the moment we crossed it, and began to descend on the south side, it was a very different story. There was not a particle of snow, and the rocks and general colour of the mountain was a dark chocolate, which in that light was quite black. If we found the ascent on Tuesday not so very formidable, we certainly found the descent to-night as difficult as the other appeared easy. There is a great difference between going 1500 feet up a steep and rocky hill in broad daylight, and coming down the same hill in the dark. Of course we had to walk every inch of the way, and lead our horses, which was worse. It took us nearly three hours, and two of the ponies had to be unloaded, and the loads carried by the men. There was no sort of track, and no moon, so we literally had to feel our way. However, we eventually got safely down to the river, and pitched the camp in the dark. It was exactly 9 P.M. by my watch when we reached the riverside, and the sun sets at 6 P.M. now.

October 16*th* (*Permanent Camp*).—I arrived here last night after a march of twenty-seven miles, and found two Kunjutis with a dâk from Younghusband, from Hunza, but no letters for us from Gilgit. I cannot understand what has happened to our letters, we have not had any since July. I found when I got home that they had got one of my wounded *Ovis Poli*, but Roche had been unsuccessful, not having had a shot since I left; he has only had one chance in six weeks, and I have had six shots, four of which were successful; one I wounded, and one I missed, so I seem to have had all the luck, such as it is. Younghusband's

Kunjutis brought us some tobacco. It was very kind of him to send men all that way, just because he knew we were out of tobacco; he sent some old newspapers also, in which Roche was terribly shocked to read of the deaths of two of his brother officers at Murree, from cholera; one of them, Major Dimond, was his greatest friend in the regiment, and they had always lived together in the same bungalow in India; the other victim, Major Cole, was the senior major. The cholera seems to have carried off a good many people at Murree.

* * * * * *

Ahmed Din arrived from Tashkurgan this evening, he reports having had great difficulties in obtaining provisions both for men and horses. The Chinese absolutely refused to let us have anything; at last, after keeping him waiting five whole days, putting him off from day to day, the Amban said he must refer the matter to his superior officer at Yarkand, and obtain his permission before supplying us with flour and corn. The fact is, the Chinese in these parts are very sore, and an Englishman is anything but a *persona grata* in their eyes at this particular juncture.

Their principal ground for soreness with the English is the treatment they consider the two Mandarins received lately at our hands, in conjunction with the installation of the new Mir of Hunza, when they were not permitted to take any active part in the proceedings. That seems to rankle much in the Celestial mind.

They dislike our being on the Pamirs, and know that we are contemplating a further expedition through the Middle and Upper Pamirs, by which means we shall get a further insight into their weakness in this country, so they are doing all they can to hamper our movements. I hear they are very wrath at my having been to Aktash and seen the destruction of their fort.

Jan Mahammad managed to get as much corn for the horses, and flour for the men, as will last us a month. The Sariq-qolis from whom he purchased it are in mortal terror of their lives for having supplied us, as the Chinese officials at Tashkurgan are sure to visit it upon their heads either directly or indirectly as soon as they find it out.

CHAPTER XXX.

History of the Kirghiz of the Pamir Region—Their Manners and Customs—Letters from Gilgit at last—My second wounded *Ovis Poli* found in the Snow.

THE Kirghiz race in this part of Central Asia are divided up into four chief tribes.

(*a*) The Niaman, (*b*) the Kipchak, (*c*) the Tai-it, (*d*) the Kissack.

The Niaman tribe is again subdivided into four smaller clans, namely, (1) the Kon, (2) Busturogas, (3) Mirza, (4) Kiak. Of these the Kons and Busturogas are Russian subjects, dwelling in the neighbourhood of Marghilan, in the Province of Ferghana, in Russian Turkestan. The Mirzas and Kiaks are Chinese subjects and live about Kiaz and the Charlung river, to the east of Tashkurgan, and in Chakaraghal, Manju, Ditagh and Bulun Kul.

The Kipchak (*b*) tribe is sub-divided into three clans, viz. (1) Sart, (2) Kirghiz Kipchak, (3) Kalta-baital. Of these the Sarts (who must not be confounded with the Sariq-qoli Sarts although bearing the same name) owe allegiance in about equal numerical proportions to

Russia and China. They live principally on the banks of the Serés river, although some of their encampments are in the Kashgar division. (2) The Kirghiz Kipchaks live mostly in the same country as the Sarts.

(3) The Kalta-baitals, who are held in great respect by the rest of the Kirghiz, owing to their antiquity and distinguished ancestry, are almost entirely Russian subjects, although a few families may be found in Chinese Territory on the Charlung river. Kalta-baital signifies "Mare with her tail cut." The story goes that an ancestor of the people of this clan accompanied Hussein, son of Ali, in A.D. 680, when he was attacked by Yezid (see page 30) on his way to Kufa, and that in the fight which took place, this ancestor's mare lost her tail with a sword cut. Hence the name which they claim to have had for the last 1200 years.

The Tai-it (*c*) tribe are subdivided into two clans: (1) Kara Tai-it and (2) Sart Tai-it.

The former live in Karakul (Pamirs), Karatash, and some in Andijan (Ferghana), and are consequently all subject to Russia.

The latter live in Murghabi, Rangkul, and the Alai Pamir, and it is hard to say whose subjects they are, as both Russians and Chinese claim the three above-mentioned districts. The refugees from Aktash (see page 102) also belong to this clan. There are also a few families of this clan, who call themselves Kizil Bash, in the Alai Pamirs, but they again, although bearing the same appellation, must not be mixed up with the *real* Kizil Bash tribe, who live in Afghan-Turkestan and on the frontiers of Bokhara and Russian-Turkestan and who are all Shia Mahammadans.

The Kissack (*d*) tribe are divided into three smaller clans, viz. (1) Bostan, (2) Kiddarshah, and (3) Khangdeh.

The Bostan clans are half Russian and half Chinese subjects. They are to be found in Sariq-qol Tagharma, Shahidula, the Taghdumbash, and Alai Pamirs, also in Andijan (Ferghana). (2) The Kiddarshah live also in Andijan, Rangkul, Murghabi, and the Alai Pamir, (3) the Khangdeh are entirely Russian subjects, living on the Alai Pamir. There are only five families of this clan residing in Oitagh. There are other subdivisions of this great Kirghiz race, but they are not of any great importance. In Ili in Chinese Territory and in Russian Turkestan, there are many other important tribes, viz. the Taghay, Andigina, Boghu, Sarighbaghish, Cherib, Chungbaghiz, and Kochi; but as they do not live in this part of Central Asia, I can get no reliable information regarding them.

* * * * * *

The Kirghiz breed camels, horses, cattle (yaks), sheep, and goats. They sometimes sow a little barley, but rarely, being chiefly nomads, taking their flocks and herds from pasture to pasture, and moving their akois every two or three months, as the grass is finished. They manufacture numdahs, or thick felt blankets, and in Andijan they make carpets. They exchange these felt numdahs for cotton, cloths, boots, Russian-made iron kettles, and cotton prints. In the report of Forsyth's Mission to Yarkand, the writer of the article on the Kirghiz says: "the Kirghiz profess Islam, and are Sunni Mussulmans, but they are very ignorant of the doctrines of the Faith, and very careless in the observance of its ordinances. In fact many of them are pagans though different from the Kalmaks. They are said to be much given to drunkenness by a strong spirit they distil from mare's milk. They are very fond of hunting and are robbers by nature."

I have been told that the writer of this article had never lived amongst the Kirghiz at all, but got his information from a man in Kashgar in 1873. Perhaps they may have improved in the last nineteen years, for all I can say is that having lived constantly amongst the Kirghiz of Eastern Turkestan, Sariq-qol, Taghdumbash, and the Chinese and Russian Pamirs, for five months, and studied their habits and mode of life, I have never seen or heard of a case of drunkenness amongst them. They do make a kind of spirit from mare's milk, which is only used by the well-to-do class, and it is called "kimis." The milk is half boiled, then put in a goat skin, and some acid is mixed with it. It is allowed to remain in the skin for three or four days, then well shaken, after which it is fit for use.

They are good Sunni Mahammadans and not at all pagans as represented. They are a simple peaceful people and neither raid nor rob. Another most startling statement is made by the same writer, who says, "they are described as extremely impulsive and impatient of control, and in cases where an aggrieved party considers himself unjustly treated by his judges, it is not an uncommon thing for him to kill himself, or to tear open his shirt and gash his chest and stomach with a knife, or to snatch up his own child, and dash out its brains on the ground, thereby throwing the responsibility of his ruin upon his unjust judges."*

I had this passage read by my interpreter to many influential men of the Kirghiz tribes, to Begs, Bais, Mollahs (priests), and "the oldest inhabitant," and one and all declared that they had never heard of such a thing occurring in their lives.

Their camps are governed by Begs, who are assisted by Aksakals. These Begs are elected by the people themselves, but the appointments, in the case of Chinese subjects, have to be confirmed by the Government. These Begs dispose of all quarrels or disputes, assisted by the Aksakals. Those who have large flocks and herds are styled Bai. The writer before referred to makes another mistake, when he says, "the chief of a whole tribe is called 'Sultan,' and he is the referee in cases of appeal against the decision of the Bai, who

* Report of Mission to Yarkand, 1873 (page 60).

settles disputes in consultation with the ácsacál, or 'grey beards' (elders)."

To begin with, the Beg is the governing power in the camp, not the Bais, who, as I have just mentioned, are simply the big flock masters, and there is no such title as "Sultan" amongst the Kirghiz.

The writer had got himself mixed up with a certain Kirghiz named Alimkul, who, 100 years ago, before the Russian conquest of Ferghana, seized on Andijan, and made himself master of Khokand and styled himself "Sultan."

The Kirghiz treat their women very well and with more deference than most Mussulman tribes, but I have often noticed that the children, especially the grown up ones, are very much too free and easy with their parents. We have a father and son in our service here on the Pamirs, and by the son's mode of speech and conduct to his father, one would never guess the relationship that exists between them. But the wives are certainly not ill-treated by their husbands; they have perfect liberty of action and are never veiled. They make excellent house-wives and fairly good mothers.

The poorer class of Kirghiz get married with much difficulty, as a wife is a most expensive article. There was a wedding not far from our camp the other day, and the bridegroom-elect, who had been engaged by us in September last as a gillie, gave to the parents of the bride, as her price, one yambu (a nugget of silver equal to 160 rupees here), two horses, two camels, eight yaks, twenty sheep and a gun. To look at the bridegroom, you would say he was not worth 16 rupees, much less 160, plus yaks, camels, horses and sheep. Amongst other presents, Osman Beg gave a camel, and Mahammad Salih, who acted as my guide the other day to Aktash, presented them with two sheep. Another two Kirghiz friends of mine, Kurmoshi and Yarumbui, gave respectively a camel and a horse; but in this case they presented them to the bridegroom, and not to the bride's parents, who in my opinion had already got quite enough for the girl, although she is the only decent-looking female in this valley. I think it showed a very good spirit on the part of Osman Beg giving anything at all, as he was a disappointed suitor for the young lady's hand.

The preliminaries of a marriage are generally arranged by the three chief persons of the tribe, who are sent by the bridegroom to the girl's parents, to settle with them the amount of money and stock that he is to give. When these arrangements are brought to a satisfactory conclusion, the father of the girl presents each of these three ambassadors with a cloak (*Khalat*). They then return to the bridegroom and "report progress." After this a day is fixed for the "small marriage," when the bridegroom kills about ten sheep, puts them on a camel and carries them to the akoi of his prospective father-in-law, where all the bride's relatives and friends are assembled.

Then all the men of the party adjourn to the nearest plain on horseback, taking with them a live goat. One man goes into the middle of the plain and cuts the animal's throat, then throws it down, when all the rest of the horsemen make a rush for it. Then commences that excessively rough game I described the other day, which I witnessed on my way to Aktash. After this comes horse-racing, the prize being generally a camel or a yak.

When these sports are over, the bridegroom, accompanied by his friends, returns to his own akoi to fetch the price of the bride, armed with which he returns to the akoi of the girl's parents, pays over the money, delivers the live stock and claims his bride.

More *Khalats* are presented to the bridegroom's friends by the bride's father, and after more horse-races and lots of eating, drinking (tea), music and singing, the marriage ceremony takes place—always at night. An akoi is pitched expressly for the use of the newly married couple, who retire there directly after the ceremony, only to re-appear after the lapse of three days! After which brief but uninterrupted honeymoon the bridegroom takes his wife home to his own akoi.

October 18*th* (*Permanent Camp*).—Another piece of good luck for me. My other wounded *Ovis Poli* has been found lying dead, by a Kirghiz, who brought the head in to-day. As it has been frozen all this time, the skin on the face is hardly damaged at all, so that I can have the head stuffed. It has been buried in snow, and has thus escaped the wild dogs. Its shoulder was broken by my bullet. I have all five heads now, which is a satisfaction.

Letters from home at last. A dâk messenger arrived from Hunza with letters from Gilgit, and it was an immense relief to get them after three months of longing for them. It was most kind of Captain Younghusband tó send them on by special messenger, as he knew we were anxious, owing to this cholera epidemic at Murree and so many of our friends living there.

* * * * * *

Some of the Kirghiz head-men from Aktash, wishing to cross over into Hunza to buy grain, came and asked me to give them a pass to Captain Younghusband, as they are afraid of being turned back at Misgah by his Kunjuti outposts, as none but dâk carriers are allowed to pass. Ahmed Din wrote them a sort of passport in Persian to show at the outpost, and I signed it. I am rather curious to hear the result. The Kunjutis at Misgah know we are in constant correspondence with Younghusband and have never stopped one of our dâk messengers at present. So I hope these men will get through. They wish to become British subjects and emigrate over into Hunza in a body, as they say the Chinese will not do anything for them, but allowed them to be turned out of their homes by the Russians. They are very bitter against the Chinese and do not hesitate to call them cowards. They asked my advice as to how to set about becoming British subjects. I declined to interfere, as I do not want to get myself into trouble with the Chinese.

CHAPTER XXXI.

A Kirghiz idea of Sport—Chinese Mandarin comes to inspect the "English Fort"—Roche and the Bear—Men getting ill from the cold—Russians refuse to let Roche cross their Frontier—Arrival of a second Chinese Mandarin—Provisions at last—Despatch sick men to Gilgit—Departure for Middle and Upper Pamirs—The Wakhjir Pass—We enter Afghan Territory.

October 25*th* (*Permanent Camp*).—This last week has been spent in comparative idleness. Every bit of the ground has been carefully spied, but with the exception of a small herd that seem to have taken root on one of the large open grassy slopes in the Kukturuk valley—for they have been there without moving for eleven days—not an *Ovis Poli* has been seen over all the ground.

This small herd are as usual in an inaccessible place, as far as stalking is concerned, for they can see up and down the river for nearly two miles.

Tukta Mahammad, having made his peace with the Chinese, has been released from the surveillance under which he had been placed for his suspected Russian proclivities, and came to pay us a visit, a day or two ago.

We asked him if he could in any way account for our

having had such miserable sport, and he replied that this was the very worst season of the year we could possibly have selected to come here, as the *Ovis Poli* always keep very high up on the mountain tops, and amongst the glaciers, during these months and he considered them impossible to get. He said he had never heard of any being killed at this time of the year before, and was much astonished when I showed him my five heads, and he wondered how on earth I managed to get them. I explained to him how I had slept out on the hill, night after night, and after once seeing them stuck to them.

He evidently considered this a great waste of energy on my part, and proposed a much easier mode of procedure; "you come back in the spring," he said, "for then they are weak for want of food and are driven down by the deep snow into the bottoms of the nullahs, where I chase them with my dogs, then you can shoot as many as you please."

Needless to say I declined his offer.

* * * * * *

The cold is still intense and on the increase, the thermometer *inside* our akois going down to zero every night, while the one hanging on the outside of the akoi averages about six to seven below zero. We find it very difficult to keep warm, and begin to fear we shall lose some of our horses, as they are all loose on the hill and, having no horse-clothing, they must suffer badly at nights.

The extraordinary part of this climate lies in the fact

that the colder it gets at nights the warmer it is in the daytime. Since the thermometer has taken to going down below zero at night, it has also registered maximum temperatures of 100 to 106 in the sun's rays in the daytime, consequently the snows have been melting fast on the hills, and we have had no fresh snow-storms for some time. Had it not been for this, my last wounded *Ovis Poli* would never have been found. Yesterday a poor little half-frozen martin flew into Roche's akoi, and it is perched there on a rope that is stretched across the inside, but whether it will live or not is a question, as there are no flies or insects at this altitude or at this season for it to eat.

I was also much astonished, the last day I was out stalking, to see lots of little mice running about in the snow, in and out of the stones and rocks; and, on the same day coming home, I came across a large flock of the ram chikore. There were a great number of them scattered about all over the hill-side, besides twenty-one that I counted all together; they were, I think, migrating; leaving the inhospitable regions of the Pamirs for more congenial climes. They made a most peculiar whistling noise as they were going along, half running, half flying. They appeared to me large birds, almost as big as turkeys.

I think I mentioned some little time ago that we had built ourselves a bake and wash-house, with rough stones and mud, and also that a report had got about amongst some of those Kirghiz, who are "paid for information received," that "the English had built a fort on the Pamirs."

Although we were told of it, we never attached the slightest importance to this foolish rumour until the other day, when to our surprise a Chinese Mandarin, with an armed following, arrived here from Kashgar, fifteen marches off, and set up his camp close to ours.

He visited us and informed us he had come on "a tour of inspection," he omitted to say of what, but he inspected our camp—which, laid out as it was on military lines, might perhaps have struck some passing Kirghiz, who exaggerated our well-dressed tent-pegs into a fort bristling with guns—and I took particular care he should visit the bake-house and admire the chimney, which he did, and, after having satisfied himself as to the peaceable aspect of our camp, he departed the way he came, having inspected nothing else. So there is not a shadow of doubt that he was sent all the way from Kashgar to see what we were up to.*

If they would leave *us* alone and pay a little more

* I discovered afterwards, when we were in Kashgar, the reason of this extraordinary interest exhibited by the Chinese in our supposed Fort. It appears that the Kunjutis claimed some piece of land on the Kukturuk river, and so as The Indian Government conquered and annexed Kunjut last year, the Chinese are in deadly fear they should claim this piece of ground and get a footing on the north side of the Hindu Kush. That is one reason why they buried the boundary stone (see Chap. XXVII., Vol. ii. p. 83).

attention to Colonel Yonoff's movements, it would be the better for them.

Yesterday Roche had a most exciting chase after the same large grey bear that fairly checkmated me, and for which I have by no means forgiven him; in fact, although I have met with plenty of bears before, I would rather get him now than the best *Ovis Poli* on the Pamirs. He must be a cunning old beast, as he played Roche the same trick he played me, for he ran to cut him off in a place where, owing to the nature of the ground, he knew he must of a certainty pass him, and there waited for him; but he never reappeared, and at last the shikari, on looking up the hill to their right, saw the bear careering gaily home out of shot. The old wretch knows the country pretty well, for he had again taken advantage of a small gully and given them the slip as he did me. This time there were two of them, but the other one remained on the south side of the river. Roche's opinion of him is that he is nearly twice as large as a Kashmiri bear, and thinks he is of a very rare species. I reckoned him as large as a grizzly bear of the Rocky Mountains, and I don't think I was far out. There were nineteen ibex in a nullah close by, which Roche attempted to stalk; but again they were put off by the wild dogs, who are simply hunting the whole ground every day, so we are off.

The whole of our flock of sheep disappeared in the night, and we have men on horseback scouring the country to regain possession of our only staple article of food—our men being imbued with the same ideas as the Kirghiz—put down their disappearance to Cossacks; we put it down to wild dogs, as I happen to know there can be no Cossacks in this neighbourhood at this time, and if there were they would no more dare raid our sheep than the Kirghiz would.

We are all ready now to make a start for the Middle and Upper Pamirs, but are still awaiting our supplies which were due here yesterday, also some sheep-skin Poshtins we ordered for the men from Yarkand, two months ago, as the poor fellows would simply perish on the Pamirs this weather without some extra warm clothing.

I have been to the Kilik pass again for two reasons —one because there has been a fall of snow, and I wanted to be able to judge of the condition of the pass under heavy snow, to report to Macartney, and also because the Kirghiz gave me news of a large herd of *Ovis Poli* that were located on this side of the spurs of the Hindu Kush. So I started off in search of them and came across a fine herd of thirty-two rams, nearly all good ones; but, unfortunately for me, they were feeding on a plain between the hills, in a place where it was absolutely impossible to get nearer than 500 yards, so I contented myself by lying down and watching them through my stalking-glass.

I waited there till evening, in the hopes that they

might move; but they remained lying down, and as I saw it was useless to stop, I returned to camp empty-handed as usual.

I have not fired a shot out of my rifle for more than a month, and Roche has hardly fired a shot at all for two months, therefore we have come to the conclusion that it is about time to change our quarters.

October 26*th*.—This extreme cold weather has begun to tell upon some of the men, especially those who hail from the lower districts of Kashmir. Two or three of them are so weak that we cannot think of taking them on with us, so we have settled to send them back *via* Hunza and Gilgit.

Jan Mahammad's son arrived from Tashkurgan with a dâk from Kashgar, which included a letter from M. Petrovsky, the Russian Consul, who in a letter, couched in the most courteous terms, regrets to have to inform me that the Russian Government have sent him notice that it is impossible to permit Major Roche to cross their frontier into Central Asia: "obtenir la permission de visiter le Turkestan Russe," he writes, "est à peu près aussi difficile que d'avoir un permis de passer la frontière du Hindu Kush." So that puts an end to any idea of Roche being able to accompany me through the rest of the expedition. Amongst other letters forwarded by M. Petrovsky was one for me from the English Ambassador in St. Petersburg, Sir Robert Morier, dated May 10th, 1892. Five months and a half from St. Petersburg to Kashgar. I thought it was a very long time, until on looking at the envelope the mystery was solved, as it bore the post-marks of Singapore, Hongkong, Shanghai and Pekin.

The fact was that the letter had been, in the first instance, addressed "Kashgar, China," instead of "Chinese Turkestan, *via* Samarkand." Consequently, when it was posted in St. Petersburg, it naturally went across Europe with the China mails, then through the Suez Canal to Singapore, Hongkong, etc., and came back to Pekin with the following annotation in French on the back of the envelope: "*Probablement pour Kashgar pour le voyageur anglais Lord Dunmore.*" So it has been a good many thousand miles by sea and by land before it reached this out-of-the-way part of the world.

This refusal of the Russian Government to allow Roche to cross the frontier is a great disappointment to both him and me. I shall now have a long, weary journey through Russian Central Asia by myself, which is a prospect I cannot say I look forward to with any great degree of pleasure, especially as M. Petrovsky in his letter says that the cholera is raging all through the province of Ferghana, through which I must pass on my way to Tashkend.

October 27th.—Another Chinese Mandarin has arrived

on this Pamir, and has established his camp close to ours. His name is Haï Dolai, and he is a big man in his own estimation. Hailing from Urumtchi, he has been sent here by the Chinese Government; but his mission, whatever it is, is a secret one. Early this morning he called upon us, sending as usual an *avant-courrier* with several square inches of red tissue-paper, which constituted his visiting card, on one corner of which was his name. When he arrived himself, he was accompanied by an escort of mounted Kirghiz, who all looked as if they would rather be somewhere else. They were armed with their peculiar long matchlocks, with an instrument resembling the prongs of a hay-fork projecting at the end of the barrel. This fork forms a rest, working on a swivel, and the man who fires has to lie on his stomach. We saw a Kirghiz fire at a marmot in that position at Cheile Gombaz; but it is needless to say he missed it.

I had to entertain this Chinaman in my akoi, as Roche is very much averse to visiting or receiving visits from any Oriental, and he remained with me for two solid hours, so much so, that I thought I should never get rid of him. Of course I had to give him tea, and his pipe-bearer was in the akoi constantly filling and refilling his little, ridiculous Chinese pipe, which holds about three whiffs.

He had the same peculiar drawling hesitation in his speech that I have already noticed, especially in the case of the Amban of Kargalik, who used to remain on the drawl on one particular note, say B flat, and then jerk his voice up to F natural, and come out with his sentence, this Amban, when hesitating in his speech, lacked the musical (?) drawl of the other one, and simply said, "Jigga jigga, jigga jigga," with the greatest rapidity, which resembled much more the going off of an alarum than the articulation of a human being, and he continued jigga jigga-ing until he got the word he wanted.

Haï Dolai is an oldish man, with rather refined features for a Chinaman. I cannot say that I was predisposed in his favour, because, like all small Chinese officials, he is imbued with the arrogance peculiar to his class. We have to thank him for telling the local Kirghiz, in our neighbourhood, on no account to supply us with anything in the way of provisions for our men or horses, and he had the additional impertinence to pitch into Osman Beg for allowing us to have Kirghiz yaks to supply our camp with milk, and Kirghiz men to accompany us with other yaks when on expeditions on the mountains after *Ovis Poli.*

All this Osman Beg had confided to me in the morning previous to this old gentleman's visit, and he added that we should have to ask him as a favour for a Kirghiz guide to go with us on the other Pamirs.

That we flatly refused to do, and during my conversation with this Chinaman, I showed him my passport from Pekin, and demanded a guide as my right, adding that knowing the terms of my passport, I hoped he would make it known to all Chinese subjects, that unless I was treated with the utmost deference by Chinese officials, and got everything I wanted, I should be under the painful necessity of reporting him to the Taotai at Kashgar. This had the immediate effect of putting Haï Dolai's tail between his legs, and he informed me that he had a most excellent Kirghiz guide, called Abdul Kerim, to whom he would give orders to accompany us through the Pamirs. I said, "that is the man I have already engaged," and I only hope the interpreter put the same emphasis on the sentence that I did.

After this little sparring between Haï and me, he asked to what part of the Pamirs we were going. So I told him. He then proposed we should go together. So then I had my innings: "Oh," I said, "I am going to a part where you cannot go for fear of the Russians." Then began a discussion, and I brought out my map of the Pamirs, and made him mark the Chinese Frontier, as claimed by them, which he did. "What is the use," I said, "of your claiming this and that on the Pamirs, if you don't protect it with some soldiers," for I well knew that the Chinese force on the Pamirs existed only on paper at Pekin. No answer. Curiously enough Haï Dolai's horse happened to be ready at that moment, so the old gentleman bade me adieu, and very glad I was to be rid of a dirty old person, who spat all over my floor, and was not able to tell me why fifteen Cossacks were able to turn out a Chinese garrison at Aktash, and level their fort with the ground; or to explain why he ordered the Kirghiz of Mintaka—who hate the Chinese—not to supply our horses with fodder, or our men with flour.

I watched my friend ride off in the direction of the Wakhjir valley, with his uncouth-looking escort following him at a hand gallop. It was certainly a very picturesque sight, these wild looking horsemen careering over the plain, with this Chinaman, a prominent figure in the midst of them, the sun shining upon their many-coloured costumes, and glistening on the polished barrels of their matchlocks; while the great solemn snow-capped mountains frowned down upon the cavalcade, as if resenting this intrusion on their hitherto unbroken privacy.

I have once before made mention of the extraordinary geographical ignorance of some of these Chinamen, even those holding high official positions; and to-day I was much struck by the want of knowledge exhibited by Haï Dolai.

We were talking about the route from Urumtchi to Pekin, and after his describing the country through which the traveller would have to pass, he wound up by saying, "when once you reach Pekin, you should go on to Shanghai and see the ocean; you can have no conception of the amount of water it contains; it is far bigger than the great Lake of Lob, in the Desert of Gobi; in fact," he continued, warming with his subject, "if all the rivers in the Pamirs flowed into one basin, like the basin of the Oxus, and filled it, it would not hold as much water as there is to be seen outside the land at Shanghai." This man was evidently under the impression that I had never seen the sea.

Talk about the proverbial insularity of the average Briton, it is nothing in comparison with the limited scope of a Chinaman's horizon, for he knows absolutely nothing outside his native land, and believes that China is the only country in the world.

October 29th.—At length our things have arrived from Yarkand and Tashkurgan, under the care of our old friend Mahammad Ahmin, who seems to have taken a great fancy to us, for the moment he arrived in camp, he rushed first into my akoi, and then into Roche's, and falling on his knees embraced our feet, exclaiming in Persian to me, "Oh, my beloved master!" I received this ebullition of affection with proper Oriental imperturbability, and responded by asking him, what the d— —l made him so long on the road! Then followed a string of excuses, the main one being the extreme severity of the weather, and the great amount of snow on the different passes. As a peace-offering for his delay, the old man had brought with him a *doster khan* of fruit, mostly pears, which, although they were frozen as hard as a stone, old Francatelli managed to serve up as a stew.

We paraded the whole of the men of the caravan, and served out the thirty Poshtins, which delighted them much, as being lined with lambs' wool, they are likely to keep them pretty warm on the arduous and freezing journey they have got before them.

Now that our provisions have come, we can make a start, and get away from this Arctic region, although we are probably about to enter regions still more Arctic.

My one regret on leaving here is the bear. I feel he has *done* both Roche and myself. I *would* like to get that bear!

October 30*th.*—This morning early we despatched our sick men to Hunza and Gilgit, and a couple of horses to India, as we were afraid of taking our two Badakshan horses with us across the Pamirs, as they are not so hardy as our Tibetan ponies. I also sent my four best *Ovis Poli* heads on the old grey I bought at Srinagar, named after the General from whom I purchased him. After seeing them off, escorted by two of Younghusband's Kunjutis, who were returning to Hunza, we bade adieu to our many Kirghiz friends, who had come to see us off, and rode in the direction of the Wakhjir pass, over which we have to go to reach Bozai Gombaz.

For the first two or three miles we took the same direction as the Hunza party, they having to turn south to cross the Kilik pass, over the Hindu Kush, and we south-west for our pass.

Just as we were crossing the Wakhjir river, over the ice, we met Jumma, who had returned to tell us that the "General" had lain down on the hill-side, and refused to move.

We explained to him that it was only natural, after fifty-five days on the grass, and doing no work, that the horse should exhibit some little reluctance at first to going up a steep hill with a load on his back, but that the remedy was a very simple one, viz. for the men to unload him, and carry the *Ovis Poli* heads on their backs, dividing the load between them. With this salutary piece of advice, we left him and pursued our journey up the Wakhjir valley.

Whilst we were halted for our midday meal we witnessed a sight which, to any one fond of studying the habits of animals, especially such rare ones as the *Ovis Poli*, must have been interesting.

Coming over a glacier on the top of the hill, facing the spot where we were resting, was a herd of these interesting animals, which had evidently been disturbed by our Hunza detachment when going up the nullah that leads to the Kilik pass. I fancy they must have been the same lot that I had seen the other day when out on that ground. We watched them intently through our glasses, as they marched on in single file, headed by a fine old ram, until they came to the edge of the glacier, where there was a small precipice of ice. Just at that moment we could see that they in their turn had perceived us, so the leading ram halted, and all his followers did the same; he was evidently looking about for an exit, for he peered over the edge of the precipice, but, not liking the look of it, faced about and walked slowly back, all the others following his example until they reached a small *mer de glace,* where they seemingly held a consultation as to what they had better do, having an enemy on each side and a precipice in front of them. The result of their deliberations was evidently to pursue a policy of masterly inactivity, as they ended by all lying down in the snow, leaving one ram perched on the top of a high rock to keep a look-out. There were several good heads amongst them, but it was useless our delaying the caravan to go after them, as they were in a perfectly inaccessible place; so we proceeded up the little river and soon got into a more open country, the valley widening out as we travelled further west.

Just before sunset we found a convenient place to camp, the only difficulty being water, the ice on the river being so thick that it almost defied the efforts of our men to break it with their axes. On consulting the aneroid, we found we had ascended 1250 feet from our old camp, and consequently were at an altitude of 16,300 feet, and the thermometer at three degrees below zero.

October 31*st.*—After a night of perishing cold, we rose

to find everything we possessed frozen as hard as a stone. To attempt even the most elementary form of ablution was utterly out of the question, our sponges being like small rocks of granite and our towels like sheet-iron. We did manage to get a cup of tea, but the bottle of yak's milk we had brought with us from our old camp was hard frozen, and we had no time to thaw it.

In striking tents the iron tent-pegs broke off short in the ground at the slightest touch of the hammer, when the men tried to loosen them to pull them up. Eventually we made a start, clothed in costumes that savoured more of Arctic explorers than Central Asian, and headed straight for the pass, which was a gradual ascent of just under 1000 feet from our camping-ground of last night.

We found it very bad going and had to walk and lead our horses most of the way, owing to the frozen state of the rough ground, until we came to deeper snow, the top of which being hard frozen, made a better road.

The river presented a most peculiar appearance, as in its fall of eight or nine hundred feet there were naturally several small water-falls and rapids, every one of which was hard frozen, and in one or two instances they were very curious. At 16,580 feet, we came to the source of the Wakhjir, which is one of the sources of the Yarkand river, the other the main source being at the foot of the Karakoram pass. Soon after leaving this, we mounted a low ridge and came upon a lake about half a mile long and some three hundred yards wide; a sheet of the most perfect ice I have ever seen, resembling the most highly polished green glass. It was rumbling, and cracking, and emitting all sorts of weird, sub-glacial sounds as we picked our way along its shore two feet deep in snow and about four feet deep in rough stones and rocks, leading our horses, who relished it as little as we did ourselves. The lake lay lengthways, nearly due east and west, and when we reached the rising ground above its western extremity we were on the summit of the Wakhjir pass, at an elevation of 16,680 feet above the sea. This is the proper Frontier between Chinese and Afghan territory, and when we descended and struck the Ak-Bilis river, at the foot of the pass, we found ourselves in the dominion of the Amir of Cabul and entering the Wakhan district of the Pamirs.

The Ak-Bilis river rises in the pass of that name, which forms the boundary between Hunza (or Kunjut) and Wakhan. The course of the river at this point is from south-east to north-west, and is one of the tributaries of the Oxus.* It flows through a deep but broad ravine, and we followed it the whole afternoon, riding down its right bank on an elevated plateau, about 250 feet above the

* Colonel Grombchevsky told me afterwards at Osh that the Russians claim this as the true source of the Oxus.

stream. The scenery was very beautiful, the lights and the deep blue shadows on the snow-clad hills that surrounded us being very effective. Ever since the extreme cold set in we have had the most glorious weather imaginable, and this day was no exception. We came across a small band of Wakhis on their way to Sariq-qol camped in a snug corner near the river. Unlike the Kirghiz or Sariq-qolis, they had no news to tell us, true or false, about the much dreaded Russians. They were a rough-looking lot, but very civil, coming out to meet us with the usual salutation of "Salaam Aleikum," and shaking hands with us all round. I have been much struck with the difference between the Mussulmans in this part of Central Asia and those of Turkey, Syria, and Arabia, the fanaticism of the latter precluding the possibility of their ever addressing such a salutation to a Christian, whereas here it is invariably the custom.

As the sun was getting low I trotted on ahead of the caravan to look for a sheltered spot for the camp, and finding one about two miles below the Wakhis bivouac, we halted there for the night.

CHAPTER XXXII.

Bozai Gombaz—Chakmaktin or Oikul Lake—Source of the Oxus —The Andemin Pass—Meaning of the word "Pamir"—Snowstorm on the Great Pamir—The Victoria Lake—The Pamir River—The Hauz Darwan—Sassigh Kul—Bulun Kul—The Fish—Surmatash—Russian Encampment—Scene of the Fight with the Afghans—Blood-stained Evidences of the Engagement—The Graves of the Afghans who were killed—Camp on the Alichur.

November 1st.—Continued riding down the right bank of the Ak-Bilis, the country being much the same as that we passed through yesterday afternoon, with this exception, that the valley was widening perceptibly as we proceeded further west, and the plateau over which we were travelling rose from 250 feet to an elevation of 800 feet above the river bed. As the valley got broader so did the bed of the river, which being composed of a blue slaty sort of shingle, had all the appearance of an immensely broad, winding asphalted roadway. Its extreme breadth might have been in some places 800 yards, but it did not average more than 500 yards in width, and all this to contain what at this season of the year could only be termed a miserable little trickle of a stream, barely twelve feet wide.

It doubtless presents a very different appearance in

the summer season, when the sun melts the snows from off the many mountains that border it, of whose northern drainage it has the entire monopoly. What struck me as being a peculiar feature in the configuration of this valley, was the absence of any sort of break in the line of mountains that sloped gently down to the table-land on the north side of the river, there being neither nullah nor stream of any importance in the whole length of the range, whereas, on the south side, the hills were not only very much higher, but were broken here and there by large broad valleys opening almost at right angles to the river, each of which had a little river of its own, whose waters flowed into the Ak-Bilis.

About nine miles from our camping-ground of last night, and eighteen or twenty miles west of the source of the river, was the Kara Dara valley, a large nullah, at the extreme southern end of which was the pass which gives its name to both valley and river. The valley lies due north and south and is from three to four miles in depth.

Nearly opposite to the mouth of this Kara Dara, and on a high promontory jutting out into the bed of the Ak-Bilis, stands the old but now obsolete burying-ground of Kara Duba, over which last resting-place of former Wakhi chiefs a large and very dark-plumaged eagle was soaring.

About two miles further west another nullah, called Iri Jilga, or the crooked valley, opened out to the river;

and a little further on was the Pito Jilga, or "no road valley," and well it appeared to deserve its name, for on looking into its snowy depths the eye could rest on nothing but a precipitous phalanx of impassable glaciers, over whose glistening surfaces the foot of man is never likely to tread. On the north bank of the river, opposite this wild and inhospitable looking glen, we suddenly came in sight of what we wrongly judged to be two men standing on the summit of a rocky eminence that rose up like an island on the plateau. These turned out to be the two pillars of Molar-Tash, but whether they were originally boundary stones, or for what purpose they were placed there, Abdul Kerim, our Kirghiz guide, was in ignorance.

From this spot the view looking down the valley of the river was very lovely, with the distant hills of the Little Pamir range half shrouded by the golden haze from the setting sun, whilst in the foreground lay the little river, winding through its grey-blue bed, flanked on each side by sloping banks of green, yellow and russet grasses, the entire picture being framed by the dark and rugged outline of rocks that form the western extremity of the two mountain ranges running parallel with the river. It being too late to attempt to reach Bozai Gombaz, we camped on a gentle grassy slope overlooking the river.

November 2nd.—Last night we held a council in my

tent as to how we were to make the Victoria lake from Bozai Gombaz, as Abdul Kerim says he never heard of any one going there straight across the mountains of the Little Pamir range. Captain Younghusband's explorations in this region of the Pamirs were nipped in the bud by reason of his having been taken prisoner by the Russians at Bozai Gombaz last year, and he was consequently unable to proceed any further in the direction of the Victoria lake.

In April 1874 part of the Forsyth Expedition under Captain (now Colonel) Trotter, after exploring the Aksu river to its source, and then following the course of the Wakhan river to its junction with the Oxus at Kila Wamar, returned through the Great Pamir, taking the route from Kila Panjah to the Victoria lake and so on back to Neza Tash and Tashkurgan. So his expedition did not go the way we want to go, viz. from Bozai Gombaz to the lake across the Little Pamir range. The only other Englishman who could have crossed those mountains is Mr. Littledale, but not having the account of his journey through the Pamirs with me, I cannot tell for certain.*

We had the greatest difficulty with Abdul Kerim, who did not seem to know the lake by any name at all.

* On the 13th of February, 1893, whilst on my way back from Central Asia, I had the good fortune to meet Mr. and Mrs. Littledale at Trebizonde, they were on their way to China, *via* Russian Central Asia, and he informed me he had been over those mountains crossing the Andemin pass.

I produced the map attached to the report of Forsyth's Mission to Yarkand and followed Captain Trotter's route, but in that map the lake is simply called Victoria lake, and it was highly improbable that any Kirghiz or Wakhi would know it by that name. Then I tried Captain Younghusband's map, on which it is called Gaz-kul, or Victoria lake. Yes! Abdul Kerim had heard of Gaz-kul, in fact he had been there himself, and on asking him to describe whereabouts it lay, he pointed north-east from the camp, Victoria lake lying in a north-westerly direction. At last we discovered that what he called Gaz-Kul was the lake marked in Captain Younghusband's map as Chakmak and in Captain Trotter's, Oikul. This latter officer mentions in his report that the lake Oikul or (Chakmak) has several names, viz. the Little Pamir lake, Barkut Yassin, Chalap and Gaz-kul, or Goose lake, in Turki, Oikul. "I made repeated inquiries," he writes, "as to its proper name, and found that the Wakhis generally call it the Kul-i-Pamir Khurd, or Lake of Little Pamir, while the Sarikolis and Yarkandis give it the name of Oikul."

Then I tried another of my maps, entitled "Turkestan and the Countries between the British and the Russian Dominions in Asia," on which the lake was marked Victoria lake, or Serikul, and finally I had recourse to a small edition of Keith Johnston's 'Central Asia,' where it was marked Pamir lake, or Victoria lake. Poor Abdul Kerim was fairly bewildered at all these different names, as well he might be, and we finally settled to work our way across the mountains by compass.

So we first rode to Bozai Gombaz, or Bozai Kavr, as it is also sometimes called, Gombaz meaning an arch or dome, and Kavr, a grave. The place is usually known by the former name. Bozai was a celebrated Kirghiz chief of bygone days, who was buried at this spot, some say murdered here as well, and his tomb consists of four low walls with a conical-shaped dome for a roof. Shukkur Ali, who was with Younghusband when he was arrested by the Russians, described the whole occurrence most graphically, which I need not enlarge upon here, as it is a thing of the past; but as the "incident" gave rise to a most serious and lengthy diplomatic correspondence between the British and the Russian Governments, Bozai Gombaz may now be fairly reckoned within the category of "historical spots."

Just under the bank, on which stands the tomb, flows the little river Sarhat, which has its source about three miles south-west of the lake, which Captain Trotter calls Oikul, Captain Younghusband, Chakmak, and the Russians, Chakmaktin. This Sarhat river,* although rising in a different water-shed to the Aksu (which rises in the lake), also flows into the Oxus at Kila Wamar. The water-shed between the two is so low

* The Russian officers at Murghabi told me that they claim the Sarhat as the true source of the Oxus, whereas Colonel Grombchevsky told me they claimed the head waters of the Ak-Bilis as the true source.

as to be scarcely perceptible. The Sarhat running south-west joins the Ak-Bilis just below Bozai Gombaz, their joint waters again flow into the Wakhan and taking a bend almost at a right angle, at a place called Ishkashem, flow north into the Oxus at Kila Wamar, after receiving the waters of the Pamir river, which flows out of the Victoria lake, and those of the Ghund river which flows out of the Yashil Kul; the waters of the Mas, Kargoshi, Shakh, Charpan, and Taguz-bulak also help to swell this branch of the Oxus. The waters of the Aksu rising, as I said before, only three miles from the source of the Sarhat, flow exactly in the opposite direction, viz. north-east to Aktash then north and north-west until they join the Murghab, receiving the waters of the Chistoba, Pa-ik, Khanjola, Koshagal, Shar-bulak, Ak-Baital, Kara-bulak, and several other minor streams on the way; then, under the name of Murghab, they flow due west, past Serez and another Tashkurgan,* taking the name of the Bortang river at the latter place till they also join the Oxus at Kila Wamar. There is scarcely ten miles difference between the length of their respective courses, the distance following the course of the Aksu from its source to its junction with the Oxus being about 250 miles, and from the source of the Sarhat to the Oxus 240 miles.

* The frequent recurrence of names on the Pamirs is most confusing. There are two Tashkurgans, two Serez, two Neza Tash passes, three Gaz-Kul lakes.

The real source of the Oxus I believe to be undoubtedly identical with that of the Aksu, and some writers assert that the names are also identical, Oxus being a corruption of the word Aksu, or White-water.

On leaving Bozai Gombaz we headed north-east for the Chakmaktin, or Oikul lake, intending to skirt the spurs of the Little Pamir range until we found a practicable pass over into the Great Pamir plateau. To go straight ahead north-west was out of the question, owing to the great amount of snow on that portion of the range. We looked at the first two nullahs that opened out on our left, called respectively Ourtabel Jilga and Ak-Jilga, and could see at once there was no means of getting over the deep snow on the tops of the hills that blocked the northern ends of both of them.

Between these two valleys, that debouched on to the plain, was a small lake called Chokar-Kul, which was frozen over from shore to shore.

By this time the evening was beginning to close in, and a heavy snow-storm passing over the hills threatened to include us, but we luckily only came in for the edge of it, and finding ourselves on the north shore of the Oikul, or Chakmaktin lake, in a fairly sheltered position, we called a halt for the night. The lake which was only partially frozen was covered with wild-fowl, both geese and ducks. It appeared to us to be very shallow, as there were many banks and islands dotted about its surface. Its length, I should say, was under five miles and position north-east and south-west. We took the altitude of the lake and made it 14,230 feet above the sea level. Captain Younghusband made it 13,850 feet, and Captain Trotter, 13,200 feet. So much for Aneroid Barometers!

November 3rd.—This morning before marching we went down to the lake, and Roche took a photograph of the source of the mighty Oxus. All along the shore were myriads of little springs, some bubbling, the weaker ones frozen. When we got on to the plain of the Little Pamir, which was covered with snow, except in those places which were encrusted with saltpetre and soda, we were joined by a large yellow dog, who attached himself at once to the caravan and seemed delighted to find himself amongst human beings. He was dreadfully thin and must evidently have been lost by some Kirghiz or Wakhis. We adopted him at once and gave him the name of Pamir.

After riding along the foot of the hills for about twelve miles, we suddenly opened a nullah that seemed to promise well, as it appeared much more open at the northern end than the former ones. So we turned off sharp at a right angle and headed due north, and followed it up for about five miles, until we came to a large basin in the hills, where five nullahs met. By this time it was snowing hard, and a pitiless north-east wind came tearing down upon us, so we had no choice but to stop where we were for the night. It was not a very inviting spot, as there was no sort of shelter, and any wind that chanced to blow must of necessity have caught us, with those five nullahs debouching on to this basin.

Just before pitching our tents, a large spotted wolf crossed our camping-ground, but was off before we could get a shot at him.

November 4th.—This morning the thermometer showed a minimum temperature of 8° below zero, inside the cover of Roche's tent, so we had had a pretty cold night of it. All our ink has frozen and burst its stone bottles, although shut up in a bullock-trunk, but one iron inkstand still remains to us. It is not of much use, as the ink is always hard frozen, but it gets periodically thawed by the cook, who puts the whole thing into a pot of boiling water, just before we want to use it, but as it freezes again as soon as one begins to write, we have had to give it up and have recourse to pencils. As to attempt painting in water-colours, it is absolutely out of the question, as the paints freeze quicker than the water.

We made a startling discovery this morning, and one that fills us with consternation! Amongst the stores we received the other day, tea, our one and only beverage, was conspicuous by its absence, also tobacco, although we had ordered both; of the former, we have but one pound left, of the latter, half a pound, and it will be a month before we can get either, at Kashgar. We have a little cocoa left, but when that and the tea are finished, we shall be reduced to drinking hot water, as we brought nothing to drink in the shape of wine or spirits, except two bottles of brandy, which remain in the medicine chest in case of illness. To drink cold water will be impossible, as there is no such thing to be had, nearly every stream and spring being hard frozen. We have to thaw small blocks of ice every day to get water to make our tea, or else we use snow.

We have discovered an excellent method of economising our small store of tea, and that is to boil it. We have an iron teapot, which we use as a kettle, in it we put only two teaspoonfuls of tea, and filling up with hot water, put it on the fire till it boils, and we make that one brew last for the twenty-four hours. We find two teaspoonfuls when boiled, equal to about six, when made in the usual way. What is left in the teapot at night is always a solid hard frozen mass of leaves and ice in the morning, but, when reboiled, serves us for breakfast, without adding any fresh tea. Thus do we intend to make our one pound last all the way to Kashgar. Would that we could make our tobacco last as long!

I shot a hare yesterday, which is a welcome change, for we have now been eating mutton twice a day for 179 consecutive days.

In consequence of the snow-storm last night, and subsequent hard frost in the early hours of the morning, our tents were not in a condition to be packed, being an inch deep in hard frozen snow.

They had to be well beaten with sticks, to break the ice off them, it was therefore some time before we could make a start.

However, by 9.30 A.M. we got off, and within an hour from leaving the camp, found ourselves on the top of a decided water-shed, which we conjectured must be the one marked in Younghusband's map as the Andemin pass. It was nothing of a pass to cross, the approach to it being a gradual rise, and very easy ground for the caravan; we made the altitude 15,150 feet.

The hills in this part of the Little Pamir range are much lower than those in the Taghdumbash Pamir, and, although covered with snow at this season, are almost entirely free from glaciers. We passed a good many skulls and horns of the *Ovis Poli* lying about, and on the north side of the pass we saw in the plain below us a small herd of them feeding. A stream rises on the north side of this water-shed and runs west-north-west; we followed it down until we came to its junction with another, called the Chistoba, which here flows due north for a little way, and then taking a bend almost due east, joins the Aksu river at a place called Istigh.

After following the course of this Chistoba river for about two miles and a half, in a north-west direction, Abdul Kerim suddenly changed his course to north and by east. I objected strongly to this direction being taken, as I maintained we should have taken an almost westerly course at this particular spot, in order to make Victoria lake, which by my calculations could not be much more than twenty miles off, and that in a westerly direction. But a heavy snow-storm coming on put an end to the discussion, as it was so thick we could not see the lie of the country at all. We had now entered the Great Pamir, if a Pamir signifies a large, broad open plain, between two ranges of mountains, but no one seems to know what a Pamir is, or the derivation or meaning of the term. I have asked Turkestanis, Sariq-qolis, Kirghiz and Wakhis, but not one of them could tell me what the word means, or to what language it belongs. When overtaken by the snow-storm, we were riding some way ahead of our caravan, accompanied by Ahmed Din and the two shikaris, and as there was no sort of track to guide them, I began to fear we might lose the caravan on this great plain. So I posted Ahmed Din and the two shikaris at long intervals, but within shouting distance of each other (Roche and Abdul Kerim being also halted ahead of Ahmed Din), and having thus formed a chain of communication in case the snow-storm increased in volume, I rode back to look for the caravan, keeping, however, within hailing distance of the man next to me. Just at this moment there came a break in the storm, and a ray of light, which illumined the plain, showed me the caravan looming in the distance and taking a westerly course, whilst we were going north and a little east. It was lucky for us that the snow-storm broke where it did, or else we should to a certainty have lost the caravan on that great plain, especially as nightfall was approaching. We were, however, soon re-united, and settled in future, never to lose sight of each other again, as it might lead to very serious consequences in an uninhabited country like the Pamirs, where there are no roads or landmarks, nothing but an almost unexplored waste. We camped soon after this on the Chistoba river. and at 8.15 P.M. saw the eclipse of the moon very distinctly, with the thermometer at 11° below zero.

November 5th.—Another bitter night followed by a much colder morning. Roche and I have at last come to the conclusion that the winter is not exactly the season to choose either for purposes of sport or of exploration on the Pamirs. When we started this morning, there was a bitter blast of north wind blowing, with the thermometer at zero.

We rode up a stream running east-north-east, crossing a water-shed which we named the Fox pass, from the fact that we saw a fox running over the summit. This was about six miles from the Chistoba, and with our horses' heads pointing west-south-west, we came again upon the Great Pamir. It was a very clear day, and we could see the country round for miles. I therefore pointed out to Abdul Kerim that I was quite correct yesterday, when I advocated a change of course for the caravan to due west, at the junction of the Andemin and Chistoba rivers, for in following his course, we had lost half a day, and come a good fifteen miles out of our way, having described two sides of a triangle. He of course made the snow-storm his excuse, but the real fact of the matter was, he had never been here before and consequently does not know his way any better than we do.

So, along this Great Pamir—an immense broad plateau deep in snow, with a range of snow-clad hills on each side—did we ride, nearly frozen, with a pitiless wind blowing right into our faces, and with the thermometer at a lower temperature than it has yet been in the daytime. The only living thing we saw in this magnificent arena of desolation was another silver fox, to whom we gave chase, "Pamir" running him to earth.

Just at sunset, we came to one of the small lakes, the western extremity of which lies about three and a half miles from the east end of the Victoria lake. This sheet of water, or rather of ice, was about two and a half miles in length, as far as we could judge, but it was very difficult to distinguish lake from shore, both being deep in snow, and the banks very low and flat. Here I saw the common sea-gull, which surprised me not a little, considering the immense distance we were from the sea.

It was dark long before we could find a convenient spot to camp, and when at length we did, we had to pitch the tents in the snow, and as for running water for the horses to drink, there was not such a thing to be found, so the poor animals had to put up with snow. For ourselves it did not matter, as we now invariably have to use ice, carrying blocks with us on the ponies, for the cook's purposes.

November 6th.—Our camping-ground of last night turned out to be three miles from Victoria lake. It was a very cold spot; in fact, this Great Pamir is by far the coldest place we have yet met with in this region of snow and ice. The thermometer this morning was at 11° below zero inside the outer fly of the tent, so before leaving the camp we took off our stirrup-irons, which made a material difference to the warmth of our feet when riding.

We spent the morning in taking observations, photographs, and sketches of the Victoria lake and its surroundings. The lake, which in summer is about twelve miles in length, is at this season of the year only nine to ten miles long. It is nearly twice the breadth at this east end that it is at its western extremity. It lies as nearly as possible due east and west in its length. The mountains on each side meet its shores, with long and very gentle slopes, making the entire breadth of lake and plain from five to seven miles. The altitude of the lake we made to be 14,230 feet above the level of the sea, or 100 feet higher than the Chakmaktin, or Oikul lake. Both photography and sketching were accomplished under somewhat trying circumstances, as we had to work without gloves in most intense cold.

We rode afterwards along the north shore of the lake, heading towards its western extremity, a most uninteresting ride, on a dead level of frozen mud and sand, the banks of the lake being very low and fringed with bent-grass. At one spot we came across a sandy bay, much resembling the sea-shore, inasmuch as it was covered with shells of various sorts, and bore the impress of the footprints of thousands of wild fowl, web-footed and otherwise.

Here Roche and Ahmed Din made an ineffectual attempt to walk across the ice, to reach an island about 200 yards from the shore; but as the ice gave forth some ominous cracks, they returned. The myriads of wild fowl that evidently frequent this lake in the summer months have evidently migrated to a more congenial climate, as we never saw a living thing all day, either bird or beast, with the exception of one beautiful white eagle. As the whole of the early morning had been taken up with photography and scientific observations, it was but a short march we were able to do to-day, and we camped on a grassy spot by the side of the lake, but in a very exposed position.

November 7th.—Ten degrees below zero again this morning. The extreme cold is beginning to tell on some of our men, three of whom have gone sick. Consequently we did but a short march again, starting very late, as we were obliged to wait until the sun was well up in the heavens, to infuse a little warmth into our frozen systems.

We continued riding along the lake side on the same monotonous flat until we reached its western extremity, where the Pamir river flows out of the lake. This river runs north-west for a little way, then west, and finally south-west, forming a junction with the Ab-i-Panj river at Langar Kisht, and then flowing north into the Oxus.

Captain Wood, R.N., who first discovered the Victoria lake fifty years ago, gave it then as the source of the Oxus.*

We followed this river for about eight miles, and then camped for the night on its banks.

November 8th.—The temperature is rising slightly as we are descending to a lower altitude, the thermometer last

* Captain Wood was probably unaware of the existence of the Aksu river.

night only registering 40° of frost, or 8° below zero. On waking this morning we made the startling discovery that twenty-three of our horses were missing, so we despatched half-a-dozen men on horseback to scour the neighbouring country in search of them. It was late before they returned, having luckily found them all, consequently we made but a short march again, camping by the side of the river.

November 9th.—The hopes in which we had indulged —that as we were getting to a lower elevation above the sea-level, so the temperature would rise—have been rudely shattered, as we had 43° of frost again last night, or 11° below zero.

Although this temperature is nothing really abnormal, still we all seem to feel the cold very severely. Personally I feel it ten times worse than I ever have before, either in the Arctic regions of Spitzbergen, or in Canada, where I have frequently marched with troops, with the thermometer ranging from 30° to 40° below zero. It is just the difference between an absolutely still cold and a cold with wind like we have here. In the early morning the men cannot use their hands either to strike the tents or load the ponies, so we have to wait until the sun imparts to us a little of its grateful warmth, in consequence of which we never march before 9.30 or 10 o'clock A.M., and as the intense cold sets in between half-past four and five o'clock in the evening we always halt, if possible, at that hour for the same reason. The result, therefore, is that our marches now are very short ones.

This morning we left the Pamir river, and rode up a very stony nullah, due north for eight miles, until we reached a kind of circular plateau, 14,900 feet, in the midst of wild, stony hills without any sign of vegetation. In front of us was a high ridge of 15,250 feet, which we took to be the water-shed, but on reaching the summit saw that we were mistaken, and that about three-quarters of a mile further on was a narrow pass, between two high rocky hills, on reaching the highest point of which we halted to take a few observations and photographs. From the top of this pass we had a very fine view of the mountains of the Alichur Pamir and the country lying to the northwards. This pass is not marked on any map, nor has it got a name, and I believe I am correct in stating that we are the first Europeans who have explored it—always excepting bands of Cossacks and Kirghiz, who have at one time or another over-run the whole Pamir region.

On the very summit of this pass was a small but perfectly square frozen lake, and its peculiarity lay not only in its rectangular shape, but in its close resemblance to an artificial reservoir, its sloping sides having been paved by nature with flat stones fitting closely together, giving it all the appearance of a piece of first-class solid mason-work.

We took the altitude at 15,720 feet, and named the pass the "Hauz Dawan," or Reservoir pass, Hauz being the Persian as well as Kirghiz for an artificial tank or reservoir, and I have marked it as such on the new map I am preparing of the Pamirs.* The descent was rapid and abrupt, being 2200 feet to the foot of the pass, and a perfect chaos of rocks and stones, which had been dislodged by the ice, met the eye at every turn. At last we reached the valley, which was fairly broad, and with a deep sandy bottom, the hills bordering the eastern side being precipitous rocks and cliffs of yellow gravel and sandstone, while those on the western side sloped gently down to the valley, being broken here and there by broad flat glens, with patches of coarse yellow grass growing at long intervals on their sandy slopes. There was no water to be seen at this season of the year, on either side of the water-shed, although I noticed a dry rocky stream-bed on the north side. On the south side, as we made the ascent of the pass, there was not even the semblance of a watercourse, dry or otherwise. We had to ride some way down the valley before we found water—or rather ice—and this was from a little frozen rivulet in a gully between the hills on the east side.

As this was the Prince of Wales's birthday, we drank His Royal Highness's health, and although the toast

* The Russians at Murghabi also adopted the name Hauz Darwan, and marked the name and locality of the pass on the new map that was in course of preparation when we were in their camp.

was drunk in tea, I venture to think that the wishes for his health and prosperity were quite as hearty as if the toast had been drunk in the best of champagne.

November 10*th*.—After another 10° below zero night, we started down the valley, riding for about two miles, until it widened out into a regular broad sandy desert. We then altered our course from north to north-west, when after another two miles we suddenly found ourselves on the brink of an enormous basin of sand and gravel, which lay 300 feet below us and contained four lakes, the nearest to us being about three miles long and one mile broad. This was the Sassigh Kul, or Stinking lake. It was not frozen over, and the hills were reflected in its deep blue waters as if in a mirror. Its shores were white with saltpetre for a long way inland, and many parts of this sandy basin were encrusted with the same saline deposit. Descending into this basin, we took the altitude of the lake and found it was 13,400 feet, then riding in almost a southwesterly direction we left another smaller lake called Tuz Kul, or Salt lake, on our right hand, and found two more in front of us, the first of which was about two miles from the Sassigh Kul. This lake was called Kargoshi Kul, or the Hares lake, and to the south of it the Kargoshi pass, which is a very low water-shed, was visible.

We might have crossed the mountains by this pass,

but we should have had to go a long way west down the Pamir river first, and our object was to find a new pass between the Karghoshi and the Besh-Gombaz.

All around now, as far as the eye could reach, was a vast desert of hill and plain; the former gravel and rock, the latter sand and stones, and not a blade of green visible. In fact, since leaving the Victoria lake, the whole aspect of the country has undergone a complete change, as all vegetation has ceased to exist, and no snow is visible except on the tops of the far-away hills. Leaving the Kargoshi Kul on our left, we headed west with a little north in it, and mounted a low, sandy ridge and came upon the fourth lake, which was almost dry. This lake was 150 feet higher than the other three. Traversing its frozen bottom of sand and mud, imprinted with thousands of footmarks of wild-fowl, we ascended again, entering a narrow defile, half blocked by a recent landslip of huge rocks and boulders. The summit of this defile, which can hardly be promoted to the rank of a *bonâ-fide* pass, was 14,100 feet, and although it does not appear on any of our maps, it is in the summer undoubtedly a water-shed of some pretensions, and as such I have marked it as a pass on my new map. As there were a great number of *Ovis Poli* heads and skulls lying about, we named it the Guljia Darwan, after the aforementioned animals.

From this pass we had a good view of the hills of Shighnan and Roshan, and, taking a northerly course, descended into a vast plain destitute of grass, and arrived at the southern end of the lake called Bulun Kul, where we pitched our camp near two mud edifices, the site of an abandoned Afghan outpost. Altitude of Bulun Kul, 13,200 feet.

November 11*th*.—This morning, whilst we were at breakfast, some of the men who had been down to the lake for water returned with marvellous tales of the amount of fish they had seen swimming about in the small patch of open water near the shore, and still more astounding were the accounts they gave of their size and dimensions. According to Rassoul, one that he saw he described as being "quite as big as Ahmed Din," the other men were more modest in the estimate they made of their proportions, saying they were not more than four feet long. So we hastened down to look at these piscatory monsters, and certainly saw plenty of fish moving, but nothing much larger than an ordinary sized trout.

As we had neither the time nor the inclination to go a-fishing with the thermometer below zero, we left these fish to share the unfrozen portion of the lake with a lot of small divers, which did not look worth powder and shot. After waiting for the caravan to come up with us, we all pushed on in the direction of Surmatash, skirting the shore of the Bulun Kul until we came to the river which runs out of it into the larger lake of

Yashil Kul. In none of the maps are these lakes made to have any connection with each other, whereas they are in point of fact almost one, the little river which connects the two not being more than half a mile in length, and with very little fall.

The Bulun Kul is about half a mile across from north to south, and its form can best be described as kidney-shaped. It lies south-east of the larger lake of Yashil Kul, and it is at its north-east corner that the river flows out and connects them. After arriving at the junction of the two lakes, we rode along the east shore of the Yashil Kul in a northerly direction for about a mile when we had to leave the shore and ascend on to a large, flat table-land, after crossing half a mile of which we found ourselves on a promontory jutting out into the lake and facing due west.

The lake, the altitude of which we made 13,120 feet above the sea level, is the next largest in the Pamirs to the Karakul, being about sixteen miles in length, but its breadth varies a good deal, owing to the indentations of the shore. It lies as nearly as possible due east and west in its length, and is a very much finer sheet of water than the Victoria lake in every way. The snow-clad mountains surrounding it are much more lofty and much grander in their rugged outlines, and rise almost precipitously from the water's edge, unlike the long, low undulating grassy spurs that slope so gently down to meet the waters of the Victoria lake.

The Ghund river, which rises at the west end of the Yashil Kul, flows into the Ab-i-Panj river, and is thus one of the many tributaries of the Oxus. The name of the promontory aforementioned is Surma-Tash, meaning the Black-stone.

What the history of the Black-stone is, Abdul Kerim was unable to tell us; all he knew about it was that "the Russians had put it upon a horse and carried it away." That some legend is attached to it, there is no doubt, but these Kirghiz are strangely ignorant regarding anything in the shape of folk-lore belonging to their own country.*

We were now on the spot where the Russians camped the night after the much to be regretted "affair" of the 22nd June, 1892, with the Afghans (a few months previous to our being there), and the marks of their encampment were perfectly fresh; broken bottles, cigarette ends, etc., all lying about, amongst other camp *débris*. But the most gruesome sight was that of the Afghan great-coats, which had been taken off the bodies

* I saw the stone afterwards in the Museum at Tashkend, and got the translation of the writing of it, which is as follows: "On the crest of the mountains 10,000 men laid down their arms. The Chinese soldiers, coming from the four points of the compass, then went unopposed as if penetrating into an uninhabited country. The two ringleaders, therefore, seeing that further efforts would be in vain, took to flight, whilst our soldiers in the pursuit resembled tigers and leopards, chasing hares and foxes. Before our soldiers had advanced far after them, and when they were still crossing the mountains, our men were in good fighting order."

of the dead by the Kirghiz, and had been left lying on the ground as useless, between the scene of the engagement and the camp. These coats were all blood-stained, and on examining them closely, we could guess pretty clearly how each of their ill-fated owners had met his death. One of them had no less than seven bayonet thrusts through it; another had the left arm almost severed through at the elbow; and the collar of a third being saturated with blood, led one to suppose that its wearer had been well-nigh decapitated.

What was the exact numerical strength of the Russian force was not known to Abdul Kerim, although his father-in-law was amongst those few Kirghiz who had an encampment on the spot, and witnessed the fight.* To attempt to throw any light upon the subject from the tales told me by the Kirghiz, is impossible, knowing their inability to make any computation of numbers, whether it be men, miles, or hours. I prefer, therefore, to wait until I arrive within the Russian lines at Murghabi, where I am pretty sure to hear the Russian side of the question, and until I have heard both sides, it would be most unfair to give any opinion on the matter. What we do know is that the Afghans were

* I was told afterwards by the Russian officers that Colonel Yonoff had only an escort of nineteen Cossacks, and the officers who were present with him were Colonel Grombtchevsky, Captains Sheremetieff (son of the Governor-General of the Caucasus), Gourko (son of the famous General), and a young officer of Cossacks who commanded the escort.

well-nigh wiped out, as out of fifteen, fourteen were killed, including their captain, Golam Haidar Khan. The dead Afghans were all buried in one grave, on a little hillock on the battle-field, just above the river.

Their grave is an oblong, composed of four low walls, built of rough stones. The bodies are not interred, but are buried (if one may use the expression) above ground, all huddled up together inside these four walls, and covered with two large *numdahs* (felt cloths), over which some mud had been thrown, and a few large stones placed on the top of it, to prevent any beast of prey from scraping up the corpses.

IN MEMORIAM.

At morn the river of the Alichur
Lay glinting in the beams of summer's sun;
A gentle streamlet winding through the plain,
Whose waters mingling with the placid lake
Of Yashil Kul—along their western course,
To join the mighty Oxus—flow.

At noon
When scarce a breath was stirring in the air,
Below the heights of Surmatash—a camp
Of Afghan soldiers on the river bank
Is all astir—for on the distant plain,
Half hidden in a cloud of dust—they see
The glitter from the lances of the foe.

At eventide the sunset's golden rays
Fall slanting on a bloody battle-field,
Where Cossack horsemen in the chill embrace

Of Death, and swarthy Afghan swordsmen from
The plains of Cabul, side by side lay stretched—
A heap of corpses neath the summer sky.
*   *   *   *   *

Ye widows, in your humble homes upon
The Cabul plains, and by the steppes of Don,
Ask those in power if a frontier's price
Is worth of human life such sacrifice?

The Russians carried off their dead, but the number lost is only known to themselves.

After taking a series of photographs of this now historical spot, we turned our horses' heads eastwards, and rode for about three miles over a wide plateau of gravel and sand, with the Alichur river flowing down below in a ravine on our left.

At a spot where the river takes a bend to the south, we descended into a sheltered hollow, and camped on its left bank for the night.

CHAPTER XXXIII.

The Alichur Pamir — Nezatash Pass — A Cossack Patrol take Rassoul for an Afghan—Murghab River — Russian Officers ride out from the Fort to meet us—Entry into Russian Fort—Hospitality of Russian Officers—Russian Pamir Frontier— Death of one of our Horses from the Cold—Departure for Rang-Kul—Reception by Russian Officers at the Fort—The Garrison drinking the health of Queen Victoria and the Emperor of Russia—Extreme Cold—Departure for Chinese Frontier—The Ak-Bhirdi Pass—Arrival at Bulun Kul.

November 16th (Russian Camp Murghabi).—I have been unable to write up my diary for the last few days, owing to my right hand being bound up in glycerine bandages, as my fingers were covered with large cracks, from the effects of the intense cold.

A pair of nice warm gloves would command a large price in our camp just now! I never felt anything to equal the cold on these Pamirs; the slightest breath of wind seems to pierce one to the very bones, and as we never have it less than eight to ten degrees below zero every night and morning, and always with more or less wind, it has become well-nigh unbearable.

On Friday night we had some snow, but not enough

to put the temperature up, or to stop our marching the next morning.

We have been riding along the banks of the Alichur river, which flows through an immense plain, without a particle of shelter from the icy winds that sweep down from the mountains. Freezing blasts that make one long to be at home in a comfortable house, with a nice warm fire at which to toast one's toes from out a large cosy arm-chair. An Indian tent is not exactly conducive to warmth in a climate such as the Pamirs boast of in winter.

On Sunday we camped at Bash-Gombaz, and we pushed on the next day, passing Chadir Tash,* which is a large rock in the centre of the Alichur plain or Pamir, resembling the Sphinx of the Pyramids of Egypt, without its head, and arrived at the Nez-a-Tash pass at such an unseasonable hour, that we were forced to camp there, whether we liked it or not. It is not a very high pass, being only 14,500 feet, but the icy winds we had to put up with amply compensated for its lack of altitude, and made it much colder than many of the highest we have had to cross. We were within twenty-five miles of the Russian head-quarter camp, and the next morning a Russian patrol paid us a visit.

The first we heard of them, was from Rassoul II, one of our pony-men, who had wandered some way from

* The Afghans claim Chadir Tash as their Eastern Boundary on the Pamirs

camp, in search of a stray horse. One of the Russian patrol rode up to him, and, addressing him in Persian, asked him what business he had there, to which the man, who understood a little of that language, replied saying he belonged to our caravan.

The Russian soldier then said, "I don't believe you; I can see that you are an Afghan, therefore I shall shoot you." By this time the patrol had come near our camp, and the Russians, seeing the man really belonged to us, left him alone, after frightening him out of the little stock of wits that he possessed. Hearing from our men that we were bound for Colonel Yonoff's head-quarters at Murghabi, they rode off in that direction, presumably to give the Russians notice of our approach.

We rode that day as far as a place called Kara-su, a short march through a country absolutely destitute of any sort of vegetation, there being not a blade of grass to be seen. The hills, which were very high and rocky, and not lacking in grandeur, were of a peculiar reddish hue, utterly unlike any other part of the Pamirs through which we had hitherto ridden. Our route lay through broad open valleys of sand and gravel, almost level; there was no snow on the ground, and not a drop of water, so we had to carry blocks of ice with us again.

This morning I sent off Ahmed Din, Ramzan, and Chota Islam, to the Russian camp, with a letter to Colonel Yonoff, a translation of which I gave to Ahmed Din. The letter apprised him of our approach.

As we had no Russian Passports,* or the faintest conception of where the Russian frontier was supposed to commence or end, I instructed Ahmed Din to find out whether they would allow us to cross the river, and if not, where we could pitch our camp. Whilst our envoys were galloping off to the Russian head-quarters, we followed slowly in their wake.

We halted for our midday meal on the banks of the Murghab river, and being in full view of the extensive plateau which stretches away east for miles, we soon perceived a horseman in a cloud of dust, coming our way at full gallop. This proved to be Ramzan, who was the bearer of a letter scrawled in pencil by Ahmed Din, in which he wrote that he had been very well received by the Russian officers, three in number. Colonel Yonoff was absent, and Captain Savonoff, who was in temporary command, had opened my letter, and had begged him (Ahmed Din) to say that he and Captains Reiffeld and Brjesickis would ride out to meet us.

About an hour after we had received this communication, we perceived six horsemen on the plain, riding our way. This proved to be the three officers above named, each accompanied by a Cossack orderly. Roche and I

* I found out later on that instructions had been sent from St. Petersburg, by order of the Emperor, that I was to be allowed free passage all through Russian Central Asia, without any passport, and this had been communicated to the different governors of each province in Russian Turkestan, the Pamirs, etc.

RUSSIAN FORT AT MURGHABI.

[To face p. 175, Vol. II.

immediately mounted our horses and rode towards them. Our meeting was most cordial, and we mutually introduced ourselves. Not one of them spoke a word of French or German, but luckily I was able to speak enough Russian to make myself understood, and to act as interpreter for Roche. We all rode back together to their head-quarters at Murghabi, and on the way, one of the officers asked me if I knew Captain Younghusband. I replied that I knew him very well. "Ah," he said, "I know him also; I had the pleasure of being present when we *met* him at Bozai Gombaz;" and "I," added another, "had the pleasure of *meeting* Davison at Yashil Kul." *

When we arrived at the Fort at Murghabi, these officers would not hear of our pitching our tents, on the contrary, they led us to two large akois (yourts, as they call them here), which they had prepared for us, in which were brick fireplaces, and after having supplied us with everything we could possibly require, they informed us that dinner would be ready whenever we wished for it. While I was unpacking my things and preparing for that unheard of luxury on the Pamirs in winter, namely a tub, Brjesickis came in and asked if there was any dish we preferred in particular, as they were at that particular moment rich in vegetables, a caravan of pro-

* This was in 1891, when Younghusband was arrested by the Russians, and Davison was also made a prisoner and sent to Osh and Marghilan.

visions having just lately arrived from Marghilan. My reply was that, as long as he did not give us mutton, we did not care what we ate, but as we had been eating that meat daily, and generally twice a day, for 191 consecutive days, we were getting rather tired of it. As to vegetables, we had not tasted such a thing since Yarkand in August. So after a good clean up, Roche and I went to the akoi, where they had their mess, which was Brjesickis' bedroom.

Everything in the akoi, although most comfortable, was of the simplest description. His cupboards were old wine boxes, lashed up to the walls, and at dinner, Roche and I were given the seats of honour, which were afforded by his bed, the other three sitting on a stool and two empty boxes turned bottom upmost. The dinner, which was prepared by a Kirghiz cook, was most excellent, and we simply revelled in potatoes and cabbage. The civility and cordiality that these officers evinced towards us was very marked, and their hospitality is the same as I have always met with before when travelling within the dominions of the Czar.

They seem to anticipate our slightest wants, and, with a delicacy one rarely meets with, they find out from Ahmed Din if we are short of anything, and then we find it lying on our tables. For instance, when they found out we were short of tobacco, lo, and behold! a box of tobacco, a book of cigarette papers, and a cherry-stick holder, with amber mouthpiece, lies on each of our tables when we re-enter our akois to go to bed. I occupied two akois, one leading into the other, and they told me they were Colonel Yonoff's late quarters.

November 18*th*.—Our most hospitable hosts will not hear of our going away, so we are still here, and have made great friends. Last night at dinner, Captain Savonoff proposed the Queen's health, and I responded by proposing the Czar's.

* * * * * *

Roche went out fishing to-day with Reiffeld, and I remained in camp with the other two officers and had a look round.

The position the Russians have taken up at Murghabi is in the bend of the river, not far from its junction with the Aksu and Ak-Baital.

The so-called fort is situated on the river bank, about thirty feet above the water, and is surrounded by a wall five feet high, with a ditch seven feet deep, and a glacis. The circumference of this entrenched position is about 500 yards; inside the walls are located 180 men, all living in akois with outer mud walls and having brick stoves, so that they are most warm and comfortable, and there is not such a thing as a tent in the whole place. The officers' quarters I have already described. The inside of the fort is a mass of stores of all sorts, piled up and lined out with military regularity.

The Cossacks' horses remain outside feeding on the plain in the daytime with the sheep and cattle, but at night are brought into the fort and tied up in lines.

In the evening the two fishermen returned half-frozen, having, nevertheless, captured seven fish, which they had got in a net. We had them the next night for dinner, and very good they were, but to what tribe they belonged we could not tell. Having no scales and being covered with small irregular spots on their smooth skins, we were rather inclined to think they were some species of Asiatic trout.

As this was our last evening in their camp, we sat up with our most kind and agreeable hosts until nearly midnight, which for the Pamirs is a most frightfully dissipated hour, and during this time we initiated them into the mysteries of the game of Ludo, with which they were so taken, that I promised them that whenever I arrived in any town, sufficiently civilised to provide such an article as a Ludo-board, I would send them one to Murghabi, to assist them in whiling away the hours of the long winter evenings.

We spent the morning in making preparations for the march to Rang-Kul, Brjesickis insisting on accompanying us as far as the Ak-Bhirdi pass, the Chinese Frontier. After breakfast, Roche took some photographs of the officers and men, and after a hearty breakfast, we bade adieu to Reiffeld, who had to remain in camp, being on duty, and, accompanied by Savonoff and Brjesickis, we rode out of the fort, followed by an escort of Cossacks. It was not a good day to see the country, as the hills were enveloped in mist, and a slight snow shower was falling. Our route lay over a vast plain of sand and gravel for three or four miles, when we suddenly turned off short to the left, heading due north, and rode up the valley of the Ak-Baital river. The river bed was perfectly dry, and the mountains bordering the valley were of the most curious formation and colour. Having absolutely no knowledge of geology, I will not attempt to describe the different strata which exist in these hills, but will confine myself to stating that they are decidedly sulphureous, as we saw immense beds of sulphur on their slopes as we rode along. I should also think these hills were full of copper, by their colour. We caught up our caravan, which had started early, about four P.M. and we found we were another pony short, as one died last night from the cold. My only wonder is that more have not succumbed to the cold since we came on to the Pamirs. However, we cannot complain, as this is only the third we have lost since leaving Leh, in June last, and by the time we reach Kashgar these hardy little animals will have carried our loads 1700 miles, and over some of the highest passes in the world.

Captain Savonoff, having seen us so far safe on our road, left us to return to his head-quarters at Murghabi, and it was with genuine regret, I hope on both sides, but on ours at any rate, that we bade each other adieu; we felt indeed that it was impossible for us to express to him our gratitude for all the many kindnesses he showed us during our sojourn in his hospitable camp. So having consigned us to the care of Brjesickis, he turned his horse's head towards the Murghab river, and rode off back to the fort accompanied by his escort. At sunset we halted and camped for the night in the Ak-Baital valley, where there were a few Kirghiz encamped. These were the Kirghiz whose original habitation was at Surmatash, but after the fight the Russians removed them to the Ak-Baital valley.

November 20th.—Before marching this morning, Roche took a very picturesque group of Kirghiz children, standing and sitting outside their parents' akoi, one pretty little girl of six carrying her baby brother on her back.

Just as we were leaving, I overheard a very amusing conversation between Roche and Brjesickis. The former was asking the latter in French the meaning of the name Ak-Baital. Brjesickis, whose knowledge of the French language was limited to about half-a-dozen words, one of which was "Cheval," understood the query and was thinking for a long time how to translate the Kirghiz word "Baital," which means a *mare*, into French. He knew that Roche understood the meaning of the prefix Ak (white); but how to convey the translation of the word "Baital"? At length a bright thought struck him, and he exclaimed triumphantly, "'Baital'—*Madame Cheval!!*"

* * * * * *

It was much warmer than usual when we started the two caravans off—as Brjesickis has his own caravan of camels—and, following them about an hour later, rode in a northerly direction until we came to the spurs of a small line of hills that jutted out on the plain, when we suddenly changed our course to east, riding round the base of this little range.

Here the weather, climate, atmosphere, and everything else, seemed to undergo a radical change for the worse, the whole plain being covered with snow, and the temperature falling down to the neighbourhood of zero, so intense was the cold. The wind rose, blowing right into our faces, chilling us to the very bones; it was what Brjesickis called a gentle breeze for the Rang-Kul Pamir, so we were enabled to form some sort of idea of what a gale would be, coming over that enormous plain, sweeping down from off the ice-clad mountains that border it.

After a most monotonous ride of three hours, we came upon a long narrow sheet of frozen water called the Chor-Kul, on the southern shore of which is a very peculiar rock, where we dismounted to make a closer examination. It is called the Lamp Rock, as it has a small cave near its summit which is pierced right through, the light showing through a little aperture, giving it all the appearance of a lighted lamp.

On the north side of the lake was a nullah, opening out on to the plain, at the northern end of which is the Kiaz pass, one of the passes used by the Russians to get to Karakul, but not their principal one, which is the Ak-Baital pass, and over which, as Brjesickis informed us, a Russian caravan of 700 horses, with provisions and stores, besides some mountain guns, were expected to arrive in a day or two at head-quarters on the Murghab. On reaching the end of the Chor-Kul, which is from six to seven miles in length, we came upon the Rang-Kul, a smaller lake, with only about the distance of a quarter of a mile between it and the Chor-Kul, and no stream or any water connection between the two. They are two distinctly separate lakes, and not one large one, as represented in nearly all the maps.

It was now beginning to get dark and there was no moon in prospect, but the snow lit up our path for us, and after riding on for another two hours at a good sharp trot, we met a Cossack orderly, who had been sent out to show us the way to the Fort of Rang-Kul. We soon came in sight of some camp fires, and, after a long cold ride of twenty-eight miles, were very glad to find ourselves inside the precincts of the fort, where we were received most hospitably by Lieutenants Repin and Timovaieff. They had prepared an akoi for us, and very warm and comfortable it was, after crossing that excessively airy plain. Our caravans did not arrive till past ten P.M., so we laid ourselves down upon the floor and slept till they made their appearance, thus was it nigh on midnight before we had finished dinner.

Neither of these two officers spoke any other language but their own, so I had to act as interpreter for Roche again, but he and Brjesickis got on capitally together without any assistance from me.

November 21st.—This morning, being a glorious sunny one, we were enabled to get a splendid view of the country surrounding the fort, which is a smaller edition of the one at Murghabi, being only about 300 yards round the walls and ditch, and containing but thirteen akois, built up with mud walls and provided with brick stoves, which are much more necessary here than at Murghabi, there being a difference of twenty degrees in the temperature in favour of the latter, as regards warmth. This fort is situated at an elevation of 13,525 feet above the sea-level, on the edge of an immense, perfectly level plain, which stretches north, east and west for miles. The whole plain was white with snow, as far as the eye could reach, although many of the surrounding hills were only capped with it. This peculiar feature in the landscape, the Russian officers told me, was attributable to the ever-prevailing winds, which, catching up the snow on the hills, drifts it all on to the plain. In the forenoon we were taken round the men's quarters, the bakery, etc., and very warm and well-cared for the soldiers seemed. The garrison consists of about twenty infantry soldiers, under Lieutenant Timovaieff, and twenty-five Cossacks, under Lieutenant Ripen.

In the afternoon of the second day we spent with our kind hosts, the weather gave us some sort of idea of how cold it could be, as the thermometer fell to 10° below zero in the afternoon; so we had recourse to various expedients to keep ourselves warm. First we had Russian peasant dances, then Cossack dances, all to the music of an accordion. Then I tried to teach the officers the figures of a reel, and hummed the music of the old Highland tune of "Gamhaidhe sinn an rathad mór" to the Cossack who played the accordion, and which he picked up very quickly, and, such as it was, we danced it to keep ourselves warm, lots of the Cossacks joining in. That was the first Highland reel ever danced on the Pamirs, I should say, to Russian music. As we were going to march the next day, a rather imposing and certainly interesting ceremony followed, namely, the drinking of the healths of Queen Victoria and the Emperor of Russia, the whole garrison saluting and cheering at the toasts. We were genuinely sorry to leave our hospitable quarters and the cheery good fellows who had been our hosts, but December was fast approaching, and I had a long way to go yet before attempting to make the passage of the Tian-shan mountains, which are not easily crossed in the depth of winter; Major Roche had to return to Kashmir before the passes were closed from Gilgit, and Kashgar also had to be reached first. So the next morning we started, and marched to the foot of the Ak-Bhirdi mountain, crossing the Kok-Beless pass 15,270 feet *en route*, from the top of which we had a splendid view of the great Mustagh-Atta, whose rugged ice-bound peaks rose some 25,800 feet into the wintry sky.

By this time the sun was getting low, and the temperature lower, so we all adjourned to the mess akoi, where we spent our last evening with these most hospitable and cheery officers. Nothing would satisfy Brjesickis, but that they also should be instructed in the game of Ludo, to which he has taken such a fancy, so we had out the board, and played game after game when dinner was over. As we intended to leave early in the morning for the foot of the Ak-Bhirdi pass, we all separated for the night at the modest hour of 9.30 P.M. with mutual expressions of friendship and goodwill.

November 22nd.—This morning we found the registering pin of the thermometer stuck fast in the glass tube at 20° below zero; it had evidently been trying to go lower, but the instrument only marks −20, or 52 degrees of frost, and it was with great difficulty we got it right again with the magnet. We dare not put it out again at night, even under the fly of

Roche's tent, where it was last night, and where the temperature must have been somewhere close upon 30° below zero.

Our ponies played us the same trick as they had on the Pamir river, thirty of them having run off in the night, so it was very late before the men we sent to search for them brought them back into the fort; it was consequently midday when we parted from our kind hosts, and accompanied still by Brjesickis rode off in the direction of the Chinese Frontier.

Our route lay over the great plain which for want of a better name we may fairly call the Rang-kul Pamir. On it we passed three different lots of sheep, camels, and yaks. The first herd we saw, numbered not less than a thousand sheep, a few yaks, and a goodly array of camels; the other two lots were not so numerous, but still very large. They were all the property of the Kirghiz, and Brjesickis told us that each lot belonged to single individuals. The Kirghiz in this part of the Pamirs are the richest of all, those on the Taghdumbash Pamir being the worst off of any, while the Aktash people, of whom I have made mention before, are mostly well-to-do.

After leaving the plain we rode up a gentle mountain slope until we reached the summit of a little pass called the Kok-Beless, 15,270 feet, and, descending about 300 feet, rode up the valley of the South Ak-Bhirdi river (now quite dry), a narrow glen full of long grass.

From the top of the Kok-Beless pass we had a glorious view both ways. Looking back we saw, as in a panorama, range upon range of snow-clad mountains extending back almost as far as Shighnan and Roshan, and in front of us the snowy line of hills we have to cross to reach Chinese territory again. Over the tops of the aforesaid range towered the great Mustagh Atta, whose rugged, ice-bound peaks rose nearly 26,000 feet into the grey wintry sky. About sunset we reached the foot of the Ak-Bhirdi mountain, where Brjesickis, with commendable forethought, had sent on a small akoi for our joint use, feeling sure that, after our experience of last night's cold, the temperature at this altitude would be of such a nature as to preclude the possibility of our sleeping under canvas with any degree of comfort.

November 23rd.—We passed a very uncomfortable night in the little akoi. None of us were able to sleep, owing to the difficulty of respiration. Brjesickis attributed it to the high altitude; but I explained to him that, after having been for several weeks in Western Tibet, at altitudes ranging from 17,000 to 19,000 feet, it was not likely we should be affected by an elevation of only 15,000 feet. The fact was the cold was so intense that we were obliged to seal up the akoi hermetically and to have a large fire of dried camel's dung burning all night, in the centre of it, between our three beds; and as there was no possible exit for the smoke, which had an excessively pungent smell, I think that and the intense cold combined would sufficiently account for our discomfort. What the cold was outside I cannot say, as, after the experience of the night before, we determined not to put the thermometer out any more, for fear of its bursting, so we hung it up inside the akoi within six feet of the fire, and in the morning we found it had been down to 2°, or 30° of frost, which was tolerably severe, considering the akoi was a very small one, and that three men, none of them particularly diminutive, had been sleeping in it, with a big fire burning all night on the floor in the centre, added to which the whole thing was shut up, with the exception of one hole in the roof about as big as a man's head to let the smoke out.

It took some time to prepare any breakfast, everything being hard-frozen. Our blankets were white with small icicles, where our breath had touched them, and my beard was the same. The men suffered a good deal, saying it was a much colder night than the previous one, when the thermometer was between 20° and 30° below zero.

About 9 A.M. everything was ready for a start, and with the big mountain of Ak-Bhirdi looming in the morning mist in front of us, we rode off, after taking an affectionate leave of Brjesickis. He did not attempt to embrace us, as one of the Rang-kul officers did to Roche, who, not knowing the Russian custom, was most indignant at being kissed by a great hairy man, while I, who did know their ways, submitted like a lamb.

The so-called Ak-Bhirdi pass is, in reality, no pass at all, according to the usual accepted term, it being the actual summit of a mountain, 17,330 feet above the sea-level, over which our caravan had to make its way zigzagging up its precipitous side, finding their own way as best they could.

Abdul Kerim had never been over it, and Brjesickis told us we were the first Europeans to cross it, as none even of the ubiquitous Russian officers on the Pamirs had ever been that way.*

Excessively precipitous and rocky, and covered with snow, it was with the greatest difficulty that we got our ponies up to the top, the last 1500 feet being as bad as the Grim pass in China, that we crossed last July.

The day was a bitterly cold one, the thermometer standing at 3° when we left the camp, so it may be imagined what it was up on the summit of the mountain, 2000 feet higher, with a biting north-east wind blowing the loose snow with pitiless force into our faces. However, we managed to get over the top without any bad accidents, although several of the ponies tumbled about and lost their loads, and had to be reloaded; but we found the descent on the Chinese side ever so much

* I have since writing this been informed that Captain Bower crossed this mountain.

more precipitous, and with nearly three times the amount of snow.

To ride down was absolutely impossible, and to attempt walking in our Tcharooks (long felt boots) was nearly so, yet we had to do it, and lead our horses as well! The frozen snow and sheets of ice we met with, were so slippery—for us shod, as before-mentioned, against frost-bite—that in one very steep place I had to crawl down on my hands and knees backwards, so as to face my horse, and thus be able to avoid his slipping down on the top of me, for, when I had my back turned to him, he more than once came slithering down on all fours, knocking me over. I had one very bad fall into a big hole—luckily for me full of snow—and as my horse came down on the top of me into the same hole, I was stunned for a minute or two; but I soon came to, and got all right, and my horse and I scrambled out and went on again. We were all on different parts of the mountain, each picking his own way down, entirely independent of each other, and being in a blizzard of wind and snow were mostly out of sight of each other all the time. Still, we all managed to meet together in safety, at different intervals at the bottom of the hill, after three hours of this hard work, and by the aneroid we found the descent was only 2930 feet. I certainly thought it was more. The ascent only took two hours and thirty minutes, but the descent a little over three hours, and so by the time the baggage-animals got down to the bottom of the hill they had had quite enough—so had we; five hours and a half of climbing up and crawling down such a mountain as the Ak-Bhirdi, in deep snow, we considered quite sufficient for one day, we, therefore, on reaching the valley, settled to stop at a small Kirghiz encampment that we found there. These hospitable people as usual gave up one of their akois to us, as every one of our men was far too "done up" to start tent-pitching.

On entering our akoi, we found five ewes, with their newly-born lambs, in full possession. We did not mind them, but made a good fire, and then had something to eat, of which we stood in much need, having tasted no food since the very early morning, and it was close on sunset.

Several of the Kirghiz came into our akoi to have a look at us, and squatting round the fire warmed their hands, and, utterly regardless of our presence, chatted away to each other, which rather bored us, as we were both very tired, and I had a splitting headache in consequence of my fall. However, as night came on, they dropped out one by one, and at length left us in peace. After visiting Ahmed Din, who was down with fever, and administering to him twenty grains of quinine —he asked for it strong—we turned in to try and snatch a few hours rest in the very draughtiest "bedroom" man ever lay down to sleep in; with a high wind outside blowing over the snow, the thermometer at 20°

below zero, and very queer companions, in the shape of live stock, all around us, the discomfort of the whole being augmented by an atmosphere of smoke from the usual pungent fuel, so thick that we could barely see each other across the akoi.

November 24th.—We passed not only a very cold, but most restless night owing to the noises made by the various animals inside and outside our akoi.

Dogs barked, snarled, and fought with "Pamir," most of the night, he being a stranger in the land. The camels that were tied up close to us gave forth that weird shriek peculiar to their species: yaks grunted after the manner of their kind, grunts that would have filled the soul of many a pig with envy; and the sheep and lambs inside and outside our akoi made night hideous with their plaintive alternate maternal and filial bleatings. It made us hate mutton more than ever!

There was one particular feeble bleat that was most annoying, and kept waking us up just as we were getting off to sleep, and it was not until this morning that we were able to discover from whence it came. Roche made the discovery, when searching about the akoi in the early morning for the usual sack in which the Kirghiz invariably keep a stock of dried camel's dung for fuel, as he wanted to make up the fire. Seeing a sack hanging up on the side of the akoi, close to the head of his bed, he was about to take it down when, lo and behold! the sack not only *moved*, but *bleated*, and there, inside it, was a newly-born lamb, and the little wretch had been crying for its mother all night.

Leaving a small donation with the Kirghiz family, who had not only given us up their akoi, but had also presented us with a couple of sheep, we rode down the North Ak-Bhirdi river for about sixteen miles, in a north-easterly direction, descending 3220 feet till we reached Bulun-kul, where there are two Chinese forts—one at each end of the lake. We were much astonished at there being no Chinese outpost at the foot of the Ak-Bhirdi pass, near the Russian Pamir Frontier, and we had our passports ready all day, thinking they would be asked for.

It was a glorious day, and the scenery was very fine, the great ice-clad mountain of Bulun-kul, nearly 20,000 feet high, making a grand centre to the landscape all day long. On arriving at the south-west end of the smaller lake of Bulun-kul, we were met by Mahammad Isa, who had been sent by Mr. Macartney from Kashgar, with the flour for the men and the grain for the horses, that we had ordered in October last; he also brought a bundle of newspapers, and one letter for me from Hunza from Younghusband. The newspapers were all September ones, and we devoured them with great interest, being much amused with some of the articles and paragraphs relating to the Pamirs, the inaccuracies of the statements of the various correspondents regarding the movements of the Russians, Chinese, and Afghans, being only equalled by the lamentable ignorance they displayed of the geography of the country. I cannot refrain from quoting a few of them, just to show the specimen of trash which is served up for the public to digest, not only in England, but in Europe as well, many of these paragraphs being copied into English newspapers from Foreign sources, from Berlin, Vienna, etc.

Newspaper Paragraphs.	*Comments on Same.*
"Colonel Yonoff reports that from several towns in the Pamirs, the natives have come to him to pay their respects and to ask to be united to Russia."	There is not a single *house* nor *village*, much less a *town*, on the Pamirs.
"I hear from a well-informed quarter the Czar received the news of Colonel Yonoff's *two* actions with the Afghans with great indignation. Accordingly the Colonel had orders not to extend his explorations beyond the Karakoram, which is regarded in Asia as the frontier between the Pamirs and India."	Colonel Yonoff had but *one* fight with the Afghans, in which there were less than forty men engaged on *both* sides inclusive. The Karakoram is 300 miles as the crow flies from the *nearest* point of the Pamirs, and 500 miles from Colonel Yonoff, who would have to cross the Hindukush and go through 250 miles of British territory to reach it. The Karakoram is the Frontier between China and Ladak (Kashmir), not between the Pamirs and India.
"The Chinese had arrived in	There has not been a *single*

Newspaper Paragraphs.	*Comments on Same.*
the Pamir territory 500 strong and fixed their head-quarters at Shindi. "Hearing the Russians were advancing on the Chinese Pamirs, they advanced eastward 250 strong, against the Ak-Baital pass, to await the Russians there. The Russians, however, had chosen Tash-korum pass, and when they advanced against the village of Aktash, the party of Chinese from Shindi opposed them. A fight ensued, which ended in the signal defeat of the Chinese. Meanwhile, the Russians fortified their position at Aktash."	*Chinese soldier* on the Pamirs during the year 1892, except a non-commissioned officer and eleven men at Aktash. Shindi is a village in Sariq-qol, about seventy miles east from the Pamirs, with a high mountain range between them, and if the Chinese *had* advanced *eastward*, they would have gone towards Yarkand, and in the contrary direction to the Pamirs. The Ak-Baital pass is 120 miles from Shindi, with *six* mountain ranges between them. The Tash-korum pass is 130 miles from Aktash, with *eight* mountain ranges between them. No fight has *ever* taken place between the Russians and Chinese on the Pamirs. Aktash is not a village. It is a large white rock on the plain of the Ak-su river, and there is not a house within many a hundred mile of it. So far from fortifying themselves at Aktash, the Russians pulled the Chinese fort down and then retired unassailed on Murghabi.
"Pamir is a country infested by wild tribes."	*The Pamirs* are not infested by wild tribes, but are the summer grazings of a quiet, peaceable, nomad tribe called Kirghiz.

Newspaper Paragraphs.	*Comments on Same.*
"It is apparently admitted by both parties that 1000 Afghans were encamped in the neighbourhood of Somatash, and that the	The Afghans had eighteen men at Surmatash.
Russian commander advanced with an equal number of men."	The Russian commander had an escort of nineteen Cossacks. 37 men instead of 2000!!

These specimens are gleaned from only a few newspapers published in September. What other rubbish may have been written during the rest of the summer and autumn months, Heaven only knows!!

CHAPTER XXXIV.

Detention at Bulun-kul by Chinese Officer, on suspicion of being Russian Spies—Two Chinese Forts—The Gez Defile—Chaos—Curious Bridges—Ingenious Corn-crushers—A City of the Dead—We take the Law into our own Hands—Arrival at Kashgar—Curious Death of another Horse—An Apology demanded from the Chinese Government for our treatment at Bulun-kul—Destruction of our "Fort" on the Taghdumbash Pamir by order of the Chinese Government.

November 25th.—This morning as we had a longish march before us through the beginning of the Gez defile, which has been described by Mahammad Isa as a fearful place to get the caravan over, we repacked our passports in our despatch boxes, as we had been two days already in Chinese territory, and no one appeared to want to see them, and sent Ramzan on early with the baggage and tents. We having slept in a Kirghiz akoi, proceeded to have our breakfast comfortably, meaning to overtake the caravan in the afternoon.

After breakfast, and just as Roche was about to take some photographs, a Chinese officer from the fort, escorted by fifteen mounted soldiers, armed with swords and carbines, and accompanied by two standard-bearers, with their colours furled, rode up to our akoi, and entering it in the most unceremonious, not to say impertinent manner, sat himself down on the floor, and, in a hectoring tone, asked who we were, and where we had come from. We gave the desired information through an interpreter, upon which he demanded to see our passports. We explained that we had had our passports ready to show all yesterday and all this morning, but as no one asked to see them, and we were in ignorance of there being a fort here, we had packed them up again, and they were with the caravan, which by this time must be a long way ahead.

He then said he must send after the caravan, and bring it back, as he wished to see our passports. We told him that was impossible, but proposed that he should ride with us, and catch it up, when our passports would be forthcoming. No, he insisted on the caravan being brought back, as he said that we were Russian officers in disguise.

We told him we were English officers, and that our passports had been examined by the Amban at Yarkand, and that we knew orders had been sent to the Frontier that we should be treated with the utmost deference by all Chinese officials.

He replied he knew we were Russian spies, and that if we did not send for our passports at once, to prove that we were not, he would send us back again to the Pamirs under escort. We protested again, but the more we did so, the more insolent did he become, until at last he placed his soldiers round the akoi, and said we did not *move* from that spot until he saw our passports.

Seeing that we could do nothing with this man, and that we were virtually his prisoners until we could show our passes, we sent Abdullah on horseback to gallop after the caravan, and bring back our despatch boxes which contained them.

Meanwhile I told this Chinaman, whose name I discovered to be Ching-Wang, that when I got to Kashgar I would report him to the Taotai for insolence, and that, although we recognised the fact that he was quite within his rights to insist on seeing our passports, yet there were two ways of asking for—or even insisting on—the production of them.

After a long wait, during which time I had the satisfaction of summarily ejecting this Chinese officer from our akoi, Abdullah returned with our despatch boxes, and we gave Ahmed Din our two passports to show Ching-Wang, but after he was in possession of them, the ignorant brute could not read a word of his own language. So he still detained us, while he spelt out every word of the two passes, assisted by a second Chinaman, who confided to Mahammad Isa afterwards, that Ching-Wang "was a very bad man."

After having satisfied himself that we were not Russian spies, he rode off without a word of apology, preceded by his two standard-bearers and accompanied by his ill-dressed, and worse mounted rabble of fifteen horsemen. Finding ourselves at liberty again, we also mounted our horses and rode off, passing the Chinese fort at the south end of the Bulun-kul, where Ching-Wang resided, breathing soft curses as we passed, and vowing vengeance against him when we arrived at Kashgar. For eight miles we skirted the shores of the lake, which was frozen over in places, but was evidently very shallow, more like a big marsh than a *bonâ fide* lake. In summer I should think it must be more of a gigantic quicksand, with thousands of small springs bubbling up all over its area of several thousand acres. It was the most peculiar combination of sand and water I ever saw. In some lights it looked like a large sheet of frozen water, and in others like a sandy basin. Heavy gusts of wind came from off the mountains, which lay to the north-west of it, which were composed of loose shifting sand, driving the same on to the ice, and covering large portions of it two or three inches deep. Then again a counter-blast would come and, carrying off the sand, would reveal a huge sheet of ice. In some maps no lake is marked at all, in others a large sheet of water, ten miles long, is depicted, while in the Russian survey it is given as a huge marsh.

There is no question about the Ak-Bhirdi river flowing into it, neither can one doubt the evidence of one's own sense of sight, when one sees a large and rapid river, like the Gez, flowing out of the north-east corner of it; but what the middle of it is like, whether dry land, quicksand, or water, no one seems to know. I examined it from the shore with a powerful telescope, but the colour of the water and the sand were so identical, I could not tell which was which. At the north-east corner of it is the second Chinese fort, called Taghdumbash Fort, which is commanded by Jung-darin who, however, was absent at the time we visited the fort, which contains thirty-five soldiers, twenty of them being Kirghiz and fifteen real Chinamen.

This fort is very picturesquely situated on a promontory jutting out into the lake, where the River Gez flows out of it, and is overlooked by some high mountains, with three very distinct *mers de glace* half-way up their snowy sides. Leaving the fort on our right we entered the defile before alluded to, and found Mahammad Isa had not exaggerated its difficulties.

The river runs through a deep narrow gorge on the left of the track, which is impossible to see in some places, and which leads over miles of stones and rocks, all heaped up in wild confusion, intersected every now and again by deep gorges, and almost impassable dry watercourses; all the result of recent landslips. Owing to our detention at the first fort by Ching-Wang, we were late in entering this defile, and as the caravan was a long way ahead, we had to ride on in the dark to overtake it. There was not a square-yard of ground where a camp could have been pitched, except on the spot where the caravan had halted, and it was late at night when we came suddenly upon the camp-fires; and very glad we were to see them, as making our way over that awful ground in the dark was excessively dangerous.

November 26th.—It blew a gale all last night, and what between the force of the wind, and the ponies trying to obtain a little shelter under the lee of our tents, and, loosening the ropes as they stumbled over them in their endeavours to protect themselves against the gale, we got very little sleep, expecting every minute to hear the ridge-poles snap, and then to have the whole thing carried away. The wind this morning was still very high, and we did not look forward with much pleasure to the continuance of our march through this awful defile especially as Mahammad Isa informed us that the part, through which we had to pass to-day, was infinitely worse than what we had to encounter yesterday, as there were two or three very dangerous places, where big stones came falling down from the rocks above, without any warning.

As if in confirmation of the above statement, a loud rattle was suddenly heard to the right of the camp, and looking up I saw a mass of stones and rocks, dislodged probably by the ice, come tumbling down the steep incline of the hill, just as we were preparing to mount our horses. The track in many places was entirely obliterated by these frequent landslips, and we found it very difficult to pick our way over these big boulders and rocks. We passed a good many dead horses, grim evidences of the dangers of this weird defile, which is certainly one of the worst places we have yet had to contend with, owing to its length. We have had worse places to negotiate before, but in a few hours it was generally all over. This defile, on the contrary, is a three days' job, and it seems to get worse as we go on, instead of better. At one period of the day we were riding high up above the river, on the edge of the precipice overhanging it, on a rough track not three feet wide, with the chance of loose stones and rocks coming down on to the top of us from the hill above on our right. Then every now and again, violent gusts of wind would come unexpectedly round corners, and almost take the ponies off their feet. In fact, at one place, a fearful squall knocked Roche's pony down on to its side, while he was on its back, but luckily this did not occur in a dangerous spot. Twice Mahammad Isa, who was leading, turned round and shouted to us to whip up our steeds, and ride as fast as we could when passing a dangerous place, on account of falling stones.

Thus did we struggle on all day with this gale off the snow mountains, freezing our very bones, until at last we came to a dead lock, in the shape of a mountain torrent, which crossed our track and which was dammed up below by huge blocks of ice, thus forming, a large pool of water, much too deep for the ponies to cross.

To remain there for the night was absolutely impossible, and to return back quite out of the question, so we determined to try and let the imprisoned water off. With that object, we set men to cut away the ice with axes below the pool, which was neither an easy nor a very safe job, as there was a high waterfall just below the ice-dam, and there was just the chance of the ice on which the men were standing, being loosened by the cutting of the channel, and being carried away over the fall. Our men worked away with a will, and after about an hour's hard work cut a good-sized channel through the ice-dam, and released the dammed-up water.

That of course had the desired effect of making a ford, and when we thought enough water had run off, and it was sufficiently shallow, we sent one man across on an unladen pony to try it. The water being over the pony's shoulders, we waited a little longer for it to fall still more, and eventually got the whole caravan of fifty-five ponies across without wetting a stitch of the baggage. This of course delayed us a good deal, so when we reached the first eligible spot, we halted for the night, having taken all day, from early morn. till sunset, to accomplish eleven miles. Close to our camp was a small and beautifully clear stream of running water, without a vestige of ice near it. This puzzled us not a little in this land of ice and snow, until Mahammad Isa invited us to put our hands into the water, when we found it quite warm, there being a large hot spring about 400 yards above us. The temperature of the water was 87° Fahrenheit.

THE HOT SPRINGS: GEZ DEFILE, CHINESE TARTARY.

November 27th.—We are still in the Gez defile, which, widening as it does at this point, is opening out fresh beauties to our appreciative eyes at every turn, as we proceed further eastward. The scenery has become so savagely grand that we have ceased to grumble at the roughness of the country over which we have to travel. We crossed the river three times to-day over wooden bridges, that appeared to us at a distance as if they were suspended in mid-air, so high were they constructed above the half-frozen torrent that swirled and tumbled over blocks of ice beneath them. Rickety contrivances they were too, when we came up to them and had to cross them, simply two rough beams stretched across from rock to rock, with a few small logs thrown across them, most insecurely lashed together with withies. Each pony had to be led across singly and with great care, as the bridges were not only very narrow, but would not carry the weight of two laden ponies at the same time, and if a gust of high wind struck them at right angles, they swayed to and fro in a most alarming way. It thus took over half an hour for the caravan to cross each one of these flimsy structures.

After riding for about three hours down the right bank of the river, we came to a huge precipitous rock that seemed to block our progress, but rounding its base we suddenly came upon a scene which will live for ever in my memory. To attempt to describe faithfully its chaotic magnificence would be almost as impossible as to reproduce it on paper or canvas with pencil or brush.

Had I the artistic talent of a Gustave Doré, and the fervid imagination of a Jules Verne combined, and were I then to set myself to paint an imaginative picture of Chaos—represented by the wildest of wild rugged mountains, whose snowy peaks towered over rocks of the most fantastic shape and outline, with huge festoons of icicles hanging from their jagged edges; ice-bound torrents and frozen waterfalls, huge boulders thrown about in the wildest confusion and with no sparing hand; the whole having been subjected to some mighty convulsion of Nature—even *then*, I doubt whether the result would convey any idea of the savage splendour of this scene of chaos.

After gazing for some time with awe and wonder upon this enthralling picture whose weird beauty was enhanced by a diaphanous haze which floated gently over it all, we rode on in the direction of the distant blue hills that marked the termination of our day's journey.

November 28th.—The place where we camped last night was called "The Jungle." There were certainly a few stunted trees and a fair amount of brushwood about the place, and the trees were real wild ones, not artificially planted, like the willows, poplars and fruit-trees of the plains of Chinese Turkestan, so we appreciated them accordingly, not having set eyes upon natural wood, except a few poplars, since May 14th at

Baltal, in the Western Himalayas, 198 days ago. The place, besides being honoured with the appellation of "The Jungle," was also called a Chinese Frontier Outpost, which accounted for the tattered flag that floated proudly over one of three roofless mud huts. Up one side of this banner was emblazoned the name of the Chinese Emperor, and in the centre was a dragon, whose body was represented as being in such painful contortions from his efforts to catch hold of his tail with his teeth, that it made him look like a large, fried whiting.

On the reverse side of the flag were the words in Chinese characters, "Frontier Outpost." It was a curious place for a frontier outpost, considering the Frontier the Chinese claim is about 150 miles from this spot, and even the Frontier the Russians have been kind enough to leave them is four to five marches off. We also looked in vain for the soldiers who guard this important post, but they were like its roof—wanting. The people, however, were inclined to be hospitable, for they offered Roche and me the two remaining mud huts to occupy for the night, but when we went in to inspect them we settled to pitch our tents, after seeing their dilapidated roofs, and I could not help humming to myself the old French nursery ditty of—

> "Caderousel a trois maisons
> Qui n'ont ni poutres ni chevrons;
> C'est pour loger les hirondelles," etc.

For here were the *trois maisons*, all decidedly in want of both *poutres* and *chevrons*, and I have no doubt but that the *hirondelles* lodge there also in the proper season.

Here we also met a Kirghiz from Tashkurgan, and on asking him if he brought any news from the Taghdumbash Pamir, he told us that as soon as the Chinese were quite sure we had left our old camping-ground at Kukturuk for good, they had set to work to demolish our "Fort," viz. the bake and wash-house.

To-day we marched down the side of the Gez river, leaving the defile behind us, and emerged on to what appeared to be a level stony plain, with high red sandstone cliffs on each side, but it proved to be all part of the Gez river channel, which in summer—if it fills up its bed—must be about half the size of the Mississippi. Like most of the rivers in this country, it has, at this season of the year, six to eight small channels, which we were perpetually crossing all day, five of them by means of bridges, the rest we were able to ford. These bridges were most primitive and somewhat alarming. Two beams were stretched across the river, almost touching the water; across these beams, brushwood was laid, with no spars underneath to support it, and on the top of the brushwood, which was not tied together, were placed large round stones. How the whole thing managed to hold together was to us a marvel. If in crossing one of these extraordinary structures, a pony happened to put his feet between the stones, they naturally went through the brushwood into the water. But that did not seem to matter in the least; the caravan got safely over all the five bridges without any casualties. We have long since ceased to be astonished at anything we see in this country, and take everything as a matter of course; nothing short of a volcano, or a first-class earthquake, could disturb our equanimity now!

About sunset we reached a spot near some mines where resided a Chinaman in charge of a gang of workmen, who combine the manufacture of charcoal with the output of copper. Here we halted for the night, and a very cold spot it was. We were in hopes that as we descended to a lower altitude, we should come in for some warmer weather, but the thermometer still clings lovingly to zero, notwithstanding the fact that we have got out of the five-figure altitudes, and are now at an elevation of only 6500 feet above the sea-level.

The next morning we rode over what appeared to be a large stony plain, but owing to the misty state of the atmosphere, it was impossible to judge of what the country was like. We halted at a little village called Tash-balyk, where we were able to procure milk, eggs and fowls. We had not set eyes upon either of the two latter delicacies for four months, neither had we seen a real house since we left Yarkand, so we began to feel quite civilised. On the way from Tash-balyk to Borah-khitay we passed some of the natives of a small village, crushing corn with a very simple, but none the less ingenious machine worked by water-power.

The corn is placed in two holes, on an elevated platform, made of a sort of rude concrete. Two large wooden arms, with hammer-shaped tops, are fixed in grooves, balanced in such a way, that when set free their own weight would cause them to fall down; the hammer-ends fitting exactly into the holes containing the corn. A wooden cylinder with large teeth, something like the barrel of a musical box, revolves by water-power, and every time one of these teeth comes round to a certain spot, it strikes the end of one of these wooden hammers, giving it a cant upwards, the tooth, having thus done its work, revolves, and the wooden-armed hammer falls by its own weight into the hole, crushes the corn, is struck again at the next revolution of the cylinder, which brings it up again out of the corn-hole to a vertical position, when it drops again, and so on. There were two of these wooden-arms working alternately, and Roche photographed them. After having minutely examined this primitive contrivance, we continued our journey, riding through villages and over cultivated fields, until we reached Borah-khitay.

We rode up to a house in the village, that we understood to be a rest-house, meaning to ask for shelter for the night; but the inmates fled at our approach, and locking themselves in, absolutely refused to parley with us. Finding neither blandishments nor threats were of any avail, we sent men into the village to fetch some one to come and reason with them, but not a man was visible; every soul in the place had pursued the same tactics, for some reason or another, and had disappeared.

It resembled a city of the dead; except that we knew it was really full of living idiots. Eventually we forced our way into the house, and finding an empty mud-walled room, took instant possession of it. An excellent stable was also appropriated by us for our ponies, which had the effect of bringing on to the roof of the house an elderly female, who by her frantic gestures was evidently not in the best of tempers. She refused to supply us either with forage for the horses or firewood for ourselves. Both were absolutely indispensable, especially the latter, as we could not cook without it, or boil our kettle, to say nothing of the need of a fire for the men, as well as ourselves, to get warm at. So seeing some nice trees round the house, we took the law into our own hands, and ordered our pony-boys to use their axes, and we soon had a tree down, and as much firewood as would last us a week. We also were compelled to break open the corn-store and help ourselves.

December 1st.—We discovered this morning that

the house, of which we had taken forcible possession, was one reserved for high Chinese officials *only*, when travelling that road, and it was entirely from fear of the Chinese, that the inmates had shirked the responsibility of offering us food and lodging. However, having cut down a tree for firewood, and broken open a corn-store to feed our horses, and taken a room to lodge in without leave asked or obtained, it did not matter much to us, as we had taken all we wanted; so leaving some money for the corn we had used, we marched out of Borah-khitay, and shaped our course for Kashgar. After passing through a cultivated country, and many villages, each with its little bazaar, we eventually reached the Kizil-su river, crossing which, we found ourselves on the island formed by the loop of the aforesaid river, and another called the Tuman. Whilst crossing the island we saw myriads of wild geese, ducks, cranes, storks and all kinds of wild fowl. Crossing the other river, we came in sight of the walls of the city of Kashgar, which, being a large fortified place, looked rather imposing with its battlements, bastions and watch towers, lit up as they were by the glow of a fine sunset. Just outside the walls we were met by Mr. Macartney, who had ridden out to escort us to his hospitable abode, situated outside the city walls.

Soon after we were comfortably settled in his house, the caravan arrived, and the ponies and baggage being all in the outer-yard, the men were busy unloading them, when a brute of a Chinese horse, that was tied up to a post in the same yard, and belonged to a soldier who had been sent by the Taotai to find out who we were, lashed out, and kicking one of our best ponies in the head, killed him as dead as a stone on the spot. It was bad luck for the poor beast, just as he had finished his journey of close on 1800 miles, without ever being sick or sorry, to meet with his death in such an ignominious manner.

This accident brings our loss in horse-flesh up to four. One having fallen down dead on the Karakoram, another killed over a precipice on the Grim pass, the third having succumbed to the cold on the Pamirs, and the fourth killed, as mentioned above. The Yarkand traders told us that they lose 20 per cent. of their horses, in crossing the passes between Yarkand and Leh; therefore our average up to the present time of four out of fifty-six is a very small loss, considering our ponies have done more than treble that distance in mileage, besides fourteen extra passes, and three months of severe weather on the Pamirs.

One of the first things Macartney did, after our arrival, was to write a letter to the Taotai demanding an apology from the Chinese Government, for the treatment we had received at Bulun-kul. He had already heard of the occurrence, but was waiting to hear our confirmation of the report, before he took action. He told us also about the excitement in Kashgar, when the news arrived that the English were building a fort on the Pamirs; the Taotai insisting on sending a Mandarin down there with orders to destroy it.

Macartney tried in vain to reason with him, assuring him that he had seen the edifice in question, when he was in our camp, and that it was not a fort, but only a bake-house with a chimney. But notwithstanding, the Mandarin was despatched, and was shown the building, and returned to Kashgar, and made his report to the Taotai, but what that report was, no one knows; suffice it to say, that the obnoxious structure has been demolished, and Chinese rights have been upheld, to the satisfaction of a Government that allowed a handful of Cossacks to destroy a *real* Chinese fort on the Pamirs, and ignominiously to kick out its garrison, without demanding satisfaction from the Power that sanctioned it.

CHAPTER XXXV.

Early History of Kashgar—Kashgar, "*extra muros*"—Visit the Russian Consul—Dividing the Caravan—The Mosque of Hazret Afarc—Russian Commercial Privileges—Treaty of St. Petersburg of 1881—Visit Li, the Taotai—A Chinese Dinner.

THERE are two cities at Kashgar like there are at Yarkand. The Kuhna Shahr, or old city, and the Yanghi Shahr, or new city. The former is a small fortified town, built in the year A.D. 1514 by Mirza Abubakar on the high ground overlooking the River Tuman. Like all other cities in Central Asia, Kashgar has repeatedly changed hands.

The earliest records of the ancient city are during the Han Dynasty, 2000 years ago, when the Chinese conquered the country, at the time when the Roman and Chinese Empires were separated only by the Caspian Sea.

The name Kashgar may possibly be derived from the "Kasia Regio" of Ptolemy, described by him as being "in the country of Scythia, beyond the Imaus."

Nothing authentic is known of its history from that date (B.C. 96), until we hear of another Chinese invasion,

A.D. 634, when they became masters of Eastern Turkestan, including Kashgar, then called Sulu.

In the eighth century the Kashgaris assisted the Queen of Bokhara to repel the great Arab invasion from the West, when the Moslem Faith was partially introduced into Turkestan by the invaders.

In the tenth century, the Mahammadan Creed became the recognised faith of the country, having been forced upon his subjects by the reigning sovereign, who was a prince of the house of Baghra Khan.

The Moslem Creed received a severe check to its spread by the invasion of the country by Jenghiz Khan, but on his demise, the Chatay Khans, who were themselves converts to the faith, re-established it on a firmer basis than ever.

In A.D. 1390, Kashgar fell into the hands of Timur, and for the next 100 years had a series of troublous times.

In A.D. 1514, Kashgar, then called Aski-Shahr, was besieged by Sultan Said, who with a large army had invaded the Province. Mirza Abubakar, who commanded the defenders, seeing that he could not hold the city, destroyed it, and, when peace was restored, built a new one, the Kuhna Shahr of to-day being the result.

In A.D. 1572, the Chatay Khans fought amongst themselves, and the country being split up into several different factions, the collapse of their dynasty was the inevitable result.

For the next 200 years, Kashgaria was the scene of perpetual strife between the Ak-Tagh-luks and the Kara-Tagh-luks which was terminated in 1759, when the Chinese again invaded the province, introducing at the same time Chinese settlers. For close on seventy years they managed to hold it, notwithstanding many revolts on the part of the Mahammadan population, until at last, in the year 1827, Jehangir invaded the province and captured the city.

In 1828, the Chinese again recaptured it.

In 1829, another revolt, headed by Yusuf, brother to Jehangir, in conjunction with Mahammad Ali Khan, proved so far successful that the Chinese were forced to make many concessions to the Mussalmans.

Then followed seventeen years of peace and tranquillity under the rule of Zahir-ud-din, but in 1846 another Khoja revolt took place, under a man called Kath-Tora, who, however, only managed to hold the city for the short space of seventy-five days, when it was again recovered by the Chinese.

The year 1857 saw the last of the Khoja revolutions, which also lasted only two months, and nothing occurred to disturb the peace of Kashgar until the great Tungani Insurrection of 1862, when the Kashgaris, headed by Yakub Beg and Buzurg Khan, rose against the Chinese, whom they turned out of the province, when Yakub assumed the reins of government and proclaimed himself ruler of the whole country.

In 1877, the Chinese again repossessed themselves of Kashgaria, and have held it ever since.

* * * * * *

Whatever it may be like in summer, Kashgar in winter is as desolate, dirty, and uninteresting-looking a city as can possibly be imagined. Inside the walls, the city is divided into two quarters, viz., the Chinese and the Mussalman, and outside the gates reside the only three Europeans in the place: The Russian Consul, Mr. Macartney, and a Dutch Missionary, of the name of Hendriks, and, if the latter is as successful in his profession as he is as an amateur barber, he ought to do well; for, as Kashgar does not boast a proper barber, Père Hendriks not only volunteered to cut my hair, but operated most successfully.

One's first impression of Kashgar, "*extra muros,*" is that it must have been quite lately subjected to a severe shock of earthquake, because from the city walls to the river there is little to be seen but a series of yawning abysses; roads, or rather apologies for such, full of gaping chasms; remains of old mud walls, tumble-down mud houses, obsolete mud cemeteries; acres of mud tombs of a more recent date, varied here and there by unsavoury heaps of filth and rubbish; and it is always either swimming in mud or smothered in dust, and what offends the eye still more is the one uniform melancholy tint of dirty drab that pervades the whole picture, absolutely unrelieved by a particle of any other colour.

Inside the walls, the streets are narrow and filthy, so are the bazaars, but unlike other Oriental cities, in which there are generally some picturesque scenes to be found, even in their squalor, Kashgar is absolutely devoid of anything approaching the picturesque, either in the architecture of its buildings or amongst the mass of humanity that throngs its bazaars. It much resembles Yarkand, although the last-named town is much larger, but Kashgar possesses one great advantage over her sister city, in that it is much healthier, there being none of those pernicious tanks—which are nothing more nor less than fever traps—in Kashgar that are met with at almost every turn at Yarkand. The people also look much more healthy than the Yarkandis, their ruddy complexions forming a marked contrast to the sickly washed-out faces one meets with in the bazaars of the larger city. Goitres, too, which abound in Yarkand, are seldom or never seen on the Kashgaris. That of course must be mainly attributable to the unlimited supply of pure water that flows under the city walls.

Yanghi Shahr, or the new city, is five miles from the old town, and was built as lately as 1838. It is a large oblong fort, running north and south, and is entered only by one gate. The walls are massive and high, and topped by turrets, while on each side are projecting bastions to protect the curtain by a flank fire. It is surrounded by a wide ditch.

During my sojourn in Kashgar, I made the acquaintance of M. Petrovsky, the Russian Consul; he and his wife Madame Petrovsky were most kind and hospitable. He has a guard of forty Cossacks, with two officers, and they are quartered in barracks adjoining the Russian Consulate. The Consul himself never goes out walking or riding, except with an escort of Cossacks. There are no other Consulates in Kashgaria, Russia being the sole country represented. After the first conversation I had with M. Petrovsky, or "The Consul," as he is generally termed in Kashgar—in which he gave me much valuable information regarding my proposed expedition through Russian Central Asia to the Caspian—I came to the conclusion that I should be obliged to give up all thoughts of going east to Maralbashi first. Time would not allow me to go there and through Russian Turkestan as well. So as I considered the latter the more interesting part of Central Asia to visit, I determined to devote all my spare time to travelling in that direction. This determination on my part necessitated the splitting up of the caravan, as Roche was going to Maralbashi, not having a Russian permit for the Central Asian Frontier.

So one afternoon we drew lots for the caravan horses, taking twenty-five each, he hoping to be able to sell his lot in Gilgit on his way back to Kashmir and the Punjab, and I with the very faint hopes of finding a market for mine at Osh in Russian Turkestan. So

M. Petrovsky hearing I wished to part with my caravan on arriving in Ferghana, wrote to Colonel Grombtchevsky, the Governor of the Osh district, informing him not only of my intended arrival, but also of my intention to sell my ponies, tents, etc., and asking him to be good enough to let it be known in Osh.

Amongst other excursions that I made in the neighbourhood of Kashgar, was one to the Mosque of Hazret Afarc, who was looked upon more as a saint than a sovereign by his people in this province, and who was buried in this mosque in A.D. 1693.

Riding out of the city by the North-gate, or the Yarwakh Darwaza, Macartney and I proceeded for about two and a half miles in a northerly direction, passing through a vast cemetery, very well kept and containing some handsome tombs.

This enormous graveyard lay to the right and left of the road for at least a mile and a half, and extended as far as the mosque, and thousands of tombs lay all around its outer walls. The mosque is a handsome building with a tower at each of its four corners, being topped with a large dome covered with green-glazed tiles. Each tower is cased in green and yellow tiles in broad alternate stripes, while its walls and the sides of its gracefully arched porch are also faced with tiles of blue and white patterns, much resembling those constantly to be met with in the old Moorish houses in Algiers. The mosque is surrounded on two sides, by a grove of the handsome

Tarik tree, one or two of which were very fine specimens. Over the porch, where the top of the arch meets the line of flat-topped roofs which form the support for the dome, were two large ibex heads, and on the top of the wall which surrounds the building was a veritable *chevaux-de-frise*, composed of the horns of *Ovis Poli*, ibex and other wild animals. Facing the centre of each wall outside the building were four altars, also built of green tiles, on which were piled hundreds of horns pyramidally.

This custom seems to prevail over all this part of Central Asia, as we have come across many such pyramids of skulls and horns, in various places, commencing in Western Tibet and in the Kuen-lun mountains, as well as in the Pamirs.

Close to this mosque are the remains of the tomb of the ill-fated Yakub Khan, whilom ruler of all Kashgaria, who was poisoned in 1876 (*see* vol. i., p. 318), and buried here with the pomp and ceremony befitting his high station.

I say the remains of the tomb, because the Chinese, after reconquering the province, exhumed the body after having with senseless sacrilege destroyed the tomb, and gratified their savage instincts of revenge by burning the corpse, "*because he was a rebel*"; and nothing now remains to show where the body of this once all-powerful sovereign rested, except a small mound of mud and a handful of bricks.

Leaving the consecrated spot where Hazret Afarc's

royal remains repose in peaceful splendour, and the desecrated spot where the head of another dynasty's remains were sacrilegiously and brutally treated, we rode back to the city, as we had to hold a little Durbar in Macartney's house, all the Hindu merchants living in Kashgar having expressed a wish to come and offer their respects and salaams to the English Sahibs.

Each man brought a *doster-khan*, in the shape of fruits, all more or less frozen; tea, sugar-candy, and in one instance the offering was augmented by the welcome addition of two boxes of Russian cigarettes. These Hindu merchants were nearly all from Shikarpur, and after a little palaver with them, they bowed themselves out and were succeeded by a detachment of Kashmiris.

They one and all complained bitterly, and with reason, of the high customs duties they have to pay on articles of merchandise they import from India.

The laxity of official Chinese morality in Kashgar is such, that the customs officers levy whatever duty they choose on Indian goods, notwithstanding there is a regular tariff. The duty as laid down in the tariff schedule is collected and handed over to the revenue department, but the excess duty which these rapacious Celestials impose, at their own sweet will, goes into their own pockets, and the poor Hindu merchant does not dare complain, knowing that he will get no redress, as the Indian Government have got no properly accredited agent in Kashgar, either as consul or resident agent.

The importation of Indian tea is absolutely prohibited, I suppose because the Chinese have found out how much better it is than their own.

The Russian merchants and traders, on the other hand, enjoy many rights and privileges that British and subjects of other nations are debarred from. They have no customs duties to pay on any goods from Russia proper, or from Russian Central Asia, thus enjoying the "*blessings*"—in this instance—of free trade.

These excellent terms are to be found in the treaty of St. Petersburg of 1881, and the manner in which they were obtained can be explained thus :—

In 1877, whilst the Chinese were in the act of regaining by force of circumstances—more than by force of arms—possession of those provinces of Eastern Turkestan, that now go by the name of "The new Dominions," to wit, Kashgaria, etc., and thereby upsetting the rule and government of Yakub Beg, the Russians took the opportunity of seizing the province of Ili, that lies to the north-east of Kashgaria, giving the Chinese to understand that as soon as they were able to prove to the satisfaction of Russia, that they were in a position to hold and properly govern their newly acquired possessions, then would Russia relinquish her hold over the province of Ili, and hand over part, or perhaps the whole of that district, back to the Chinese. When matters became settled on a sure footing in Kashgaria, the Chinese Government called upon Russia to carry out her undertaking, with regard to the province of Ili, and to hand it over to them. The Russian Government replied that they were quite prepared to hand over the province after a slight rectification of the Frontier, but must in return have a *quid pro quo*, in some shape or other, to their benefit. Therefore, amongst other concessions, one of which was the establishment of Russian consulates in Ourga, Tarbagatai, Kashgar, Sou-Tcheou and Tourfaw, the Chinese had to agree to Clause XII. being inserted in the Treaty of St. Petersburg of 1881, which enacts that "Les sujets Russes sont autorisés à faire, comme par le passé, le commerce en franchise de droits dans la Mongolie soumise à la Chine, tant dans les localités et les aïmaks où il se trouve une administration Chinoise, que dans ceux où il n'en existe point. Les sujets Russes finiront également de la faculté de faire le commerce en franchise de droits dans les villes et autres localités des provinces d'Ili, de Tarbagatai, de Kachgar, d'Ouroumtsi et autres, situés sur les versants nord et sud de la chaine du Tian-chan, jusqu'à la grande Muraille. Cette immunité sera abrogée lorsque le développement du commerce nécessitera l'établissement d'un Tarif Douanier, conformément à une entente à survenir entre les deux gouvernements. Les sujets Russes pourront importer dans les susdites provinces de la Chine, et en exporter, toute espèce de produits, de quelque provenance qu'ils soient. Ils pourront faire des achats et des ventes, soit au comptant soit par voie d'échange;

ils auront le droit d'effectuer leurs paiements en marchandises de toute espèce."

* * * * * *

On Tuesday, Mr. Macartney had made arrangements that I should visit the Taotai Li-Tsung-Pin (I make use of the first personal pronoun, because I could never persuade Roche to visit anybody), and as we had already received an ample apology from the Chinese Government for our detention at the Frontier, with an assurance that the culprit, "Ching-Wang," should be severely punished, there was every reason I should go and visit the chief official of Kashgar. Had the apology not been tendered, I should not of course have visited the Taotai, and the matter would have then been placed on another, and more serious footing, as Mr. Macartney would have referred it to the Government of India. Things, however, having been satisfactorily arranged, I made my preparations to pay the Taotai a visit of ceremony.

No clothes that I could produce, amongst the small stock which constituted my wardrobe, would please Macartney, who said that a Chinaman judged a European by his outward appearance entirely, and he regretted very much, that I had not brought some uniform with me!

Fancy taking a uniform over the Karakoram and into the Pamirs!

At last, to please him, I consented to array my person in an old uniform great-coat of Younghusband's, with a political officer's brass buttons and an imposing cape on it.

It being two sizes too small for me, it was therefore very tight and uncomfortable; but I thought of the old lines, "Dulce et decorum est pro patriâ mori," and bore the discomfort with Christian resignation, being told it was for my country's good; so the whole of this original and grotesque costume being supplemented by a Tartar fur cap, I was pronounced at last as "fit to be seen," and, mounting our horses, we rode through the bazaars, preceded by Macartney's chuprassie, Jaffar Ali, clothed in a bright scarlet *halat*, and followed by an admiring rabble of the youth of Kashgar. Being market day, the streets and bazaars were crowded, and locomotion was difficult, but we eventually arrived in safety at the Taotai's Yamên, which being an exact counterpart of those I had already visited at Kargalik and Yarkand, needs no further description.

Passing through the inner chamber of a sort of pagoda, reserved only as a passage-way for guests of the highest distinction, we reached a large hall in which stood the Taotai himself, got up in his very best, waiting to receive us.

He is an oldish man—in fact, for a Chinaman, a very old man—portly and with a jolly sort of look about him, as if he was in the habit of "doing himself pretty well." He advanced to meet us and shook hands most cordially, Chinese fashion, and then conducted us to an inner chamber and seated us on a raised dais, covered with red cloth, with a table in the middle of it, on which he placed with his own hands, most reverently, two cups of tea, much in the same way as a priest places a holy vessel on to an altar, and then seating himself on our right, the conversation commenced by his putting to me the usual Chinese query, as an opening to a dialogue, of "How old are you?" After having put him in possession of this piece of valuable information, he commenced making profuse apologies for the manner in which "my excellency" had been treated by a Chinese officer at the Frontier, etc., etc.

Undoubtedly Macartney was right, and Younghusband's great-coat was working wonders, as I saw the Taotai's eyes wandering with unfeigned admiration up and down the two rows of brass buttons.

After the usual interchange of remarks about the weather, which I find that as a topic of conversation, when every other one fails, holds its own in Central Asia equally with Europe; the Taotai conducted us to another spacious hall, where eight Chinese servants stood round a table laid for three. On seating myself, I found opposite to me a small saucer, two chopsticks, a diminutive soup-ladle, and a small china cigarette ash-tray, which turned out to be a wine-glass. The dinner began by the Taotai helping me, with his own chopsticks, to a slice of tongue and some apricot jam mixed. Then the Chinese "butler" came round with a brass jug, like an Arab coffee-pot, in which was some steaming liquid. This he poured into my little ash-tray, which held about two thimblesful and, on accepting my host's invitation to drink with him, I found the liquor bore a strong resemblance to very sweet hot toddy, it being a concoction distilled from rice. After partaking of the small dishes, which fashion much resembles the Russian one of taking "Sakouska," before sitting down to the more serious business of dinner proper, the servants brought in the different dishes, each being contained in a small tureen of most lovely shape, there being constantly four of these on the table at the same time, and each one of a different pattern.

The first dish to which the Taotai helped us, with his own hands, was shark's fins, called in Chinese *Yu-tchaih;* next came pigeon's eggs, then deer's skin, after which a very well cooked duck made its appearance; then followed bamboo shoots, and last, but not least, one of China's greatest delicacies, viz. "Sea-slugs," called in Chinese *Hai-sun.* The bread we had to eat was brought up hot, and in relays, but very doughy, and at the first bite I gave it, out came a quantity of brown juice, which squirted about all over the table-cloth; this seemed to afford much amusement, not only to our host, but to the servants standing about, who waited upon us, not strictly in conformity with our English ideas of serving. One especially attracted my attention, for his sole duty seemed to be to loll with his arms hanging over the back of an arm-chair and smoke cigarettes. Another's duty resembled more that of a nurse's, for it consisted of perpetually wiping the mouth and clothes of the Taotai with a damp cloth, as the old gentleman slobbered in a most infantine way. At length this banquet came to an end and we took our departure, visiting another Chinese official on our way home. To our horror, this man had also prepared a feast for us, and we were forced to sit down and pretend to eat again. We managed to get away early from this party and at length, much to my relief, got home; and as I sat and smoked my pipe over the fire, I wondered how a mixture of bamboo shoots and sea-slugs would agree with my health, but strange to say they had no ill effects.

Two days after this, the Taotai came to Macartney's house to return my visit, arriving with beating of drums, clanging of gongs, and accompanied by the most fantastically dressed escort I ever saw off the burlesque stage.

He had a very bad cold on his chest and a sore throat, so I presented him with a bottle of Elliman's Embrocation, showing him how to use it. I also offered him a teaspoonful of cough mixture, but had to swallow one myself first, as he was evidently afraid of being poisoned.

The next day I was invited to dinner by Wan-Chun-Men, commonly called "Wang," the officer commanding *all* the troops in old Kashgar city.

On arriving at his Yamên, we were received by a guard of honour, the beating of gongs, the braying of discordant trumpets and, worst of all, with a salute of three guns which were fired off *à la mode Chinoise*, right under our horses' noses, which one of Macartney's young horses, that I was riding, resented by plunging right into the middle of the guard of honour. On dismounting, we were preceded as usual by a man bearing aloft in his right hand our large, red, Chinese visiting-cards, and, at the entrance of the inner pagoda, the distinguished warrior himself came forward to welcome us. He had invited five guests to meet us, and after being duly presented to each of them in turn, we proceeded to the dining hall and sat down to the longest dinner but one * that I ever had anything to do with, always excepting public banquets, political or otherwise.

We sat down soon after midday (we were invited for twelve o'clock), and it was close upon six P.M. when the repast came to an end. But I feel I should not be doing justice to my excellent friend, "Wang," nor to his cook, if I omitted to mention the number of the dishes and the names of those that I can remember, of each of which both Macartney and I were forced to partake, or risk giving offence.

* The exception I make is in favour of a dinner given to me, many years ago, by a certain Armenian, Prince Mirzoeff, in Tiflis, which lasted nearly twice as long as Wang's.

As it was a very cold day—much snow having fallen the previous night—we had a fire *under* the table, in the shape of a large chafing-dish, full of live coals placed on a low stool, which was really a very sound idea, as the table was large enough to permit of plenty of room for a person's legs underneath it, as well as the fire, which at the same time imparted a grateful warmth to the whole body; a highly necessary thing, in a large draughty hall, with snow falling in such close proximity that it occasionally drifted into the room under the ill-carpentered doors.

The dinner commenced in the usual way with shark's fins, then followed a number of dishes of the sausage family, varied occasionally by eggs and ducks, cooked in different ways. What between the larger dishes, and small plates of hot dough, with all sorts of juicy surprises inside them, both sweet and savoury, but all with a decided tendency to "squirt," like a haggis, we had already reached No. 14, when, to my great relief, a dish was placed on the table, which I took to be stewed pears, coloured with cochineal, and caused me to hope that, as sweets were beginning, so perhaps dinner might be ending. But to my horror I found that my pears were pig's feet, and so far from dinner coming to an end, it was hardly begun, for dish succeeded dish, until we reached No. 23, which latter was certainly very good, being the favourite dish of a Chinaman, namely, lotus seed. Then came the second act in this

Prandial drama, which commenced by the servants removing the entire top of the table, leaving only the legs.

This had a most ludicrous effect, for it left us all sitting in a circle round the fire; however, a new top soon replaced the old one, and we commenced again, this time with sea-slugs, lotus roots, and bamboo shoots, etc., after which, sweets and tobacco. At that period I made up my mind that it was *really* all over, especially as we had arrived at dish No. 35; but again I was misled by appearances, for although the pipes and tea-cups were removed by the servants, yet more hot wine was poured out, and evidently some important dish was expected, for a profound silence reigned over all, as if an Archbishop was about to say grace.

The door opened, and a solemn-looking Celestial placed a dish reverently on the table. It did not strike me with awe, for I only saw some dark-brown fried chips of sorts; but Macartney told me this was the greatest delicacy in China, and also indicative of a desire on the part of our host to show us the very greatest honour possible. To furnish that small dish at least five little pigs met an early death, for it was the crackle of the skin of sucking-pig, and a very good dish it turned out, and so the Chinamen considered it, for by the rapid manner in which it disappeared I should say that any one Chinaman at that table could easily have accounted for a whole sty. Small bowls of soup brought us to No. 37, when at length this extraordinary repast terminated. Wang's secretary promised to send me the next morning a list of the thirty-seven dishes, with their names in Chinese; but he must have forgotten all about it, as I never received it.

* * * * * *

We have had snow now for two days and two nights, and so heavy has been the fall, that doubts are expressed as to the feasibility of my getting across the Alai mountains, as there are several passes, including the Terek Dawan, which in winter is sometimes impassable. However, I am making all preparations to leave on Monday next, having the ponies re-shod and purchasing provisions for man and beast.

I am only taking eight men with my caravan, including Ramzan, who will continue with me in Russian Turkestan.

M. Petrovsky was good enough to offer me an escort of Cossacks to accompany the caravan; but I declined to accept for various reasons. The one thing I do want is a cook; but there is not such a thing to be found in Kashgar. Old Francatelli (Rassoul) goes to Maralbash with Roche, as we had to divide up the camp-servants, so I shall have to cook for myself, as none of my seven Tibetans know anything beyond boiling a kettle, and Sehr Singh, my Sikh, can only make chupatties.

CHAPTER XXXVI.

Departure for the Alai Mountains—Deep Snow on the Road—Minyul—Quicksands—Kizil-ui—Aksalir—An Earthquake—A Hawking Party—Ulukchatt, Chinese Frontier Fort—Russian Frontier Fortress of Irkeshtan—A Cossack Escort—Three Passes—Christmas Eve on the Terek—Horses Frozen to Death—Severe Cold—Christmas Day in the Alai Mountains—A Christmas Pudding—Arrival at Osh—Reception by Sart Officials—Colonel Grombtchevsky—Sale of Caravan Horses and Tents—Parting with my Faithful Tibetans.

December 13*th.*—I left Kashgar yesterday, about mid-day, Roche leaving at the same time for Maralbashi. It was melancholy work parting, and being forced to split up the caravan, but there was no help for it, as he was not allowed by the Russian Government to cross their Central Asian Frontier. I shall be very lonely without him, after seven months' constant companionship, and amongst many other things, shall miss the old familiar tunes that he used daily to whistle on the march, especially the two in which he was most proficient, the Gaiety 'Pas-de-quatre,' and Chopin's 'Funeral March.'

* * * * * *

Macartney and Ahmed Din rode out with me

yesterday, as far as Zong, which is a Chinese outpost for Kashgar, and as the former was personally acquainted with the officer in charge of the post, we went in and partook of the inevitable cup of tea, after which I bade adieu to my two companions, and started off on my solitary journey.

I do not know what I shall do without my faithful and invaluable interpreter, Ahmed Din, as I am not very strong in Hindustani, and my men, Ramzan included, only speak it as a foreign tongue, and except a little Turki, speak no other language but their own (Tibetan).

* * * * * *

Having started late yesterday, I made but a short march, and timed the caravan as they trudged along through the deep snow, and found they were doing barely two miles an hour, as the snow balling in the ponies' feet caused them to stumble a good deal, and materially retarded their progress.

We have only about 300 miles to travel with the caravan, but how many days or weeks it will take in the deep snow, I know not, for I fear the mountain part of the journey will be extremely difficult, if this weather lasts. After riding all the afternoon, skirting the base of a low range of hills, we arrived about sunset at a little village called Sulok, where I called a halt for the night, just as it came on to snow again.

This morning we had a bright sun, and a very sharp

frost, in fact, the glare off the snow was so blinding, that we all put on our snow spectacles. We continued along the foot of the same range of hills; the country on the left hand, which was a vast plain, looking like a frozen sea, so level was it, and with apparently a boundless horizon, owing to the mist that hid whatever might be beyond it.

MINYUL.

We passed a flock of ram chikore running about in the snow, but having no gun with me, they failed to interest me. I brought only one weapon with me except my revolver, and that, my 450 Henry Express, as I cannot drag a lot of guns and rifles with me through Russian Turkestan; and the 450 Henry takes little or no room. At noon we passed an old fort, called Andijan Kichik, and three hours afterwards we left the plain, and striking the Min-yul river, rode up the little valley for another two hours, until we reached the large rambling fort of the same name, where we halted for the night.

It was the perfection of a winter's evening, and I came in for one of those glorious sunsets, for which this part of Central Asia certainly ought to be famous, and would be, were it only better known.

The great beauty of these sunsets lies in the extreme delicacy of the colouring. On the Pamirs I have often seen evening tints in the sky, the colours of which I do not believe that any landscape painter in the world could give a name to, and the after-glows, which would almost answer to our twilights in Europe, are so exquisite in their refinement, that it were absolutely impossible to attempt to describe them.

When I say that an autumnal sunset on the west coast of the highlands of Scotland is crude and harsh in its colouring when compared with one of these, then perhaps I shall make myself better understood.

After dismounting I walked up to the top of the ridge overlooking the fort, and the view that met my not unappreciative eye was supremely lovely. On the right was a range of hills, whose high needle-shaped peaks caught the glow of the setting sun, which tinged the snow, that seemed to lie so softly upon them, with a colour which I can only describe as that of a "la France" rose.

On the left towered high sandstone cliffs above the little river, in whose half-frozen waters the evening tints were faithfully reflected, and beyond lay the plain, surrounded with hills of graceful outline, the whole arrayed in its winter garb, one glorious dazzling sheet of pure white, against a sky of the most delicate turquoise.

December 14th.—Before leaving camp this morning, I took the altitude of the fort, and found we had been imperceptibly ascending, the aneroid marking 5730, which is 1300 feet higher than Kashgar. On crossing the Min-yul, the three leading ponies of the caravan broke through the thin crust of ice, which covered a treacherous quicksand on the brink of the river, and they sank in so deep, that we had the greatest possible difficulty in extricating them. I believe, had it not been for their loads, which kept them up, we should have lost them altogether. As it was, it delayed us a good deal, but luckily we had made a very early start, having a long march through the snow before us. About midday, we passed the old and new forts of Karanghalik, very picturesquely situated in a broad valley, through which wound the little river, the hills on either side being of sandstone.

At this spot we had to cross the stream a second

time, when we again had some little difficulty, as the river was only two-thirds frozen, the other third, that is to say, the middle of the stream, being open water, with a very strong current flowing through the ice. The ponies would not face it for some time; we got them over the ice easily enough, but the downward plunge into the strong, running water, frightened them. We did not know the depth, but a Kirghiz we had with us said that caravans always managed to get across, but then caravans in this country are composed chiefly of camels, and a camel would cross many places in safety, where our little Tibetan ponies would drown. However, after a good deal of pushing and pulling, and shoving and beating, we managed to get one pony into the water, and then the rest followed, but most of the baggage got a wetting.

It was a glorious day, without a cloud in the sky, but fearfully cold, every bit as bad as the Pamirs, in fact, last night was simply perishing.

Except for a north wind blowing, which cut like a knife, it would have been very pleasant travelling, as the scenery, although not exactly beautiful, was very interesting, being utterly unlike any other part of Chinese Tartary, through which we had hitherto travelled. It was sunset when we rode past Kan-jugan, and very late when we arrived at Kizil-ui, where we halted for the night. Tura Khan, the Beg of the Kirghiz of this district, came out to meet us, and offered me the hospitality of his house, and such as it was, needless to say, I accepted with grateful thanks; anything to avoid sleeping in a tent with the thermometer at twenty degrees below zero. Taking the altitude, I found we had ascended 1470 feet, being at an altitude of 7200.

Before leaving Kashgar, I bought, amongst other purchases of stores, some fresh eggs, and a jar of honey. The eggs froze as hard as stones the first day, which proved a great advantage in two ways, as first of all, they could not break, and secondly they kept beautifully fresh. The honey has also come in very useful, as Ramzan forgot to buy any sugar, and Kashgar tea, without milk or sugar, is a trifle bitter. So last night I tried putting a spoonful of honey into my tea, and it proved a gigantic success; in fact, I prefer it to sugar, as it not only takes away all bitter taste, but imparts to the tea a most delicious flavour.

December 15th.—Prices in this part of the country are almost as absurdly cheap as they used to be in Kashmir. This morning, Ramzan asked me how much he was to pay Tura Khan for all we had had for men, ponies, firewood, and the room I slept in. I thought it would be interesting to see how much they asked. So after a little while Ramzan returned with it all entered in his pocket-book. One sheep, three loads of firewood, hay for twenty-four horses for one night, and some bread, thirteen and a half tongas; a tonga being threepence. Altogether three shillings and fourpence halfpenny.

I offered the Beg a gratuity in excess of this startling account for the use of his house, which consisted of a single room, built of mud, with no windows, but a hole in the roof, which served for light and air, but he would accept nothing. These Kirghiz are undoubtedly the most hospitable people in the world. We have been living amongst them now, ever since we left Shahidula last July, and amongst the many hundreds with whom we have come in contact, we have never yet met one who has not shown us the greatest civility, and in most cases extended to us the most genuine and disinterested hospitality.

Being another lovely day, following a bitter cold night, I walked a good part of the way until we came to the foot of the Kan-su pass, which is a very mild affair, crowning one of a little low range of hills that surround the plain of Kizil-ui. On entering this basin, it appeared to the eye at first as if there was no possible exit, but winding up a sort of corkscrew path, we suddenly found ourselves on the summit of this small range, and a very curious view there was from the top. Looking over to the north-west, it appeared to be an absolutely impossible bit of country to get over, range succeeding range of low, but very precipitous-looking hills, as far as the eye could reach.

At the foot of the pass on the north side, after a steep descent, we came upon a small plain through which flows the Kan-su river, on the high banks of which was a tumble-down looking edifice, where caravans are in the habit of resting, and as there was neither wood nor water within twenty miles of this spot, I settled to stay there for the night. Just before turning in, Ramzan came and asked me if I had any medicine for Shukkar Ali, who had a very bad cough; so I gave him some black-currant lozenges, and within the space of half an hour, he returned to say that all the men had bad coughs. The fact was, Shukkar Ali found the lozenges were sweet, and imparted the news to the rest, and as the Tibetans love sweets more than anything, they all started coughing, in the hopes of being doctored after the same fashion, so, having plenty of lozenges, I served out two dozen, to their great delight.

December 16th.—This morning, while the men were busy loading the ponies, I amused myself watching a most independent young person, in the shape of a Kirghiz maiden, preparing her camel for a journey. Having led it out of the serai, she made it kneel, then packed it with baggage, and, after having adjusted the load to her satisfaction, she jumped up, and sitting astride the animal, started off all by herself, to her destination. The women in this part of the country seem to be just as independent as the men, and they dress so like them, wearing the same long boots and sheep-skins, that it is difficult to distinguish between the two at a distance, especially as they are not veiled, but wear little fur caps, and not the enormous white headdress of the Kirghiz women of the southern Pamirs and Sariq-qol.

The scenery, as we proceeded further west, was certainly more curious than beautiful. Our route lay through miniature mountain ranges of sandstone, from fifty to one hundred feet in height, reminding me very much of the country we came into, after leaving the desert of Shaitan-kum, between Yarkand and Tashkurgan. We met several small caravans of camels, and in each instance, one of the horsemen riding with them, carried a hawk on his wrist. They are great falconers, in this part of Central Asia, and use these birds for hawking hares, partridges and chikore.

One valley we rode through was carpeted with wild mint, and, as there was little or no snow in it, the perfume, which was not at all unpleasant, pervaded the whole air. Nearly all the valleys and plains were covered with short scrub and broom, and occasionally a few trees, chiefly willows, fringed the banks of the small streams, all of which were hard frozen. To my astonishment, the more we ascended, the more the snow decreased, until at last we only found snow in those valleys or gorges that never see the sun in winter. At one spot a very curious sight revealed itself, in the shape of a long, high ridge of sandstone cliffs, with buttresses jutting out on to the plain, with a bright red stratum about twenty to thirty feet deep, running through them in a perfectly horizontal line, taking in the tops of the buttresses, and making them look exactly as if they were artificial and painted.

After riding through a series of short plains, and shorter valleys, we eventually entered a very narrow winding gorge, with broad ledges of rock running obliquely across the path, forming steps which reminded me of those streets in Constantinople that lead from the waters of the Golden Horn up to the tower of Galata, and which are practicable for foot passengers only.

In one part of this gorge, where there had been a recent landslip, I saw some beautiful fossils. Emerging on to a plain, we came upon a good-sized Kirghiz encampment, where we were joined by the Beg of the Aksalir Kirghiz, who had ridden out to meet us, the Taotai of Kashgar having very civilly sent a Jigit in front of my caravan, to give notice of its arrival, as far as Ulukchatt, the Chinese Frontier.

Following the lead of the portly Beg, we arrived at Aksalir, just at sun-down, and passing the picturesque old fort, now in ruins, rode up to his akoi, which he kindly put at my disposal.

Hardly had I been in it half an hour, before a pretty severe shock of earthquake threatened to bring the whole structure down about my ears. These akois being destitute of flooring, of course one felt the shock all the stronger. About an hour later, while I was eating my dinner, a still stronger shock took place, upsetting several plates off the table, and scattering the logs which were burning in the fire, in the centre of the akoi, much to the detriment of the numdahs that the Beg had spread on the floor in my honour, to do duty for carpets. Luckily there were but these two shocks, which frightened my men out of their senses, as it was quite a novel experience for them; and then all was quiet, with the exception of the dogs, which barked as only Kirghiz dogs can bark at night, which means for several hours at a stretch. I know now why Kirghiz dogs are always fast asleep during the daytime. Altitude of Aksalir, 7180 feet.

December 18*th*.—I spent a truly wretched night; not only was it fearfully cold, and the Beg's akoi full of holes, and consequently horribly draughty, but there was one particular dog which barked without ceasing nearly all night; not an honest bark, but a most irritating nagging sort of snap, and always in the same key. He kept coming nearer and nearer, until at last he fairly got on my nerves, and I could stand it no longer; so at three A.M. I got up, and taking my revolver, sallied forth, with every intention of killing the brute, if I could only get near enough to shoot him. It was a bright starlight night, and at last I saw the fiend silhouetted against a bank of snow, and proceeded to stalk him; but my revolver refused to work, the oil in the locks was hard frozen, and the trigger would not pull.

So I went back to my akoi, and got my rifle, and when I returned I found the dog there, barking away as hard as ever. I fired at him, but missed him, as it was too dark to see the sight of the rifle; but the loud report, which sent him scurrying off, had unfortunately the pernicious effect of rousing every dog in the camp, and instead of only one barking, about fifty started to make night hideous with their noise. Sleep was, therefore, quite out of the question, so I made up my fire, and wrapping my plaid round me, smoked a pipe, and warmed myself at the blazing logs, and ruminated.

At daylight we made a start, marching up the valley of the Aksalir river, through a small jungle, full of chikore. It was so cold that I walked all the early part of the day, until about noon, when we mounted a high ridge on the top of which was another old ruined fort. The whole of this part of the country must have been bristling with fortresses in the old days, but they are now all in ruins. From this old fort an extraordinary view came in sight. I counted eleven distinct ridges, on the top of each of which were perfectly level plains.

It was, in fact, a series of gigantic terraces, as far as the eye could reach. We were delayed a good deal, by one of the ponies falling ill, and we had to shift his load on to one of the others, and even then the poor beast could hardly move, so all hopes of reaching Ulukchatt were out of the question.

Just before dark we came into a regular forest, and finding water (frozen), we halted, and I pitched my tent in a nice warm-looking spot, under some big trees, and making a huge fire, just in front of the tent, cooked my dinner, and sat over the fire afterwards, and smoked in real luxury and enjoyment. Oh, the pleasure of being in a real wood again of large trees! While I was sitting there, two Cossacks rode through the camp, and, finding they were going to Kashgar, I wrote a few lines to M. Petrovsky, and gave them the letter to take with them.

December 18th.—Another delay this morning! Seven of the ponies strayed in the night, and it took a long time to find them, as the jungle was not only thick, but extended for nearly two miles.

Eventually they were captured, and we made a start. It was another glorious day, and much warmer than heretofore; these varied climates and temperatures that obtain in different localities in this part of Turkestan are to me riddles. We are 4000 feet higher than Kashgar, and 2000 feet higher than Minyul, both of which we left under deep snow, and the latter with a temperature of 20° below zero, Fahrenheit, and here there is not a particle of snow on the low ground, and the temperature to-day has been about the same as on a fine frosty winter's day in England.

After emerging from the jungle, we mounted a high ridge of sandstone rocks, coming down on the other side upon a beautifully wooded valley, with a large river running through a low broad shingly strand, down to the edge of which sloped banks covered with low brushwood, which fringed the borders of a good-sized jungle of forest trees.

This river turned out to be the head waters of the Kizil-su, which flows past Kashgar, and loses itself, some say, in the sands of the great Desert of Gobi, and others say it empties itself along with the great Tarim river into the lake of Lob, in the same desert. We had to find a ford for ourselves, as our Kirghiz guide had not reappeared, his horse having been amongst those that strayed last night, and he was still searching for it, and I would not wait for him.*

On riding through the jungle a large (game) bird rose out of the covert, so close to me that I was able to see that it was of very dark plumage, something like a black-cock, and quite as big, and its heavy noisy flight was similar to that of a capercailzie. Of course, just because I have no gun with me, I see plenty of game, the jungle

* As a matter of fact we never saw him again.

being full of jungle-fowl, chikore and partridges. I am told there are pheasants and wild turkeys, but I have seen none as yet.

We rode past large clumps of high, graceful feathery grasses, something like the Pampas grass, and some of the trees in this forest were very large, but I could not put a name to them. After travelling through the

ULUKCHATT.

monotonous insignificance of the low bare sandstone hills of the two previous days, it was a great relief to find oneself in such a beautiful and expansive bit of wooded country.

In the afternoon we came in sight of the Chinese Frontier fort of Ulukchatt, 8380 feet above the sea, beyond which lay the high rugged snow-clad range of mountains that form the boundary-line between the

Central Asian dominions of the Czar, and those of the Emperor of China. As a fort, Ulukchatt is much more pretentious than any I have yet seen belonging to the Chinese in Eastern Turkestan. It is situated on the plain, and stands some little way up from the river, but why it is built twenty-five miles from the Frontier, is a problem only solvable by a Chinaman.

On arriving before its portals, we were surrounded by a motley crowd of Chinese soldiery, Tunganis, and Kirghiz, in every sort of costume, and I was informed by a Chinese soldier that I must show my passes to the Amban, who commands this Frontier post, before I could be allowed to proceed any further. I therefore sent a Kirghiz into the fort, to say that I wished to be conducted at once into the presence of the Amban, as I was in a hurry to get on, but the messenger returned with the answer that the Amban was at his dinner, and could not be disturbed, and that I must wait till he had finished.

This I flatly refused to do, and told the messenger to inform the Amban that if he did not choose to look at my passes *at once*, I should proceed without further delay, and report him to the Taotai at Kashgar, for keeping me waiting. The arrogance of these small Chinese officials is as well known as is the courtesy of those holding higher positions, and I had been long enough in the country to know that the only way to deal with this class of gentry, was to pay them back in their own coin, only with interest, especially in this case, where I knew the Taotai had sent on a message to say I was coming.

So my threat had the desired effect of bringing out of his den a fat bloated Chinaman, more like a porpoise with a pigtail, than a soldier, who informed me he was the Amban of the fort, and cringingly added that the edifice in question was entirely at my disposal, and he hoped I would remain as his guest for the night. I replied that I was much beholden to him for his offer of hospitality, but that I was in a hurry to get on, and as the day was yet young, I could do a few more miles before halting. He assured me that there was no wood to be had on the road, until we reached the Kirghiz encampment of Yegin, which was sixteen miles off, so at last I consented to pitch my tents near the fort, because, after seeing the filth and dirt with which he was surrounded, no power on earth would have induced me to accept his offer of shelter for the night, inside the walls. So I camped just far enough from the fort, to get free of the rabble that hang about its gates, and just as the evening gun was fired, a present of three camel-loads of hay was brought me with the Amban's compliments.

December 20th.—Yesterday, after leaving Ulukchatt, we continued riding along the banks of the Kizil-su, and camped last night at Yegin (9230 feet), near the

Kirghiz, from whom I got a bottle of yak's milk—a great luxury!

This morning I started for the Russian Frontier fortress of Irkeshtan, which was reputed to be quite a short march, so I did not hurry myself about getting the caravan off, but, finding that a party of Kirghiz were going off on a hawking expedition, I joined them to see the sport, telling the caravan to go on, and I would catch them up. We were a party of seven, and started off to catch hares and partridges on a large plain; the hawker, a young Beg, riding on the left, on a piece of elevated ground, while we other six scattered ourselves over the plain, on his right, and acted as beaters. I rode next to the young Beg, who carried the bird, a fine specimen of the Peregrine falcon and, for some time, we saw nothing in the shape of game, until coming suddenly round a bend of the river, I put up four wild duck, and thought of course the Beg would fly his hawk at them, but no such thing; he waited until a covey of partridges rose between me and the next man on my right, and then let the bird go, but the small birds were too quick for the big one, of whom they had a good start, and he failed to catch them up. Then came rather an amusing scene, viz. the Beg trying to regain possession of his falcon, which, being only a borrowed bird, did not know the man who was hunting him. It took some time, but by dint of great perseverance, and a little raw meat, he eventually got the bird on

to his wrist again, and we started off in pursuit of more game. We rode on for some time without seeing any hares, and the Beg at last gave it up as a bad job, as he had to return to Yegin, so we parted, he having prattled away all the morning to me, in the Kirghiz tongue, and I nodding my head at intervals (probably at the wrong time), without understanding one single syllable of his interesting conversation.

The predicted short march to Irkeshtan turned out to be a longer one than usual, and the sun was just setting, when we came in sight ef the Russian fortress, which, situated as it is, on the top of a high promontory overlooking the river Chuk-su, with its long low white walls, and flat-roofed white houses, resembles a lighthouse more than anything else, barring the light tower. This fort was built in 1884, and stands at an elevation of 9930 feet above the sea-level.

I rode up to the gate, but the sentry would not have anything to say to me, as he probably took me for a Kirghiz in my tcharooks, sheep-skin coat, and fur cap, but when I addressed him in Russian, and told him to let the officer commanding know that the Englishman's caravan had arrived from Kashgar, and that I was the Englishman, he communicated the fact to another Cossack, the result being that the officer in command (who was only a lieutenant) came out himself, and begged me to dismount, and enter the fort.

He and his wife entertained me most hospitably,

and gave me a barrack-room to sleep in, and we dined together, and finding that he had served under Colonel Yonoff, on the Pamirs, we talked Pamir "shop" until bedtime. They were a very homely couple, and had but one room, in which they and their two children slept and lived, and took their meals; the wife herself doing the cooking and baking, and even waiting upon us at meals as well.

In the middle of dinner, Ramzan came in to inform me that the caravan ponies, that were picketed below the fort near the river, were in danger of being attacked that night by wolves, as he and the men had seen lots of those animals prowling about. As there was no room for the ponies inside the fort—every available space being occupied by the Cossacks' horses—I told him to take my rifle and some cartridges, and fire a few shots through the night to scare them off. The officer told me they were very much troubled by wolves and wild dogs there, and could not keep any sheep in consequence.

December 21*st.*—I had, what is termed in India, a "*Europe* morning," that is to say, finding myself in a comfortable room, with a nice warm stove, I lay in bed till ten o'clock, after which I had the extremely rare luxury of a hot-bath, and a change of raiment.

I had as my attendant a corporal of Cossacks, a lean, wiry little fellow, with a merry twinkle in his eye, who was most communicative, and exhibited the greatest interest in Sehr Singh (who is as black as a coal), examining his hands, and rubbing the backs of them, evidently thinking that the colour would come off. He told me he had never seen any man darker than a Kirghiz before; the Sikh took it very good-humouredly, only grinning from ear to ear. After breakfasting with my kind host and hostess, I made ready for a start, meaning to do a half march, the men, the ponies, and myself, having had a good rest. The weather looked very threatening, it was already blowing half a gale of wind, and snowing heavily on the mountains. The officer protested against my starting in such weather, and prophesied all sorts of fearful results from the "Bouran," as it is called in this country, which is neither more nor less than a severe blizzard, straight into which, he assured me, I was about to ride.

It did not require any great amount of weather-wisdom on my part, to perceive that the "Bouran" was travelling from east to west, and I was going due north, and by the time I reached the mountains, it would have passed over my track. So I made a start, and although my entrance to the fortress yesterday was humble in the extreme, yet my exit to day was—although I say so, that shouldn't—supremely imposing, being attended by an escort of thirty Cossacks, commanded by my host in person. It was a pretty and interesting sight, watching the caravan winding through the hills, followed by the Cossack escort, on their little shaggy Tartar horses, riding in fours, the rocks echoing back the music of their wild songs, which were extremely tuneful and very well sung. It appears the Cossacks always sing when on the march, and some of these men had good voices, and as they all sang in parts, the result was well worth listening to, and as we were riding some little way behind, we heard it better than if we had been in front. When the evening began to close in, the officer bade me adieu, and returned with his men to the fort, while we continued plodding on through snow, again ascending very perceptibly, as the path was beginning to get steep and slippery, and the hills deeper in snow.

About sunset, we came upon a little unfrozen spring, and thinking it would be more prudent to halt where we were sure of water, than to proceed further—with the probability of finding none—I ordered a halt, especially as the wind was beginning to rise, and snow to fall. The only difficulty was, to find a place level enough on which to pitch a tent, but at last, having shovelled the snow off a small bank, we found just room enough for my tent, and there we remained for the night, having come up 1200 feet from the fort. Altitude, 11,130 feet.

December 22nd.—The snow got deeper and deeper,

as we ascended and the cold became intense, and a strong wind blew all the loose snow into our faces. We were now in the heart of Alai mountains, having crossed a pass called the Kok-bel this morning, and a very stiff pull it was up to the top (12,120 feet), and the descent was very slippery, there being a great deal of ice. We spent the whole day winding through narrow defiles all deep in snow, and in the evening crossed another pass called the Ek-zek, 11,900 feet, and we had just enough daylight to get down on the other side, where we found a river of running water, called the Kok-su, and there we halted for the night.

December 23rd.—Hardly had we marched one mile up the Kok-su this morning, before we found another very precipitous ascent staring us in the face, and this was the Borak pass, 11,480 feet. These passes appear very insignificant when judged by their altitudes, especially after those that we had crossed in the Himalayas, and Karakoram ranges of 17,000, 18,000, and up to 19,000 feet; but it must be borne in mind, first, that the latter are only crossed in summer, and now we are in the depth of winter; and secondly, to cross the Himalayan and other passes, to which I refer, the start is from Ladak, already at an elevation of 11,680 feet, whereas in this case the start is from Kashgar, only 4300 feet elevation. Therefore, the ascent of these passes is, in proportion, much greater than the others, plus the extreme difficulties engendered by the presence of deep snow and masses of ice.

The two small passes we crossed yesterday, and the Borak to-day, were much harder work for both men and ponies, than the Karakoram; in fact, the descent of the Borak pass to-day was very bad, for not only was it very precipitous, but most frightfully slippery; so much so, that even with the help of an alpenstock, it was all I could do to get down, and then only after several falls. The ponies tumbled about freely, but only one came to such serious grief, that I doubt whether we shall get him to Osh alive.

At the foot of this pass, we struck the South Terek river, which flows through a very narrow gorge, the perpendicular cliffs on each side almost meeting, about 700 feet above it, forming an arch, and nearly shutting out the daylight. We led our horses through this dark defile for about half a mile, walking on the frozen river itself, after which, we emerged again into sunlight, and also into a narrow glen, very deep in snow, and following the course of the river for the rest of the day, camped in three feet of snow, at the foot of the great Terek pass.

December 24th.—Christmas Eve. Neither the Russian Consul at Kashgar, nor the officer in command of the fort of Irkeshtan, exaggerated the cold of the Alai mountains in winter, even when the latter told me the temperature had been constantly known to fall as low as forty degrees below zero, Fahrenheit, on the Terek mountain, for the cold last night fairly outdid anything we encountered even on the Pamirs. Sleep was impossible, not so much from the intense cold, but in consequence of some of the ponies stumbling over my tent-ropes all night, in the endeavour, poor things, to get a little shelter, from the icy blasts that came sweeping down the mountain side. I got up three or four times in the night, to drive them off, for humanity has its limits, and I drew the line at having my tent brought down about my ears, in the middle of such a night as that.

At daybreak I looked out to see whether the men were stirring, as I knew we had a very long and arduous day before us, and the first thing that I saw, was one of the ponies lying dead close to my tent, having been frozen to death during the night. I aroused the camp, and we found two others lying frozen but not dead, only unable to rise. Curiously enough, the one that was so bad yesterday was not amongst the dead or dying: on the contrary, he was apparently quite well again.

This caused a delay, and we held a council of war, as to what to do. To leave the two half-frozen ponies behind, was to leave them to a lingering death, and to shoot them would be more humane. But as they were good, healthy, hardy ponies and might perhaps recover when warmed, and thawed by the morning sun, it seemed a pity to sacrifice them, without giving them a chance,* so I settled that they should come slowly on after the caravan, if the sun in any way revived them, and I would wait for them on the other side of the pass. So, leaving two men with them, I made a start, and hardly had we gone half a mile before we saw on the rocky hill opposite to where we had camped, a small herd of ibex, consisting of two males and three mahdines. I had a good look at them through my telescope, and saw that one of the males had a very fine head, so I thought I would have a try for him; but after a careful examination of the ground through the glass, I came to the conclusion that even if I could get on to the top of the hill, which was very doubtful owing to the deep snow, I could certainly never climb the precipitous place, on the top of which they were standing, and without this I could never get a shot at them. The big male was on the very top of a rock that crowned the summit of the mountain, and very grand he looked; his brown coat standing out in deep relief against the blue sky, both colours being intensified, by the contrast of the pure whiteness of the snow that lay beneath. Seeing it would be but a waste of time and energy on my part, to attempt to stalk them, I most regretfully left them and proceeded to make the ascent of the great Terek pass, which is evidently the "Karakoram" of

* They never recovered.

this part of the country, by the way people talk of it. It was very deep in snow, and in some places where it had drifted, the ponies were almost up to their necks and took some getting out. The ascent was nothing, being only 2650 feet from where we had camped, the summit being 14,430 feet; but the descent was awful, 5300 feet straight down, which took seven hours and forty-five minutes, the last 1000 feet being done by moonlight. In some places it was simply large sheets of ice; I had to walk the whole way, and could not even lead my pony, as it was just as much as I could do to get down myself.

It was perfectly lovely by moonlight, and although the most difficult descent of any pass we have hitherto undertaken, yet the scenery was so lovely, it amply atoned for the difficulties we encountered. As its name Terek (tree) indicates, it is wooded from a certain altitude. About 3000 feet from the summit, I noticed the first trees, stumped pines growing out of the rocks which tower on each side of the pass. At 4000 feet from the summit, the trees were larger and of various kinds, mostly of the *Juniperus*, *Cedrus*, and *Cupressus* tribes.

I stopped to examine some of them minutely, as I was anxious to discover what they were, but found they were mostly strangers to me. Altogether, I should say there were seven species: the first bearing a very close resemblance to the *Thujopsis Borealis;*

the second a decided *Cupressus*, much resembling the *Cupressus Macrocarpa;* the third a *Cryptomeria*, something like the *Japonica*; the fourth a *Taxodium* of sorts; the fifth a *Cedrus*, not unlike the *Deodara*, of the Himalayas; the sixth, a wild straggling *Juniperus;* the seventh an *Abies*, so like the *Abies Canadensis*, or Hemlock Spruce, that I classified it as such in my mind. It was very late, indeed, when we found a spot level enough to pitch a tent on, and thus I spent my Christmas Eve.

Christmas Day.—This day, last year, I left England on this expedition, and spent the day in the train and Channel steamer, *en route* for Brindisi. To-day I spend it in the Alai mountains of Central Asia.

Just before we struck tents, a party of three horsemen rode into our camp, and making straight for our fire dismounted, sat round it, and after warming themselves, began to converse with the men, without any preliminary solicitations on their part, or invitation on ours, always excepting the "peace be with you" salutation; in fact, they acted exactly as if they had been expected.

That is the freemasonry of the road, which obtains all over Central Asia, and to my mind, it is a very sound principle to go upon. It amounts to this: that you look upon every man as your friend, until he proves to be your enemy; whereas, the outcome of our much-vaunted civilisation in Europe is, that you look with suspicion upon every man you meet, until you have proved him to be your friend. There is an almost childlike trust and utter absence of suspicion displayed by these people, which is very refreshing after the stilted conventionalities and etiquette of Western Europe.

These three travellers were Turkestani merchants, on their way to Mecca, to worship at the holy shrine of the Prophet. I joined the circle round the fire, and, finding one of them spoke a little Arabic, conversed with him in that tongue.

He told me they were now on their way to Cabul, and thence hoped to reach Peshawar, where they would get the railway to Bombay, and embark for the Red Sea. They were much interested to hear about the railroad, for they had never seen the Trans-Caspian line, not having been at Samarkand.

When I explained to my friend that the distance from Peshawar to Bombay was about three times as far as from the Terek pass to Yarkand, he was very much astonished, but when I added that the railway-train covered that distance in four days, he looked at me as if I was making fun of him, for the caravans from here to Yarkand would take over twenty days; therefore, any mode of locomotion that could in four days bring him to a place which would take sixty days to reach on horseback—which was his only idea of travelling—seemed to him impossible.

When these worthy merchants had thoroughly warmed themselves, and had some good hot tea, they started off to make the ascent of the Terek pass, and we rode in the contrary direction. The commencement of to-day's march lay through a very narrow defile for a short way, after which we got into a good bit of track by the side of the North Terek river, down which we rode for several hours, with low wooded banks on each side of us. Coming out of this rather confined glen, we came into a more open, although mountainous country, for we were still in the Alai mountains, although we had crossed the highest of them.

Being some way ahead of the caravan, I dismounted at the end of this little glen and sat down to wait for the ponies. All of a sudden, round a corner, came a small cavalcade, in the midst of which was a very smart-looking Kirghiz in green, with a spotless white turban, and wearing a handsome Circassian sword. This turned out to be Hassan Beg, Mingbashi, in the Russian service, who had received orders from Colonel Grombtchevsky to meet me at Sufi Kurghan, and escort me to Osh, and to make all preparations and arrangements for me on the way. As I was all alone and spoke little or no Turki, and he spoke no Russian, it was some time before I understood what he wanted with me, seeing that he dismounted, salaamed, and seemed to take great interest in my proceedings; at last it occurred to me that he might speak Persian, as many of these Begs are Badakshanis, so I started airing my small stock of that language, and found I was right in my conjecture, and he was a Badakshani, and consequently spoke Persian fluently. So eventually I gathered what his mission was, and just as I had exhausted my limited vocabulary of the Persian tongue, Ramzan and the caravan made their appearance and we got on all right.

We then rode off together in the direction of Sufi Kurghan, which was reached quite early in the afternoon. Here I found an akoi ready prepared for me, and soon after I had seated myself at the fire that was burning brightly in the centre, a Kirghiz brought in Hassan Beg's doster-khan of dried apricots, raisins, and pistachio nuts, the sight of which possible ingredients gave me the bright idea of having a Christmas Pudding for dinner. So calling in Ramzan, I commenced by explaining to him as best I could in the Urdu tongue that this day was the great festival of the Christian's year, and one on which all right-minded Franghis were wont to spend the first half of the day at their Mosques, the inside walls of which were decorated with green branches and made as much as possible to resemble a jungle, and the other half of the day and most of the night in over-eating themselves with the most unwholesome food their Khansamas could procure in the bazaars, and, therefore, as I did not wish to be behind-hand in following the example of my brother Franghis, but wished—in the absence of my mosque—

to keep the day as near as possible in accordance with the articles of my faith, I called upon him as a good Mussulman, to come to my assistance in the manufacture of the most unwholesome edible compound the united ingenuity of our inventive brains could devise.

So after a long discussion and close inspection of our resources, we built up between us, using the Beg's doster-khan, a Christmas Pudding, which turned out so successful that I cannot refrain from giving a minute description of its architecture.

First of all we took some dark-coloured Kirghiz flour and some baking-powder and the frozen yolks of six Kashgar eggs, which we scraped with a knife into a yellow powder, and after being well kneaded, this compound was rolled out, my telescope making a grand rolling-pin. We then stewed in a small Degchi all the Beg's apricots and raisins with some of my own honey. Another corner of the fire was occupied by a frying-pan, in which I fried the kernels of the pistachio nuts, in the only butter I could get, which I very carefully took out of a fresh tin of *Sardines au Beurre.* When the paste looked as like the beginning of a roly-poly pudding as we could make it, we poured the apricot, raisin and honey stew into the middle of it, then rolled it up and stuck the outside of it full of the fried kernels of the pistachio nuts, until the result looked like a new-born porcupine. We then proceeded to bake the whole thing as best we could, and I venture to say that no cook in Europe, on the 25th December, 1892, could have been as proud of his Christmas Pudding as I was of mine.

Although its manufacture was not the least interesting part of it, still the eating of it was more pleasurable than most enforced duties are usually, notwithstanding the slight suspicion of a flavour of sardines about it, which at any rate was a new departure in Christmas Puddings, and possessed the one great advantage and charm of novelty.

December 26th.—Had a capital morning's hawking, Hassan Beg, who is a most sporting little person himself, hearing from Ramzan that I was fond of all kinds of sport, enlisted the services of a professional hawker, to accompany us this morning; so off we went with our falcon, leaving the caravan to follow. We rode down the Terek, leaving the bright red hills of Sufi Kurghan behind us, but for the first three or four miles, saw no game. We then turned off to the right, into a large triangular basin, where three nullahs meet. Here we struck the Taldek river, a tributary of the Syr Daria (Jaxartes), whose waters flow north into the Sea of Aral.

Crossing it, we rode down its left bank until we came into a very broad, level valley, dotted here and there with large trees, over which plain we all spread and beat for chikore. At last we put up a covey, which flew to the left, towards some high sandstone cliffs, with a sprinkling of brushwood growing on their steep sides. The birds had too much of a start for the hawk to catch them at the first attempt, but it gave us a good gallop following them, and they settled in the brushwood. When we came up to the foot of the cliffs, the hawk was sitting perched on a stone, and the chikore, although not visible, were chirruping all round him in the most foolish manner. Here the hawker dismounted and began to beat the brushwood, his falcon perched on his wrist, when all of a sudden one old cock chikore rose and flew down wind over the plain. The hawker let fly his hawk with a peculiar shrill cry, a sort of Kirghiz tally ho, and then it was a really pretty sight to watch, and as it was excellent going, we had a good gallop after them, and were able to see the whole flight of the hawk, until he struck his prey. I noticed he kept above the chikore until he meant business, then gave a sort of dive underneath him, then again with a sudden twist struck him upwards, and down they both came together on the plain. By the time we came up to them, the hawk was pecking away at the chikore's head, his claws being firmly embedded in the bird's body.

We had several other hunts, but no real good flights except that one, but it served to relieve the monotony of the march, for when we arrived at the junction of the Buloh-leh river, with the Taldek, and parted from our hawker, who had to return home to Sufi Kurghan, I could scarcely believe that we had already covered fifteen miles of our road towards Kizil Kurghan.

As we crossed the frail wooden bridge that here spans the Buloh-leh, the Beg informed us that at this very spot, fifteen years ago, he was fighting with the Kirghiz against the Russians and the former lost forty-two men killed.

We arrived at Kizil Kurghan Red Fort just after sundown, and well does the place deserve its name, for the rocks above the Kirghiz encampment were simply crimson in the evening light. I never saw such vivid colouring before in Nature, and these rocks were visible for miles before we reached the camp.

December 27th.—My good little friend Hassan Beg appeared this morning, arrayed in a most martial costume. This was all in consequence of our prospective arrival at the Russian Fort of Gulcha, for he holds, as far as I can make out, some sort of semi-military position in the district of which this fort is the centre. Anyhow, the respect in which he is held is self-evident, as all along the road every Kirghiz we meet dismounts, bows down to the ground with arms crossed in front, and if the Beg extends his hand, the man seizes it in both of his, then puts both his hands on to his face, and strokes it downwards, whether he has a beard or not. In the case of having a beard, he as it were combs it right out with both hands. That is the most respectful form of salutation amongst the Kirghiz.

We rode down the valley of the Taldek, which here flows through an enormous shingly bed, and is broken up into four channels, and, on turning a sharp corner, came suddenly upon a small caravan advancing towards us, the leading horseman of which had a decidedly European look about him, although clothed like myself, more or less in the garb of the country. But I confess I was astonished when I heard him shout out, in the most excellent English, "a Merry Christmas and a happy New Year to you, Lord Dunmore."

This turned out to be the celebrated Austrian Central Asian traveller, Dr. Troll, who was on his way to Pekin, and whose antiquarian contributions to the Austrian National Museum at Vienna, on behalf of which he travels, are well known to the scientific world. Needless to say, we both halted our caravans, and dismounting, conversed for some time. He told me he had seen Colonel Grombtchevsky at Osh, who had told him I was expected there, and so when he saw my caravan he knew it could be no one else. He was anxious to hear about the Terek pass, and so I gave him all information in my power, especially about the intense cold, and did not conceal from him the fact that some of my horses had come to grief in consequence. Then, seeing him look with envious eye upon my stirrups, which I had made myself out of rope and wood, covered over with felt, I offered to give them to him, as he had only the common stirrup-irons, in which his feet would probably be frozen, but he was very loth to accept them. I explained to him that I could not possibly have any more use for them, as in three days I should be at Osh, where my riding would be over for some time. So at last we ended by effecting a barter; I being very short of tobacco, he gave me 200 Russian cigarettes for my rope-stirrups. Thus we parted, he for Pekin, I for Persia or the Caspian.

It was early in the afternoon when I reached the Russian fortress of Gulcha, which is situated in the valley of the Taldek, and stands up a little way from the river.

On riding past some of the out-buildings, I was much struck with the excessive neatness and tidiness of everything connected with the barracks and stabling. The latter especially were a model of cleanliness, and resembled more the stables connected with some large hunting establishment in the "Shires," than what one would expect to find provided for the housing of Cossacks' horses in Central Asia. Thanks to the provident forethought of Colonel Grombtchevsky, I found three akois all ready prepared for me, and as I could not possibly occupy more than one at a time, my men were in clover, as they occupied the other two.

December 28th.—Made an early start, having a long

march before us, and three passes to cross, the whole country here being under snow. Soon after leaving the fort, we crossed the Taldek river, and leaving it on our right, headed due south for about six miles, crossing the Sheli-bel pass, which was rather a difficult one, owing to the ice. Here my poor old grey pony "Srinagar," who has carried me a good many hundred miles, utterly collapsed; but the Beg, with most commendable forethought, had luckily brought a spare horse for me, in case of accidents, and so I shifted my saddle on to a very strong wiry dun pony, which carried me splendidly for the rest of the day, and Srinagar trotted by my side all the way; the poor beast was so accustomed to follow me down passes, etc., or when I was walking, that he stuck to me all day.

After crossing the Sheli-bel, and descending 1500 feet, we came into a most magnificent down country, something like the Wiltshire or Hampshire Downs, only of course on a much more extensive scale, and very much higher, but grass right up to the rounded tops of the hills, and not a rock to be seen. Here, curiously enough, there was no snow again.

Changing our course now to west, we rode for nearly twenty miles through these beautiful downs, passing a lake called Kaplang Kul, where there was a small Kirghiz encampment, in the neighbourhood of which I counted over 200 horses grazing, mostly mares and foals. From this lake we ascended 4050 feet, to the tops of these grassy downs, crossing the three Takka passes, on all of which there was a little snow. It seemed so odd to go over passes without any rocks or rough ground. The views from the summit of these downs were magnificent.

On the top of the second Takka pass, I found the ice plant growing, and also captured a curious zoological specimen in the snow; it was an animal about the size of a very large rat, with a head nearly as big as its body, and with a mouth like a fish. I had thought of keeping it as a pet, but it exhibited such vicious tendencies, fixing its little sharp teeth into my thick leather glove, that I thought it better to let it go, especially as it would probably have died, for I had no idea what to feed it on, and I don't suppose it would have thriven on tough mutton and hard biscuit, which is all I could have offered it in the shape of food.

It was late when we arrived at Langar, where I found another akoi prepared for me. Langar is a sort of resting-place for caravans, and consists of one small mud house, in which reside an old Russian peasant and his wife, from whom I was able to buy some fresh-laid eggs. Shortly after my arrival, I was met by another Beg, sent by Colonel Grombtchevsky. He also wore a uniform, and a Russian order or medal round his neck, with a red ribbon.

December 29th.—I started this morning early for Osh,

accompanied by my two Begs, or Mingbashis, each with two Kirghiz gallopers of their own, and also by Ramzan, who being evidently determined not to be outdone by the Begs in the matter of dress, had got himself up in the most extraordinary mixed costume, viz. a pair of old scarlet pantaloons that he had bought from a Cossack at Gulcha; on his legs were Yarkandi tcharooks; round his waist a Kashmir soldier's belt, hanging to which was an English Royal Artillery non-commissioned officer's sword-bayonet; an English-made Norfolk jacket; and on his head an Afghan puggary.

After a ride of twenty-four miles at a good sharp pace, I being mounted on a fresh horse, the property of the Russian Government, we reached the outskirts of the native quarter of Osh, when all of a sudden my two Mingbashis, who were riding ahead of me, drew rein, and wheeling round, formed up behind me; this was to allow three smartly dressed horsemen, in really very handsome uniforms, half European, half Oriental, with Circassian swords, and beautiful puggaries, and wearing Russian decorations, to ride up with a large escort to greet me to their city. Dismounting they shook hands with me, then remounted their very good-looking horses, with gorgeous trappings, and saddle-cloths of red and gold embroidery. These were the three principal Sart officials of Osh and, as Grombtchevsky told me afterwards, were the "Lord Mayor and Sheriffs of the city." I was so taken aback and overwhelmed with astonishment at this great honour paid me, that I hardly knew what to do.

Luckily the "Lord Mayor" spoke Russian, and we were able to converse as we rode along into the more populous part of the town, passing through the bazaars, which were lined with the native population, who salaamed low as we rode by. We at length came into a long avenue of poplars, planted in double rows on each side of the broad, well-kept road, passing many small white one-storied houses, like Indian bungalows, but built very far apart. These were mostly officers' houses, this being the commencement of the Russian cantonments, the barracks, prisons, and other public buildings, such as post and telegraph offices, bureaux of different sorts, civil and military, and some very fair shops being situated in the same area, although standing on different avenues of poplars.

We rode up to the Sobrania, where a room had been prepared for me, and dismounting, I bade adieu to the Sart officials, after thanking them for their kind welcome, and was greeted by Captain Topournine, a Russian officer, whom Colonel Grombtchevsky had asked to be kind enough to look after my wants, and most good-natured he proved to be. We took a very late lunch together, and as my caravan did not turn up till 7 P.M., I was unable to accept Colonel Grombtchevsky's kind invitation to dinner at 6 P.M., not being presentable in my well-worn travelling costume, which was a happy mixture of Chinese, Kirghiz and English.

The next morning, accompanied by Captain Topournine, I went to visit Colonel Grombtchevsky in his snug little country house, situated on a wooded hillside, overlooking the river, about a mile from the cantonments, and after lunching with him he took me for a walk, showing me over the prisons and the barracks, both of which were scrupulously clean and tidy, especially the former, and the prisoners were very well cared for. I tasted their bread and soup, both of which were excellent. Amongst the prisoners was an Arab, who having no pass and not being able to account satisfactorily for his presence in Russian Turkestan, was naturally detained on suspicion of being a Turkish spy. He began appealing to me in his native tongue to get him released, and seemed delighted to find I could understand him. On my asking him where he came from, he replied he was a native of Syria, but our conversation was cut short by Grombtchevsky's carrying me off to another ward. After visiting other public buildings and showing me round the little Russian settlement, my kind host carried me off to his hospitable house and to an excellent dinner. The conversation turning upon the Pamirs, I hazarded a question upon the Surmatash affair, when my host, who was present on the occasion of the fight, cut me short by saying in a tone which precluded the possibility of re-opening the subject — "I have entirely forgotten all about it."

So I took the hint and changed the subject. Grombtchevsky has a great liking for Captain Younghusband, whose photograph stands on his writing-table, but he was very sore about the manner in which he himself had been treated by the British officials in Kashmir, when he attempted to cross the Karakoram pass, producing from a drawer all the correspondence for me to read, and complaining that he had been left to starve as he was refused even provisions. So this time I turned the subject into more congenial channels, after which I returned to the Sobrania.

Next morning I inspected the Tarantass, which Colonel Grombtchevsky had bought for me in Marghilan, and was not altogether pleasurably impressed with the idea that it was to be more or less my home for some time to come. It was an old ramshackle-looking concern, very dear at the purchase price of 140 roubles.

However, as there is no other means of locomotion in this country except sleighs, I could not help myself. This carriage has no seats and will not hold more than one person comfortably. There is a seat in front for the driver, which can at a pinch accommodate a servant on the box, and behind them is a sort of little footboard for luggage. It also rejoices in a hood, so cunningly devised and constructed, that if the traveller puts it up and uses one of his luggage boxes as a seat, it just catches him on the top of the head and knocks his hat off at every jolt, and if he fills the bottom of the vehicle with hay or straw as I did, and tries to lie down in it, it is just eighteen inches too short to enable him to stretch his legs out.

I sold fifteen of my horses to a caravan master for less than half what I paid for them, but they were perfect scare-crows, and all had sore backs, after that hard journey over the Alai mountains, but the rest I disposed of much better, getting in a few instances close upon my purchase price. So altogether I did not do so very badly, as they had carried loads for 2200 miles over the wildest country imaginable, and over forty-one mountain passes, some of them amongst the highest in the world, during the last seven months, and by purchasing them at the outset I saved a sum of over 4000 rupees; for had Roche and I done as Prince Galitzin did at Leh, and hired at fifty rupees a month, it would have come to the large sum of 19,600 rupees for the seven months, including, of course, wages and keep of the men and horses. Even supposing we could have beaten down the owners to forty rupees a month, it would have reached the heavy sum of 15,680 rupees. I calculate my share of the ponies to have cost me as follows:—

	Rs.
Purchase of ponies	1500
Food for ponies *	676
Pack-saddles	260
Shoeing, etc.	52
Eight pony-men, food and wages for seven months	982
Clothing for eight pony-men	70
	Total, 3620.

3620 rupees, against 7840 rupees for my half of the caravan, which is taking the hire at forty rupees, and not fifty, makes a saving of 4220 rupees.

I then sold my tents and camp-equipage, saddles, etc., and got for them very nearly as much as I paid. So, after taking leave of my faithful Ladakis, Shukhur Ali, Sedik, the two Islams, the two Sonnams, and Sehr Sing, the Sikh, I started off for Andijan in my Tarantass, with three horses, having walked and ridden close on 2500 miles from the Punjab; from the 9th of April, 1892, till the 1st of January, 1893, over forty-one mountain passes, crossing sixty-five rivers, in Kashmir, Baltistan, Ladak, Western Tibet, Chinese Tartary, Sariq-qol, The Pamirs to Ferghana.

There was no snow on the road, and the weather was balmy and spring-like. We arrived at Andijan,† just

* More than half the time they were costing nothing for food, being on the grass.

† Andijan was unsuccessfully attacked in 1875, by General Trotsky, but early in 1876, the city was taken by storm by Scobelef, after which he defeated Abdurrahman at Assaki, and

as the full moon shed her glorious flood of light upon a new year, for it was half an hour past midnight of December 31st, 1892.

---

received the submission of Marghilan and Shahrikhana, and shortly afterwards Abdurrahman surrendered and the whole country became at the mercy of the Russians.

CHAPTER XXXVII.

Marghilan—Banquet given by General Karalkoff—An Amateur Pianist—The Military Governor's Garden—Khokand—Caught in a Bouran—Tarantass and Horses dug out of the Snow—Khojend—Syr Daria—Snowed-up at Murza Rabat—A Bouran—Detention of the Imperial Mails—A Start and an Upset—Arrival at Tashkend — The Governor-General's Palace — Russian New Year's Day.

January 1*st*, 1893.—The weather being so mild and beautiful, I determined to travel all night and sleep in my tarantass, which I did, arriving the next morning at 8 A.M. at Marghilan, where I again found quarters prepared for me at the Sobrania, and very comfortable I found them. Hardly had I had time to tidy up a bit before Captain Hoeppener, Aide-de-camp to General Karalkoff, called, he having been told off by that most courteous and hospitable of Russian officers, to look after me during my stay in New Marghilan. I say *new* Marghilan, because the native town of Marghilan is fifteen versts away from the Russian town. Captain Hoeppener spoke French perfectly and English fluently, as did also Madame his wife, in whose hospitable house I soon found myself both lunching and dining.

The first day of my arrival was taken up first in

going to a tailor and getting a suit of evening clothes made, as I had nothing respectable to wear, and afterwards in making visits to the head officials of the Province, commencing with General Karalkoff, Military Governor and Commander of the troops, in the Province of Ferghana; then to General Medinsky, Vice-Governor of the same Province; to Colonel Spitzberg, Chief of the Staff, and General Ssarantchoff, Commanding a Brigade. This latter officer told me lots of Indian news, including the Chitral affair, Lord Roberts' Mission to Cabul being given up, as well as that gallant officer's successor in the Supreme Military command in India.*

During my visit to the Chief of the Staff, I made the acquaintance of one of his officers, a certain Captain Bourkowsky, who afterwards turned out to be quite the best amateur pianist I ever had the pleasure of listening to.

In the afternoon I had to remain at home and receive the return visits of the Military Governor General Karalkoff, and General Medinsky, both of whom were much interested in my journey from India to Russian Turkestan, following the line of march on my maps, and asking many questions regarding the countries I passed through.

In the evening we had a very pleasant dinner at General Karalkoff's, who had also invited Captain

* Every Russian officer I met in Central Asia expressed the greatest admiration for Lord Roberts as a military commander.

Bourkowsky, and it was after dinner that I had the extreme pleasure of hearing that officer perform on a very good full-sized grand piano, of German manufacture. He told me he had pursued his musical studies in the Conservatoire at Leipzig, and he certainly did ample credit to his musical instructors. His marvellous execution was only surpassed by his beautiful touch on the instrument, and he played with such feeling that it was easy to see that his heart was wholly in his work, besides his being gifted with extraordinary talent. He was as modest as he was obliging, and played several pieces of Chopin, Liszt, Wagner, and other celebrated classical composers, till a late hour.

The next day Captain Hoeppener showed me all there was to be seen in Marghilan, and we returned to the Sobrania in time to dress for a grand dinner, given in my honour by General Karalkoff, to which upwards of thirty guests were invited. This banquet was given in the big ball-room of the Sobrania, which was beautifully lighted for the occasion, and the many brilliant uniforms served to make it a very gay scene. During dinner the massed bands of the four regiments quartered in Marghilan played very good music, and after dinner some toasts were given. General Karalkoff, in proposing the health of the Queen, styled Her Majesty as "La Reine Victoria de la Grande Bretagne, Impératrice des Indes, notre illustre voisine dans l'Asie Centrale."

I gave the Toast of the Emperor and the Army, and after the General had proposed my health in a very neat well-turned speech, to which I responded, we were all photographed in a large group, by the aid of the Magnesium Light, and the picture with an account of the banquet is, I am told by General Karalkoff, to appear in one of the Russian illustrated papers. After this we had a very musical evening, Captain Bourkowsky again playing the piano, and Captain Lewanewsky playing very nicely, and *in tune*, on a more than averagely good violin of Italian make. Amongst those who were present at the dinner were, first our host, General Karalkoff, Military Governor of Ferghana; then General Medinsky, Lieutenant-Governor of the Province; Colonel Spitzberg, Chief of the Staff; Colonel Léontieff, Commanding 15th Battalion of the Line; Colonel Cholmsky, Commanding the Cossacks; Colonel Yasewitch, Commanding Engineers; M. Gradussow, Principal Medical Officer; M. Prilechaeff, Head of the Schools; M. Prawlikowsky, Conseiller du Gouvernement de Ferghana; M. Sollogoul, also a Conseiller du Gouvernement; Captain Rondanowsky, Commissaire de Cadastre et des Impôts; Captains Koichewsky and Danowsky, both officers of the same department; Colonel Tomitch, Chef du District de Marghilan; M. Paschkewitch, Employé pour les cas extraordinaires; M. Sokolinsky, Juge d'Instruction Militaire; Captain Bourkowsky A.D.C. to the Chief of the Staff; Captain Lewanewsky

Captain in the Line; Captain Hoeppener, A.D.C. to General Karalkoff, and many others, whose names have escaped my memory.

The Governor is a great gardener, and besides being the happy possessor of a marvellous collection of roses, has a very good assortment of *Coniferæ*, and other ornamental trees, in his beautiful and well-kept garden, and grounds round the house. So I spent the whole of the following morning with him in his garden and forcing-houses. His collection of roses I should say was unique, comprising as it does considerably over a thousand different varieties.

Amongst many curious and rare trees, he showed me one large one in the garden, which was quite a stranger to me. It had a very white bark, almost like a silver birch, and we picked up some of the fallen leaves, which, shrivelled up as they were by the frost, still measured from sixteen to eighteen inches across. It bears in the month of March a beautiful bell-shaped purple flower, which has all the odour of a tea-rose. The name of this tree is the "Pavlonia Impériale" of Japan.

After lunching again with the General, I went to take leave of all my kind friends in Marghilan, preparatory to making a start for Khokand, which I eventually managed to do about 2 P.M., and after passing through alternate arid steppes, cultivated ground, and villages, I reached Khokand after a somewhat tiresome journey of twelve hours.

Khokand is a comparatively modern city, having been built about 150 years ago, in consequence of which its streets and bazaars are not so narrow and cramped as those of the older cities of Turkestan. The bazaars are roofed over like those of most Central Asian cities, with light wooden boards and matting, and there are in the city more than the usual number of mosques, some of them rather handsome, being faced with blue and white glazed tiles, mostly with Persian and Arabic inscriptions, in most cases with verses from the Koran, and roofed with graceful melon-shaped domes. From the city walls a very fine view is to be obtained of the Tchatkal mountains on the north, which face the great range of the Alai mountains on the south, the Syr Daria (the river Jaxartes of the Greeks) flowing through the valley, between the two.

Khokand, in which the whole province of Ferghana is now included, embraced in the middle of the last century an immense area of country, which was divided up into several smaller provinces and cities. The present city was built by Abdul Kerim Bek, whose son Edeni Bek succeeded at his father's death, and in 1759 gave his submission to Kian-Lung, the Emperor of China, as did also the Beks of Marghilan and Andijan, following the example of Tashkend, which province had tendered its submission in the year previous.

The 'Thai-Thsing-Thonugh-Tchi,' or Great Geography of the Chinese Empire, translated by Klaproth (in the

Magasin Asiatique,' vol. i. 82) records that "Among the gifts sent from Khokand to the Chinese Emperor, were horses that sweat blood (argamaks), great eagles and falcons for hunting, and plates of the fountain of the dragon."

Khokand was constantly at that time at war with Tashkend, and even amongst these rival factions dissensions constantly arose; sons had a playful way of murdering their fathers, and nephews thought little of poisoning their uncles, in order to become rulers themselves; after having attained which object, they in their turn become fair game for the dagger and bowl of the next lot of aspirants to power.

This went on until the commencement of this century, when Alim Khan captured Tashkend, and it is probable that he being the first to proclaim himself Khan of Khokand, it was about that time that the province ceased to pay tribute to the Chinese Emperor. Alim Khan was murdered in 1812, with the connivance of his brother Omar, who himself ten years afterwards was poisoned by his own son Mahammad Ali, who then became Khan.

In 1825 he joined Jehangir in his efforts to recover Kashgar from the Chinese, and in 1828–29, Mahammad Ali gave every assistance to Yusef, Jehangir's brother, who also succeeded in driving the Chinese out of Kashgar, but as before, on the reappearance of a large Chinese army, the Khokandians retreated, this time taking with them 70,000 Kashgarians. This depopulation of Kashgaria, and the prospect of being in a perpetual state of warfare with the Khokandians, induced the Chinese to make those concessions referred to by me (page 218), which were the outcome of the treaty of 1831 at Pekin, and which enacted that the Khan of Khokand was to have the right of levying duties on all foreign goods imported into Aksu, Ushturfan, Kashgar, Yarkand, and Khotan, and to have Aksakals stationed in those cities for that purpose, and also for the protection of the Mussalman population.

After getting into trouble with the Emir of Bokhara, who upbraided him for transgressing the Mahammadan laws of matrimony by having married two sisters and his step-mother, Mahammad Ali offered him his submission, and agreed to become his vassal. But the Emir, thinking he could do better, invaded the province, and had Mahammad Ali and most of his family put to death.

Thus in the year 1842 Khokand became tributary to Bokhara, but this state of affairs only lasted three months, for in that short period the Kiptchaks rose and turned the Bokharans out again. Then followed the siege of Khokand, which at the end of forty days was raised, and Sher Ali proclaimed himself Khan of Khokand.

Then came a long period of fighting between the Sarts and the Uzbecks, followed by the murder of

Sher Ali, and several changes in the Khanate, brought about by intrigues, poisonings, murders, etc., until at last the Russians, under General Kaufmann, put an end to the whole thing, by taking possession of the country in 1875.

* * * * * *

Leaving Khokand on a cold wintry morning, I proceeded in a snow-storm to cross the great steppe which separates that city from Khojend, and when about in the middle of this plain, the sky rapidly grew darker, the snow seemed almost to stop for a little while, so few and far between were the flakes, and all of a sudden, a dull sort of a roar was faintly heard in the distance. The driver, lashing up his horses to try and get to the next post-house, turned round to me and said, "the Bouran is coming." Just at that minute the horses got into a bad snow-drift, and the lashings of his whip and imprecations of his tongue, made not the slightest impression upon them. The poor brutes were up to their bellies in the snow, and the bouran sweeping over the plain from the north-west came right down upon us, bringing with it clouds of loose snow and sand.

The driver and Ramzan immediately got down, and scraping a hole in the snow behind the tarantass, sat and cowered under the lee of the hood and the luggage, and all I could do was to lay flat down at the bottom of the tarantass, and cover myself over with all my wraps.

Three long weary hours did it last, and when at length the storm broke, the snow was over the body of the tarantass, and I was a white mass inside. The result of all this was that the driver had to flounder through the deep snow to the nearest village, which luckily was not far off, where seven men with shovels were requisitioned, and after many hours' work we were dug out. We managed to reach the next post-house before dark, having been all day in that snow-drift, and having accomplished only forty versts (twenty-five miles) in the twelve hours.

The night looked so threatening, that after having had a cup of tea, I interviewed the man in charge of the post-house, who said it would not be safe to attempt to proceed any further that night. So I laid me down upon a hard wooden sort of couch, with a few wraps, but sleep was not easy; the wind howled round that little post-house, shaking the doors and windows, and causing me to thank my stars I was, at any rate, not travelling on such a night as that.

The next morning, there being a lull in the storm, I determined, at all hazards, to leave that miserable post-house, and try to reach Khojend. So ordering my horses I started, and in the afternoon came within sight of the city. About two miles from Khojend I saw a lot of men and camels near the roadside, all at work on something, and on coming up to them, found it was a large working party, trying to make a temporary road, as the Bouran had worked great havoc there. Trees were lying scattered about, and in one narrow place the road was entirely blocked by a very deep snow-drift, and the bridge over a small stream was also rendered useless. So a new bridge had to be temporarily constructed, and was just finished as we drove up. The horses had to be unharnessed and the carriage dragged over by men. It was a very rough and ready sort of bridge, but it served its purpose, and we got safely over the little river. After a deal of bumping over hard frozen ploughed fields, one of which was "lumped up" for melon planting, each lump a mound about two feet high, we eventually regained the road and arrived in safety at the city of Khojend, on the Syr Daria.

Khojend is an old fortified city, entered by a rather imposing-looking gateway, between two bastions, which project from the old battlemented walls, now almost in ruins. Through this gate we drove into the narrow streets and through the covered bazaars of the native quarter.

These bazaars appeared to me at a cursory glance to be very good; I suppose the fact that Khojend is the central city on the trade-route between Samarkand and Khokand may account for this. Khojend, before its annexation to the Russian dominions, was always a bone of contention between the Khans of Khokand and the Emirs of Bokhara, the latter holding it in subjection up to the year 1864, but General Romanofsky took it by assault in 1866, after the defeat of the Bokharan army at Irja. In 1872 there was a serious rising, of the Mahammadan population, which had to be put down by the Russians with force of arms, and in 1875 the small Russian garrison stood a siege from the Khokandian army, which numbered over 10,000 men, and at one time were in imminent danger of losing the town, and being all massacred, but eventually relief came from Tashkend, and the siege was raised.

The Russian quarter stands almost on the Syr Daria, little villas dotting its banks and facing the rocky mountain of Moghul Tagh, which rises out of the plain on the north side of the river. To the west of these little Bungalows, and almost overlooking the river, stands the old Citadel of Khojend, picturesque in its ruins.

I did not make a long stay in Khojend, as I was anxious to reach Tashkend, especially as the weather had completely broken up, and looked very threatening, the barometer having fallen so low, as to predict another serious storm, and the country I had now to pass through was for a long way a wild uninhabited waste, except for the post-houses, about 25 to 30 versts apart. To cross 140 versts of wild country, already under deep snow, was an undertaking not to be trifled with in the month of January.

Crossing the wooden bridge over the Syr Daria,

which is about 200 yards across, we emerged on to a bleak desolate steppe, between the mountains and the river. In the afternoon the sky clouded over again, and the wind rose, driving the loose snow before it, like the spindrift of the ocean in a white squall.

"The Bouran is coming," said the driver, and very lucky it was for us that we were close to the little post-house of Murza Rabat, for scarcely had we got into the friendly shelter of the courtyard, before the tempest came raging and tearing over the plain with perfect fury. The whole of that night did that storm last, drifting the snow into the room, where I was trying to sleep, so that in the morning one half of it was white. There was no chance of getting on that day, for the storm redoubled its fury about midday, and there was nothing left but to try and make oneself as comfortable as circumstances would permit of. But a "Station de Poste," on a steppe, in Russian Central Asia, is not exactly my idea of comfort, especially if one happens to be storm-stayed, as I was. To begin with, doors slam all day and all night with the wind, simply because they are not made to shut properly; the snow drifts in at the windows and under the doors, the stove gives little or no warmth, and the floors are of stone—innocent of any sort of covering in the shape of a carpet—on which stand hard, uncompromising wooden couches, without so much as a cushion to relieve their painful resemblance to a prison bench, in a condemned cell, and that is all that is supplied to the traveller on which to rest his weary limbs. But worse than all is the inability to get any wet things dried, and as the traveller comes out of a Bouran, considerably damper than he goes into it, this also has its disadvantages, resulting in sitting in wet clothes and wet feet, and having to sleep all night in the same draggled condition. The only article of food or drink to be obtained is boiling water from a samavar, although in some cases it is possible to get some tea and a little bread. The traveller has, therefore, to take everything with him, including tea, sugar, bread, and meat.

At Marghilan I was advised to take enough provisions for three days, and I did so, but being an old traveller, I made a little allowance for contingencies, and took enough for six days, and bade Ramzan do the same, which was just as well, as it turned out, for we were eight days on the road, instead of three.

But a good word for Murza Rabat. The man at the post-house was most attentive, and his good wife did all she could to make me as comfortable as the inadequacy of the surroundings would permit. She stoked up the fire in the stove, tied up refractory doors to prevent their banging, pinned up a sheet across the window, to keep the snow from drifting into the room, and, best of all, gave me some of her own tea and sugar when I had quite run out of my stock of both, and she also baked me some bread.

After the second day of being snowed-up, I made an attempt to start, but was obliged to return, although I had five horses attached to a sleigh. The next day I tried again in a sleigh, but the Bouran was still raging, and it was impossible for the driver to see his way at all, to say nothing of the impossibility of getting through some of the deep drifts. So again we were baffled, and had to return. By this time I had run completely out of all my provisions, and had to depend entirely upon the good woman of the house for any food she could supply me with. But her resources were rather heavily taxed, for, besides myself, there were the men in charge of three different sets of mails all snowed-up in the same place. The mails from Tashkend, going south, arrived in the middle of the fury of the storm, having been snowed-up all night on the steppe, although, in order to travel as light as possible, the mails were carried in six sleighs, with four horses each. The Marghilan mails going north to Tashkend and the mails from Samarkand also going in the same direction, were detained at our little post-house, as the fury of the storm seemed to be concentrated at that spot. There were only two rooms to contain the mail-bags, the men in charge, Ramzan, and myself. The mails were exceptionally heavy, as it was the Russian Christmas and New Year time.

At last, on the afternoon of the fourth day, the Bouran ceased, and we all got off. I cannot say that I left that post-house with any feelings of regret, but I was certainly most grateful to the man and his wife who kept it, for they did everything they possibly could to make me comfortable. As the last twenty-four hours of the storm was wind *only*, the Bouran had carried off a great deal of the snow that lay on the steppe, and with the exception of one or two deep drifts in hollows, it was good enough going. So I took my tarantass with five horses attached, three in the wheel and two leaders, with a man riding postilion, and made a start. Everything went smoothly for the first hour, until we got into a deep drift, and with great difficulty got out of it. The next one we came to, the driver thought he would "rush" it, so he lashed his horses and went at it *ventre à terre*, but, alas, there was a deep invisible hole in the road, full of snow, just before we reached the drift, and the two wheels on the off side of the carriage just fitted nicely into it, and over went the whole concern! Nobody was hurt, although the driver and Ramzan were shot off into the snow, but I remained pinned into the tarantass, which, falling over as it did on the right side, sent all the things I had inside flying out into the snow, except myself. With great difficulty I managed to get out, as the carriage was turned almost completely over, but eventually I crept out, and then we had to right the vehicle again, which had suffered a little from the smash, but not as much as one of my yak-dans, which was split up, and half full of snow, the sleeve of a shirt and the toe of a boot protruding out of a hole big enough to assure me that everything I had inside, would be wet through. However, we started on again, and drove for twenty-five miles, but got no further that night than the next post-house, which, to my consternation, I found was crammed full of snowed-up passengers going South, mostly Sarts. There were already eleven people in the only two rooms and I was forced to stop, as the mails had taken every horse in the stable. So in that wretched post-house, crowded up as it was, I had to remain, and wait, not only all that night, but the next morning, till some horses arrived to take us on.

My patience was pretty well exercised, and I thought of Job, and wondered if he had ever been in a *bouran* on the steppes of Russian Central Asia!

At last some horses arrived, and then it was a fight as to who should have them, but on my producing a small paper out of my pocket, with the signature of General Karalkoff attached to it, six horses were put at my disposal at once, and leaving the wounded tarantass behind, to follow when the road was clear for carriages, I embarked in a small sleigh with half the baggage and three horses, and Ramzan in a ditto with the remainder.

On our arrival at Uralska, I found that the Governor-General had been expecting me for some days, and had most courteously sent some officials to meet me at that

x 2

place, but after waiting for three days they had returned to Tashkend.

However, the Aksakals of the place all congregated on my arrival, and presented me with a doster-khan on behalf of his Excellency, after partaking of which, I resumed my journey, arriving at Tashkend late that night.

The next day, at the invitation of the Governor-General, Baron Wrewsky, I took up my abode in his most hospitable house, arriving just in time to be present at the Russian New Year's Fêtes.

CHAPTER XXXVIII.

Ancient History of Tashkend—Tashkend the Capital of Russian Turkestan—The three Provinces—(1) Syr Daria; (2) Ferghana; and (3) Samarkand — Population — Manners and Customs — Cotton Cultivation—A retrospect of Russia's advance in Asia since the XVIth Century—The Governor-General's Palace—New Year's Festivities—Blessing the Colours of the Regiments in Garrison—Arrival of an Ambassador from the Emir of Bokhara with New Year's Presents for the Governor-General —The Emir's Telegrams from St. Petersburg—Snowed-up—Journey to Khiva Abandoned—Departure for Samarkand and the Caspian Sea.

Of the ancient history of Tashkend, very little is known except that, like all other cities in Central Asia, it was perpetually changing hands, although it mostly remained in the possession of the kings of Bokhara and Samarkand. Still we find that in the fifteenth century Shebhani Khan captured it, amongst other cities that the great conqueror took from the possessions of those sovereigns who succeeded Tamerlane in the Suzerainty of Bokhara, and Samarkand. Previous to this, however, Tashkend was in the possession of Tchingiz Khan, who at that period over-ran the whole of that part of Central Asia.

At the close of the sixteenth century, when Abdulla

Khan reigned over Bokhara, Tashkend was captured by the Kirghiz, who retained possession of it for over 100 years. In 1758 the Province of Tashkend gave in its submission to Kian Lung, Emperor of China, and, in the commencement of the present century, it was captured by Alim, the Khan of Khokand (see page 289), in whose hands it remained until General Tchernaieff, in 1864–65, added it as well as Tchemkend to the dominions of the Ak-Padisha (White Czar).

Tashkend is the principal city of Russian Turkestan, and as such, is the seat of Government. The Russian portion of the city bears a strong resemblance to that of other cities in Central Asia, as do its native bazaars and streets to those of Andijan, Marghilan, Khokand, Khojend, etc. In the Russian quarter there are the same wide streets, with double rows of the white poplar standing sentry on each side, with almost painful military regularity, the same little one-storied white houses with their mud roofs, some of them shops, others private houses, and in the centre of the city, midway between the Sart (native) town and the Russian, is situated a large open square, in which stand the old Greek church, and the more modern cathedral, which is a handsome octagonal building of freestone, surmounted by a large dome, on the top of which is the usual golden cross, which marks in Russia all orthodox places of worship.

The population of Tashkend numbers 144,081 souls,

exclusive of the military, which number 11,919 officers and men.

During the summer months, society in Tashkend emigrate to the mountains in the same way as all Anglo-Indians, who are enabled to do so, go to the hill stations in India or to Kashmir.

Russian Turkestan is divided into three provinces: (1) Syr Daria, with Tashkend as the capital; (2) Ferghana, with Marghilan as its chief town; (3) Samarkand, with the city of Samarkand as its seat of Government. Each of these Provinces has a Lieutenant-Governor, and Baron Wrewsky, the Governor-General, rules over all.

The Oblast, or Province of Syr Daria, is divided up into five Oujesd, or districts, and one otdel, or section; the population of the Province numbering 1,143,584 persons.

The otdel of Amu-Darjinski	containing	149,610
The oujesd of Kasalinski	"	128,375
" " " Perowski	"	105,253
" " " Tchemkendski	"	206,948
" " " Aulieatinski	"	180,731
" " " Tachkendski	"	237,147
	In all,	1,143,584.

FERGANSKAJA OBLAST.

Oujesd Kokandski . .	107,526 males	104,806 females
" Margelanski . .	97,337 "	98,040 "
" Andijanski . .	64,698 "	59,350 "
" Namaganski . .	104,112 "	93,097 "
" Ochski . . .	23,973 "	22,361 "

Or a total of 785,600.

SAMARKANDASKAJA OBLAST.

Oujesd Samarkandski	254,195	290,686
Samarkand (city)	34,016	
Penjekent (city)	2,479	
Oujesd Katta—Kurghanski	153,400	168,684
Katta—Kurgan (city)	15,284	
Oujesd Djizakakski	132,930	146,339
Djizak (city)	13,049	
Oujesd Chadjentski	68,460	106,711
Chadjent (city)	28,826	
Oura-Tube (city)	9,425	

Or a total of 712,420.

Thus the entire population of the three provinces amounts to 2,641,604.

The inhabitants of Tashkend are mostly Sarts, but Tajiks, Tartars, Kirghiz, Jews, and a few Hindus, are to be found in the city, the two latter races plying the trades almost exclusively of usury.

Lending money upon usury is strictly against the Mahammadan law, but still, for all that, there are besides the Hindus, some Mussalmans, who make a practice of it, having recourse to all sorts of roundabout dodges to keep as near as possible to the letter of the law, and so quiet their consciences, although the result is sixty per cent. after all. Schuyler, in his work on Turkestan, mentions a tradition so grotesque in its blasphemy, that I cannot refrain from quoting it. After describing one method of lending money, resorted to by Mussalmans, he says: "Another method is for the lender to buy of the borrower some piece of property, as a house or a horse, for less than its value, paying him at the same time the amount of the loan. A paper is then drawn up before the Kazi, in which the lender promises to resell the property to the borrower for a sum that will equal the money lent with the interest added. Mussalmans, however, perfectly well understand that these methods are the direct evasions of the religious command; and amongst the traditions as to future punishment, is one that the usurer will be sealed up in a metallic box, which will then be heated in a fire. When the usurer cries out in his torment, asking the reason of such punishment, the Almighty and All Blessed will answer him, 'You are punished because you took usury.' 'But I did not take usury; I sold a thing lawfully,' he will reply. Well then the All Highest will reply, '*I don't burn you; I only heat the box!*'"

Talking of Sarts, I found it very difficult to get any one to explain to me the difference between Sarts and Uzbeks, and as far as I can gather there is not much more difference than between a Yorkshireman and a Cockney. If a Kirghiz came and settled in a city, he would become a Sart, but if a Sart went and lived a nomad life on the Pamirs, in an akoi, I don't believe the Kirghiz would recognize him as one of themselves.

The word Sart, according to M. Lerch, merely means the inhabitant of a city. He traces the word Jaxartes and Jaxartai to a root Xartai, which is the representation of an old Iranic root, Khastra, as seen in the later Persian Shehr city. Jaxartai would thus mean the dwellers in cities, and Jaxartes, the river of cities, and the word Sart, the corruption of Jaxartai, was passed over from the Iranic nomads to the Turkish nomads, as a designation for the settled inhabitants of the lower valley of the Syr Daria, which was then thickly populated, and full of flourishing cities, probably about the time when, as tradition has it, the Nightingale could fly from Samarkand, to Khokand, and rest on the branch of a tree in a garden all the way, whereas now it is simply a howling wilderness.

The language spoken by Sarts, Uzbeks, Kirghiz, etc., is Turki, which, as I mentioned before, resembles Turkish so little, that a Turk from Stamboul would not be able to make himself understood amongst the people.

The summer dress of a Sart consists of loose baggy trousers, the same as those worn by all Orientals; over these a long shirt, with a small aperture for the head to go through, with sleeves a foot too long, so that the hands are always concealed. Over this is worn a *chapan*, which is a sort of quilted dressing-gown, with strings to tie round the waist, over which a gaudy-coloured kerchief, or a sombre-coloured shawl, according to the taste of the wearer, acts as a girdle or cummerbund. In the case of a merchant or well-to-do person, the *khalat* covers all; this is a much-coveted article of dress, as it is a sort of robe of honour or distinction, and in most cases has been presented to the wearer by some high Government official, for services rendered. On the head, which after the manner of all Mussalmans is shaved, is worn an embroidered skull-cap, round which, in hot weather, is worn the *chalmah*, or *chit petch* (forty folds), which is a turban generally of white material. Out of doors all the men wear high boots, with small high heels.

The women dress very much the same as the men, wearing the same long boots, same loose baggy trousers, and long coloured silk chemises reaching down below the knee. They are very fond of jewelry, especially necklaces and earrings.

When out walking, they wear black horse-hair veils, which completely hide the whole face, not like the Arab women, who only hide the lower part of the face, showing the eyes, or the Turkish ladies who, if pretty, wear the most transparent veils over the mouth and nose.

The ordinary means of locomotion in Central Asia, for both men and women, is riding, either on horses or camels. Carts or Arabas on huge wheels, very far apart, and without tires, but studded with huge nails, are much used in the country, and the driver, instead of sitting in the cart, which is often covered with a matting hood, sits on the horse, with his feet on the shafts, and his knees therefore in close proximity to his ears. All heavy goods, such as large bales of cotton, etc., are carried on camels, and most beautiful animals they are, these long-haired Central Asian camels, nearly half as large again as an African camel. I passed hundreds of caravans of camels during my journey through Central Asia, and was more particularly struck with one caravan, between the Syr Daria and Djizak, where the camels were nearly pure white. Their saddles and trappings, too, are very picturesque, being of bright colours and ornamented with many gaudy tassels.

The Asiatic is naturally fond of music, and passionately adores dancing, or rather the witnessing of dancing. Twenty years ago there used to be regular dancing boys, called *Batchas*, but the system of these boy-dancers has been practically abolished, and very properly so, in almost every part of Russian Turkestan, by the Russians, although I believe it still exists in Bokhara.

The musical instruments most in vogue amongst the Sarts, are the Du-tara, or two-stringed, the Si-tara,* or three-stringed instrument, both of which are like a mandoline with a very long finger-board, and these they use to twang an unmusical accompaniment to a

* Si-tara—Persian, three-stringed. Evidently the origin of the word guitar.

still more inharmonious vocalist. Tambourines are also much used, and a sort of flageolet is sometimes piped on, with equally unmusical results.

The Sart marriage laws and customs are much the same as those that obtain in Yarkand, described by me in Chapter XXIII., but divorces are not so frequent.

As in all Mahammadan countries, a man is lawfully allowed four wives, but no more, although, of course, if one dies or is divorced, the husband can fill up the place with another. Two sisters cannot be married to one man at the same time, although he can divorce the one, and then marry the other.

The cultivation of cotton has made rapid strides since the Russian occupation, especially in Ferghana, where the best cotton is produced, as well as the greatest amount.

Several officers were sent over by the Russian Government to the Cotton States of America, to study its culture in all its branches, and they have brought their experience to bear upon the native agricultural population with the most successful results.

Last year the exportation of cotton from Russian Turkestan amounted to 50,000, tons or 3,000,000 *poud,* (of 36 pounds to the *poud*), and was sold at prices ranging from six to eight roubles the *poud.* Taking a mean of seven roubles, that would amount to 21,000,000 roubles, or over £2,000,000 sterling. Before the Russian occupation, the export of cotton was about 100,000 to 150,000 *pouds* in the year, and of very inferior quality.

As we are dealing now with facts connected with the Russian occupation of Central Asia, perhaps it will not be out of place here to review shortly her gradual absorption of different parts of Asia from the earliest times. It has been to the north, the east and south, that this great Northern Power has moved. The first movement to the north was at the close of the sixteenth century, when she invaded Siberia by way of the Oural mountains. The second was eastwards, over those steppes on which congregated the different hordes of the Kirghiz, and which led her eventually into the valleys of the Oxus (Amu Daria), and Jaxartes (Syr Daria); and the third, to the south, towards the Persian and Afghan frontiers, into the country of the Turcomans, with Merv as an objective point. But it was to the northern parts of Asia that she first turned her attention, and to the conquest of those states, over which reigned at that time, powerful Tartar princes, the most important among which was the Khan of Sibir.

M. Regelsperger, in an excellent and comprehensive article on 'Les Russes en Asie,' tells us that, in the year 1558, the Czar Ivan IV., surnamed Ivan the Terrible, made a concession to the family Strogonoff, of the valley of the Kama, the Oural, and all the countries on the eastern watershed that they were able to conquer, confiding to them the care of guarding the Frontier of the Empire in that direction. Twenty years after this, one of the Strogonoff family, accompanied by a band of freebooters, composed of men of all nationalities, invaded the dominions of the Khan of Sibir, and eventually received his submission. This system of semi-official marauding met with the approval of the Czar, who gave Strogonoff every inducement to continue his career of subjugation of these wild tribes. Thus, in 1587, a new city sprang up on the site of the ancient Sibir, and was named Tobolsk, and became the capital of the Russian Asiatic dominions, and remained as such until the commencement of the present century.

In 1631 the Cossacks, to whom Russia practically owes the conquest of Siberia, if not of other parts of Asia also, established themselves at Ostrog, at the junction of the rivers Angara and Oka, and there they levied taxes on the surrounding inhabitants. Shortly after this, they took entire possession of the upper Amoor, after conquering the kingdom of Irkoutsk, and it was then that the city of Albazin was built, and the Russians found themselves threatening the Chinese.

In 1689 a treaty was made between the Russians and the Chinese, giving the latter all the basin of the Amoor, and fixing the Russian frontier with China, but to the eastwards the former power had already secured the Pacific Ocean as their limit.

During the reign of Peter the Great, Siberia was

divided into five provinces, under one Governor-General, and a Lieutenant-Governor for each province, and it was during his reign that the celebrated silver mines of Siberia were discovered. It was in 1691 that the Government were informed of the presence of silver in the neighbourhood of Nertchinsk, and they immediately took steps to verify the information, and soon after began working the mines.

In 1705 Demidoff founded the first factory for the smelting of iron and copper ore in the Oural district, and afterwards discovered more silver mines, which he made over to the Government. Peter the Great made several abortive attempts to cross the Tian Shan range of mountains with Russian expeditions, in search of gold, and he was the first of Russian monarchs to cast a loving and determined eye on Central Asia, for in 1717 he sent an expedition against the Khan of Khiva, with whom he subsequently made a treaty.

The force numbered 3300 men, under command of Prince Bekovitch Tcherkasski. When 100 miles from Khiva, he was met by the army of the Khan, and a three days' battle ensued, in which the Russians were victorious. The Khivans induced this Commander Tcherkasski to break up his force into small detachments, in order to facilitate the supplying them with food. The Khivans then fell upon each detachment in turn, and thus treacherously annihilated the whole force.

His successors, however, instead of following up his policy of conquest and annexation in Central Asia, concentrated the whole of their energies in the subjugation of the wild tribes of the Caucasus, where they were not only opposed by the native princes, but also by the Shah of Persia, who had a distinct interest in those regions.

It was by the Caucasian route that the Empress Catherine II. thought she would be able to find her way into Central Asia, and eventually to India, and after making treaties with all the hill tribes, she protected her route through Kourban and Terek by a line of strongly fortified outposts. To this Empress, Heraclius, King of Georgia, gave in his submission, and the Sultan was also forced to cede to Russia all those Caucasian provinces which had heretofore been tributary to him.

In 1799, after the Russians had repelled an invasion of the Persians in Georgia, George XIII., King of Georgia, and son of Heraclius, became the vassal of the Emperor Paul I. and in 1801 Georgia became a Russian province. On the Persian Frontier, English interests came into collision with Russian, for Persia and Afghanistan were the only two countries left between these two great powers. So the Emperor Paul made a proposition to Napoleon Buonaparte, then First Consul, for a joint expedition of Russian and French forces to attack India by way of the Caspian Sea, Astrabad,

Herat, and Kandahar. But France refused to join in the undertaking, so the Emperor determined to make the attempt single-handed. His death, however, put an end to the project, notwithstanding the fact that General Arloff had actually started with his *Corps d'armée*.

In 1807, Napoleon the First and the Emperor Alexander formulated a similar project, to attack India, with the assistance of Persia; and a French General was despatched as envoy to the Persian Court, to try and induce the Shah to join in the undertaking. On his arrival there he found that British influences predominated, and he was forced to depart the way he came, with his task unaccomplished.

In 1812, after the Franco-Russian war, Russia made peace with Persia, who, by the treaty of Gulistan, in 1813, gave up Emeretia, Mingrelia, and Daghistan, etc., to the Czar.

In 1826 war broke out again, and two years afterwards, by the treaty of Tourkmantchai, Russia became mistress of Erivan, and obtained the sole right of navigation on the Caspian Sea. A few months later, Poti on the Black Sea was also ceded to the Great Northern Power, by terms of the Treaty of Adrianople, in 1828.

Sixteen years previous to these events, Russia had entirely subjugated the Kirghiz hordes, and had entered into negotiations with their still wilder brethren the Turkomans, who at that period over-ran the whole of Central Asia, from the Caspian to the Frontiers of Persia, Afghanistan and even of China.

When in 1819 Mouravieff went to Khiva, and in 1824 a Russian caravan penetrated as far as Bokhara, the country now known as Russian Turkestan was in a most deplorable condition, the Turkomans devastating the whole territory, pillaging, murdering, and taking into slavery all the inhabitants, to such an extent that no caravans dared take the road, and trade and commerce were entirely paralysed.

The most powerful amongst the native princes, were the Khans of Khiva and Khokand, and the Emir of Bokhara, and at that time no Christian dared show his face in the country. The Tekké and Sarik Turkomans occupied the whole of the country between the Caspian and Oxus, and Merv had been captured by the Sarik Turkomans from the Persians. Kafristan, Herat, the Upper Oxus and the Pamirs, were all tributary to different Khans, who in their turn were dependent upon such powerful sovereigns and princes as the Amirs of Afghanistan, and Bokhara, and the Khan of Khokand. China, who was mistress of Eastern Turkestan, also held ill-defined relations with the Pamirs.

In 1835 Russia, being then determined to make herself mistress of Central Asia, built the fort of Novo-Alexandrovsk, and in the same year a Russian accredited envoy presented himself at Bokhara, and another at Cabul. The year 1842 witnessed the murder of Conolly and Stoddart, in Bokhara, by Nasrullah, the most cruel and bloodthirsty scoundrel that ever sat upon a throne, and he remained Emir until 1860, having reigned thirty-four years.

Russia, although anxious to put an end to all the barbarities that existed in that part of Central Asia, was not in a position to undertake a military expedition, having no base of operations, as the Caucasus was still unconquered.

In 1839, Perovski, with 4500 men, made a disastrous attempt upon Khiva, starting from Orenburg, which resulted in the loss of most of his army; but in 1841 Daniloski was more fortunate and made a treaty.

In 1844 the Kirghiz great horde were conquered and a line of forts established from Orenburg to the Lake Baikal; the Russian Frontier travelled gradually south, to protect what they already had conquered from incursions of the Khokandians, and the Fort of Novo-Alexandrovsk was replaced by a new one called Novo-Petrovsk. In 1848 the Fort of Azalsk was constructed on the shores of the Sea of Aral, and a flotilla of Russian war-ships were launched, and the following year the Fort of Kasalinsk was built on the Jaxartes. In 1853 the fort of Perovski also was erected on the banks of the same river, and in 1854 the Frontier kept moving more and more to the east, until it culminated with the erection of a fort at Vernyi, north of the lake

Issigh-kul (hot lake), to command the passes of the Celestial mountains, belonging to China.

In the same year Mouravieff conquered the Amoor, and, by the treaty of Pekin of 1860, China gave up the whole country south of the Amoor, down to Oussouri, and Vladivostock was made the Russian port on the Pacific.

In 1867 Russia exchanged the Kurile Islands with the Japanese for the island of Sakhalien. Six years previously, Tchernaieff had extended the Russian Frontier to the Tian Shan range of mountains, and three years afterwards the same General captured Aoulie Ata, Hazret, Tchemkend, and in 1865 Tashkend.

The Emir of Bokhara, having occupied Khojend, 140 versts from Tashkend, and on the south bank of the Syr Daria (Jaxartes), war broke out between him and Tchernaieff, who was forced to retreat, being short of soldiers, but in 1866 General Romanovski captured Khojend and Djizak.

In 1867 General Kaufmann was appointed Governor-General of Russian Turkestan, and in 1868 he captured Samarkand, and in 1873, Khiva. The year 1876 witnessed the repression, by force of arms, of a serious revolution in Khokand, which was annexed to Russia, and given the name of the Province of Ferghana. In 1879 General Lomakine was repulsed by the Tekké Turkomans, at Geok-Tepe, and the following year, General Skobeleff captured it. In

1881 the first portion of the Trans-Caspian railroad was made from the Caspian to Kizil-Arvat, and in 1884 Merv was annexed to Russia.

* * * * * *

As I mentioned before, I had arrived in Tashkend just in time to participate in the Russian New Year's festivities, I say the Russian, because our New Year's day had already passed and gone, twelve days previously, and the first of these fêtes commenced on New Year's Eve, when the Governor-General gave a dinner-party, and various were the amusements in which we indulged during the evening. Amongst others, was the telling of people's fortunes for the coming year, through the medium of a barn-door fowl. The guests all sat in a large circle, and at the feet of each was sprinkled some corn. A large and very handsome white cock, who had been starved for the twenty-four previous hours, was brought in and placed in the centre of the circle. He seemed somewhat dazed at first, especially as the floor was a very highly polished parquet, which caused him to slip about in the most ludicrous manner, but once firmly established upon his legs, he walked round and surveyed with hungry eye the different little heaps of corn, evidently unable to make up his mind which to go to. Every one tried to induce him to come to his or her particular heap, for the person at whose corn he pecked first would have good luck in the coming year, and in the event of its being an unmarried young lady, the superstition was that she would find a husband within the next twelve months.

Needless to say, the cock went straight up to an old married lady and made a good supper at her feet, to the great sorrow and disappointment of many younger ones still unattached. Then, when the clock struck twelve, we all drank each other's healths and sat down to a very cheery midnight supper.

The next day the Baron gave a big official luncheon to all the Generals and Heads of Departments, civil as well as military, in the large room reserved for banquets and balls and such like entertainments, on the walls of which hung two large full-length portraits of the Emperor and Empress. When the toast of His Majesty's health was given by the Baron, every one who had their backs turned, faced towards these two pictures, and remained standing while the military bands in the adjoining room played the Russian National Anthem.

A few days after this, a very interesting and impressive ceremony took place in the Cathedral, namely, the blessing of the colours of the different regiments in garrison, which takes place every New Year. The regiments (mostly Cossacks) were formed up on the big parade ground close to the Governor-General's Palace, their formation being a hollow square facing the Cathedral. After the religious ceremony was concluded inside the Cathedral, the clergy all came out, as well as the Governor-General and high officials, on to the ground, and the colours were restored to the different regiments; but what form that ceremony took, I am unable to relate, because I did not see it. The fact was, that, after remaining inside the church for some time, the heat and the crush drove me out, for not being in uniform, I was not able to accompany my host, but had to be squashed up in the crowd. When outside again I waited for half an hour, walking briskly up and down through the snow, trying to keep myself warm, in the hopes of seeing the conclusion of the ceremony, but on being told by an officer who had just left the Cathedral, that they would be another hour before they came out, I preferred to return to the Palace, as it was much too cold to stand about in the snow. After three hours' hard work, the Baron returned home, very glad it was all over.

The Palace is a large one-storied house, not quite in keeping with the popular idea of a palace, but so-called in Tashkend by courtesy, as being the residence of the Governor-General, or General Governor, as he is styled by the Russians.

It is a somewhat rambling sort of building, having been frequently added to by successive Governors, and is situated exactly in the centre of the city, as the Russian town comes up to it on one side, and the Sart town commences just on the far side of the high wall, which surrounds the garden and pleasure grounds.

These gardens must be quite lovely in spring and summer, as they are beautifully laid out, and the natural undulation of the ground is most picturesque. A river runs through the grounds, and the miniature hills and dales in this small park are planted with ornamental trees and shrubs; so—what between small cascades, long avenues of trees, which afford grateful shade in summer; flower beds, rose gardens, not to mention the palms and tree-ferns, and the more delicate plants, which now form a beautiful winter garden in the centre of the Palace, but which, in summer, are all planted out—it must truly be a sort of little Paradise.

Zoological and ornithological specimens also are not wanting, there being a large pit in which the former Governor-General kept some bears, until they took to eating the gardeners, when they were destroyed; and the present Governor has replaced them with some silver foxes, and in another cage are some kunitzas. His Excellency has also a large aviary, in which there are pheasants from the Oxus, partridges from the hills of Chimgan; orange-coloured ducks, much resembling the ruddy sheldrake; pigeons and doves, all tending to show that the extreme warmth of heart and kindliness of disposition, which characterise the present General Governor, is not confined only to the human beings under his beneficent rule, but is also extended to those dumb animal favourites that he feeds daily with his own hand.

The Palace is most thoroughly comfortable, and possesses some really handsome, well-furnished rooms, and the hospitality of the present occupier, is only equalled by his charm of manner, and his way of putting every one at their ease the moment they come in contact with him.

During the fêtes, attending the New Year, I made the acquaintance of the Ambassador from the Emir of Bokhara, who had just arrived with the New Year's offerings from his sovereign to the General Governor. Twice every year, on New Year's Day and on the anniversary of the Emperor's coronation, does the Emir send an ambassador to the Russian General Governor of Turkestan, with greetings of peace, augmented by a substantial indication of goodwill, in the shape of a host of presents of all sorts, from horses and carpets, down to jewelry.

I had the extreme good fortune to be present when these New Year's gifts arrived, and great was the excitement in the household when they were being unpacked and inspected.

Unlike our high officials in India, who are not allowed to receive presents from rajahs or native princes, the Governor-General of Russian Turkestan is not only permitted to receive them, but it is an understood thing that it is part of his perquisites, the Emir of Bokhara's gifts alone bringing him in a sum of 30,000 roubles every year.

The peculiar feature in these offerings lies in the fact that each article is *marked* with its value in roubles, and as the Emir knows quite well that almost everything will be sold, he sends merchants from Bokhara, who purchase at the sale. The result is that many of the articles that I saw sold by the Governor-General, at this New Year's time, will return again as presents on the Emperor's Coronation-day.

On this occasion, the presents from the Emir consisted of a beautiful scimitar, with scabbard of red velvet, and pure gold plaques; a waist-belt, also of pure gold. Eight horses, with gorgeous saddle-cloths of blue, green, white, and red velvet, embroidered thickly with gold and silver; bridles, headpieces, breastplates, etc., of gold, and studded with turquoises. Two beautiful halats, or robes of honour, gold embroidered, on crimson velvet. 406 silk khalats of various colours. One pelisse of Kashmir stuff, lined with Kunitza fur. Two Indian shawls, four Kashmir shawls, 300 yards of Bokharan silk velvet, 208 pieces of silk of different colours, eight large carpets; and for the ladies of the General Governor's family, a casket containing a magnificent necklace in gold, with emeralds, rubies, and pearls, a circlet for the head, and a pair of earrings, also of the same gems, also four Indian shawls. 100 yards of Bokharan silk velvet, and eighty-six pieces of silk of various colours.

No sooner had these presents arrived at the Palace

before the outer court was thronged with Sart merchants from the bazaar of the native town, all waiting until His Excellency had selected what he wished to keep for himself, when they would be permitted to enter, and purchase the surplus stock. A more orderly or respectful crowd I never saw; they all inspected and handled the different articles, and having each made his selection, they deputed one man to buy the whole lot, and then divide the goods amongst them all.

Before night every single article was disposed of, including the horses, which were sold by auction in the courtyard. I was lucky enough to secure some very valuable articles, at what I considered ridiculously low prices, as it was not in the Emir's interests to place too high a value upon goods he intended to repurchase himself.

The Emir of Bokhara was at that time in St. Petersburg, making his first visit to the Russian capital, by special permission of the Czar. The only other time he had ever been in Russia, was on the occasion of the Coronation of the present Czar at Moscow. He took with him a large retinue, and a mass of presents for the Czar, several tons weight of gifts of all sorts, amongst which were a silken tent containing seventeen rooms, a carpet so large that it took two Arabas to convey it to the Trans-Caspian Railway, and a casket of magnificent jewels for the Empress. He is evidently very pleased with his visit, for one evening Baron Wrewsky received a telegram from him, which he handed me to read, and it ran thus: "I have the honour to inform your Excellency that I dined last night with His Imperial Majesty the Czar, and had the extreme honour of leading Her Imperial Majesty, the Czarina, into dinner by the hand."

* * * * * *

My intended visit to Khiva has been given up. There are but two ways to reach it from here, one by Kasalinsk, or Fort No. 1,* which road is now impassable, owing to the snow, and the other by the Oxus, which is not navigable, owing to the mass of small icebergs, which are rushing north to the Sea of Aral on the river's swift current. The road to Samarkand also has been blocked for some days, as the river Syr Daria has to be crossed, and there is neither boat nor bridge at Chinaz, and the floating ice rushing by also, on its way to the Aral sea, has made the crossing impracticable. So I am a prisoner, and a very comfortable jail it is, in which I am incarcerated, to say nothing of the kindness and hospitality of my janitors.

January 30th.—Information having been received by the Governor-General that the crossing of the Syr Daria at Chinaz was at last feasible, after the hard frosts of the last ten days, I settled to leave my most

* This is the route Burnaby travelled. He drove in sleighs from Orenburg to Kasalinsk, and rode from Kasalinsk to Khiva, a distance of about 400 miles.

comfortable quarters, and start for Chinaz, Djizak, and Samarkand. It was with genuine regret that I parted from my dear kind host, with whom I had spent nearly three weeks, and whose kindness to me I shall never forget, and in the evening, after dinner, entered my tarantass, and bade adieu to Tashkend. It was a lovely moonlight night, and I drove all night, arriving at the crossing of the river at Chinaz at 7 A.M.

This same Syr Daria, which was known to the Greeks in Alexander the Great's time, as the Jaxartes, has its source in the mountains of Tian Shan, south of the Issigh-kul, or hot lake. Near to its source it is known by the name of the Taragai, and after its junction with the Karasai and Kurmanta, it is called the Narin. In Khokand, it joins the Karakuldja which rises in the Terek Darwan, in the Alai mountains, and down which I rode on Christmas Day. These combined waters, under the name of Syr Daria, flow south-west, and passing Khojend, take a bend north, and receive the waters of several small rivers in the neighbourhood of Tashkend, Chemkend and Turkestan. From there the river runs north-west, and passing the forts of Julek, Perovsky, Karmakchi and Kasalinsk, empties itself into the Sea of Aral on its north-east littoral, 243 feet above the level of the Caspian, and 159 feet above the level of the Black Sea.

The crossing of the Syr Daria was much easier than I had expected, the hard frosts of the last ten days having knit the ice together in such a way that it was possible to get a carriage across with very little difficulty, the only obstacle being the bank on the opposite side of the river, up which the tarantass was hoisted by natives. From Chinaz to Djisak, a distance of nearly ninety miles, there is nothing but desert.

The Russians call it the "Golodnaia," or the hungry steppe. It certainly was the most peculiar place I ever saw. I have seen deserts in Africa, but never such a place as this Golodnaia steppe. It was absolutely level, without a rock, stone or bush, to break the line. Covered with snow too, as it was, one felt oneself on a huge frozen sea, instead of on dry land. At last the eye was relieved by seeing in the distance the hills that lay behind Djisak, and about sunset I drove through the little bazaar, and reached the post-house. There I rested a while, and continued my journey at daylight. Djizak was captured by General Kryzhanoksky, in 1866.

After leaving the little city, our route lay through the gorge of Jilan-ute, through which flowed a river with so many turns and windings, that we crossed it seven different times, before emerging from the defile. On a rock, on the right of the road, is a square tablet, on which are two Persian inscriptions. I could not make them out, not being able to read Persian, but Schuyler, when he passed them, had a Mullah with him, who gave him the following interpretation of the writing, which I quote: "With the help of God the Lord, the great Sultan, conqueror of kings, and nations, shadow of God on earth, the support of the decisions of the Sunna, and of the divine law, the ruler and aid of the Faith, Ulug Bek Gurugan—may God prolong the time of his reign and rule—undertook a campaign in the country of the Mogols, and returned from this nation into these countries uninjured in the year 828." (A.D. 1429.) This Ulug Bek was the famous grandson of Tamerlane, so well known for his patronage of learning, for the observatory and college he founded at Samarkand, and for his astronomical tables.

The second inscription relates to one of the victories of Abdullah Khan, a century and a half later, and runs thus: "Let passers in the waste, and travellers on land and water, know that in the year 979 (A.D. 1571), there was a conflict between the army of the Lieutenant of the Khalifate, the shadow of the Almighty, the great Khakan, Abdullah Khan, son of Iskunder Khan, consisting of 30,000 men of war, and the army of Dervish Khan and Baba Khan, and other sons of Barak Khan. In this army there were fifty relatives of the Sultan, and 400,000 fighting men from Turkestan, Tashkend, Ferghana and Deshta-Kiptchak. The army of the Sovereign, by the fortunate conjunction of the stars, gained the victory, having conquered the above-mentioned Sultans, and gave to death so many of them that, from the people who were killed in the fight, and after being taken as prisoners, during the course of one month, blood ran on the surface of the water in the river to Djizak. Let this be known."

* * * * * *

From this gorge we gradually descended till we reached the valley of the Zarafshan, and shortly afterwards, the domes and towers of Samarkand came in view, lit up by the golden light of a grand winter sunset. Driving into this city of beautiful ruins, we left the high towers and domes of the Mosque of Shah Zindeh on our right, while to our left lay the dome of the Mosque of Bibi Khanum. On passing through the native bazaars, which are the smallest and most insignificant in every way of any that I had seen in any other city of Central Asia, we suddenly came upon the huge back walls of the Righistan, leaving which, on the right, we drove into the Russian quarter, and proceeding down the avenue Abramofski, a long broad Boulevard, at last reached a lodging house, guided there by the jigits that Colonel Galkin, Chief of the Staff at Samarkand, had sent as far as the Zarafshan river to meet me.

The next day this most agreeable officer came round to my quarters, and volunteered to accompany me round the ruins of this once most gorgeous city of Asia, an offer I accepted with much pleasure.

We first visited the Tomb of Timur or Tamerlane,

entering a court through a broken-down archway, which, judging by what is left of it, must have been once of exquisite architecture; it was covered with mosaics, and there still remain some very beautiful tiles. Over this portal is a Persian inscription: "The weak slave Mahammad, son of Mahmoud from Isfahan built this."

Inside the Mosque, the tombstone of Tamerlane lies exactly in the centre, under the large dome, which is covered with alabaster work, and the outside of which was tiled with beautiful green glazed tiles, more than half of which have either fallen off through age, or been destroyed in other ways. The sarcophagus, which has been at one time broken in half, but repaired with cement, is of dark-green marble, and is surrounded by a beautifully carved stone railing. Round the edge of the sarcophagus is an inscription in Cufic characters, giving the date of Tamerlane's death, 807 (1405 A.D.), and his various titles. Exactly underneath the sarcophagus is the real tomb, to reach which, we had to go down a narrow staircase into a crypt, most beautifully built of yellow brick, the workmanship of the brick arches being equal to anything that could be done of the same sort at the present day, and it looks quite fresh, certainly not close on 500 years old. There are other slabs in this vault, one of them covering the remains of Tamerlane's old teacher.

From this Mosque, we proceeded to the Mosque of Shah Zindeh, which was built in 1323, by Tamerlane, on each side of which are smaller mosques, now in ruins. Passing through a splendid arched gateway, faced with gorgeous tiles, we went up a long flight of steps, as this mosque is built on the side of a steep hill. On each side of the paved causeway were these small mosques, all containing tombs, and on the right is the famous well of Shah Zindeh, into which he is supposed to have leaped *after* having had his head cut off I suppose by the Christians, as Samarkand was a Christian See, with a Bishop, in the thirteenth century. The mosaic and alabaster work in every one of these small mosques, each with its own beautifully designed arched portal, covered with Persian tiles, is very splendid, even in its present state of dilapidation; what it must have been when new, can hardly be imagined, so gorgeous must have been the effect.

Leaving these we visited the *Medressé* (college) of Bibi Khanum, daughter of the Emperor of China, and favourite wife of Tamerlane. It is surmounted by an enormous dome, and is in every sense of the word a magnificent specimen of ancient Oriental architecture. From there we proceeded to the "Righistan," the three *Medressés* of which form the three sides of the great square. The first we entered was on the north side of the square, called Tillah-kari, or "covered with gold" (probably owing to the "*kibleh*" being overlaid with gold). We next entered the Shir-dar, which was built in the middle of the seventeenth century, and is a very handsome building. On the western side of the Righistan stands the Mosque of Ulug Bek, built early in the fifteenth century. It has a minaret on each side, both of which look like the Leaning Tower of Pisa, so much out of the perpendicular do they appear to the eye.

One of the great beauties of all these mosques and *Medressés*, are their fluted melon-shaped domes, covered with mosaic patterns, chiefly in glazed Persian tiles. What struck me, was the utter indifference exhibited by the mullahs and janitors, who hung about their portals, to an "infidel" going in with his boots on. In no other Mussalman country have I ever entered a mosque, without being either obliged to remove my boots, or being supplied with large slippers to put over them, like galoshes.

* * * * * *

Samarkand is famous for the gallant defence made by its little garrison of Russians in 1866. General Golovatcheff and his army were in a most critical position at Katta-Kurgan, not far from Samarkand, being surrounded by an overwhelming mass of the Amir's troops. General Kaufmann, who had just captured Samarkand, went off, therefore, by forced marches to the relief of his comrade, leaving all the men he could spare to garrison the city. Out of these 800 men left, more than half had been wounded in the assault, and many were sick. No sooner had General Kaufmann left Samarkand, than a body of 20,000 troops from Shahrisabs, who had been concealed in the vicinity, attacked the city. The little band of Russians, that formed its garrison, retreated into the citadel, where they made a most gallant and stubborn defence, against overwhelming numbers, for the space of five days.

General Kaufmann luckily returned just as the garrison, now reduced to a handful of men, had resolved to blow up the citadel and magazine, and perish in the ruins. The troops who were besieging Samarkand were under the command of Jura Bek, one of the most powerful antagonists that Russia had at that time to deal with. That was only about five and twenty years ago, and when one day at dinner, at the Governor-General's, I found myself sitting next to, and conversing with, a tall handsome man, still in the prime of life, dressed in a Russian uniform, I could hardly believe it was the same Jura Bek who had been such a bitter enemy to Russia, only a quarter of a century ago. But it was the selfsame man, now a Colonel on the Russian General Staff at Tashkend; and his son, with whom I was constantly thrown in contact, was one of Baron Wrewsky's Aides-de-camp. His name is Alacul Bek, and a very nice, gentleman-like fellow he is.

Jura Bek's history is a somewhat curious one, and worth relating, as it was told me during the time I was an inmate of the Governor-General's Palace at Tashkend, where Jura Bek's duties often brought him, besides being rather a favourite of His Excellency's, who had for his character a genuine admiration, as well as perhaps, an *arrière-pensée* of pity for fallen greatness.

Jura Bek is the son of Kalendar Bek of Shahrisabs, at whose death Nasrullah, the Emir of Bokhara, annexed his little kingdom, and took the son into his service as a sort of page of honour at Bokhara, where he remained until death removed the bloodthirsty ruffian, Nasrullah, when the young Jura Bek escaped from Bokhara, returning to his native Shahrisabs. When about twenty years of age he was, in consequence of the misdeeds of the unprincipled Muzaffar Edin, elected by the Shahrisabians Bek of the neighbouring and allied city of Kitab. In 1866 the country was enveloped in such a network of intrigue, that it is difficult to discover exactly what Jura Bek's political aspirations were. He was certainly opposed to the Emir of Bokhara, who had deprived him of his principality, and in the year 1870, about the time of General Kaufmann's advance on Samarkand, there is but little doubt that both he and Baba Bek were in secret correspondence with the General, promising him their assistance against the Emir.

After the capture of Samarkand, General Kaufmann sent for Jura Bek and Baba Bek, but the message was falsely delivered, in such terms that Jura Bek imprisoned the messenger, and made his peace with the Emir, promising him his assistance against the Russians. Thus it came about, that when General Kaufmann marched from Samarkand to the relief of General Golovatcheff, Jura Bek and Baba Bek, with 20,000 men, made an attempt to recapture the city from the Russians, which they most undoubtedly would have accomplished, owing to their overwhelming number of troops, and the sore straits to which the gallant little band in the citadel were reduced, had it not been for a false report which reached them, that after General Kaufmann's victory at Zera-Balak, he was marching on Shahrisabs. This caused Jura and Baba Bek to withdraw the whole of their forces from the siege of Samarkand, and march to Shahrisabs to encounter Kaufmann. When they arrived there, they found no Russian troops at all, General Kaufmann having after his victory at Zera-Balak, returned straight to Samarkand, arriving there just in time to save the garrison, and raise the siege.

In 1870, Shahrisabs was taken by the Russians from Jura and Baba Bek, who both escaped to Khokand, the Khan of which place treacherously gave them up to the Russians, who had them removed to Tashkend, where they remained as prisoners of war for some time. Finally they were released and placed under surveillance, and eventually, seeing that nothing was to be gained by opposing the Russian advance in Central Asia, the success of which they looked upon as a *fait accompli,* they gave their unswerving allegiance to that power, and many are the instances which have been quoted to me of their scrupulous fidelity to the Government of the Czar, even under exceptionally tempting circumstances. Jura Bek is a tall, good-looking Sart, with aquiline nose and bearded face, and his hair is only just beginning to turn grey. He does not look more than ten years older than his son Alacul, when standing side by side, both wearing the same uniform.

Baba Bek is also a colonel in the Russian army, and I saw him perpetually at the Palace at Tashkend. He is enormously fat, and as round as a ball, with rolls of fat at the back of his head and neck. In his present condition, he does not strike one as a leader of men, whilst his former companion in arms still looks a soldier, every inch of him. Both are of course Mussalmans. They have great power and influence amongst the Sart population in the province of Syr Daria, especially at Tashkend, and it is always used for good, and in the interests of the great power which they now serve. This was amply illustrated in the *émeute* of last July, the garbled reports of which reached us at Yarkand. Of these I made mention in Chapter XXXIII.

The Governor-General was at his country residence at Chimgan, in the hills, two days' journey from Tashkend, at the time of the outbreak, which was the outcome of some ill-advised cholera regulations, but as the attack was made on an officer, who is still in office at Tashkend, whom I met several times in the Governor-General's Palace, and who was answerable for the said regulations, I shall not enter into any details. Suffice it to say there were faults on both sides.

Leaving Samarkand by the Trans-Caspian Railway, of which line it is the present eastern terminus, I arrived the next morning at Bokhara, but did not remain there long enough to see anything of the city. In the afternoon of the same day I crossed the Oxus at Charjui, over a long wooden bridge. The great river was full of large blocks of ice, rushing northwards on its turbid current, and it was easy to see it was unnavigable, for it was from this point I had hoped to be able to reach Khiva. Late that night we arrived at Merv, where a very agreeable Colonel of a Circassian regiment joined the train, with whom I struck up a sort of acquaintance. He told me he was going to Tiflis, to the marriage of his daughter, and that his regiment was quartered at Merv, which place he disliked very much. Crossing the Murghab river, which flows past Penj-deh, just south of Merv, we travelled through the sands of the Kara-kum, the southern extremity of the great Khivan desert. In fact, the whole way from the Oxus to Askabad, on the Persian Frontier, which we reached at 2 P.M. the next afternoon, a distance of about 400 miles—the whole route was a vast desert of sand-dunes, an awful looking country to cross on foot, and with very little water, and yet the

Russian troops had to march over that very same desert, all the way from the Caspian Sea, for about seven or eight hundred miles eastwards.

About midday on Monday we reached Askabad, where I had hoped to procure transport animals to convey me and my baggage across the mountains that form the Persian Frontier into Khorassan, the city of Meshed being my objective point. From there I had intended to work my way south to the Persian Gulf, and so back to Karachi. But the mountains were impassable, owing to the great amount of snow, and as no transport was forthcoming, I was forced, most reluctantly, to give it up, so I continued travelling west, and passing the now famous "Geok Tepe" found myself, on February 7th, by the shores of the Caspian Sea. On the afternoon of the same day, I embarked in a very small steamer for Baku.

The sky looked very threatening, and there was a greasy look about the sunset, that betokened bad weather. In the middle of the night it came on to blow very hard, accompanied by heavy showers of snow and sleet, and the motion of the vessel in those quick short seas was very unpleasant. It reminded me of a night spent on Lake Michigan, in a gale of wind in a small steamer some years ago, but Michigan was the worst, because it was fresh water, and the Caspian is very salt, so there is a certain amount of buoyancy in the latter.

We arrived at Baku the next morning, where again I was doomed to be disappointed, as the vessel that leaves for En-zili had sailed that morning, and there was not another for a fortnight. En-zili is the port on the Caspian for Teheran, to which city I had had all my letters addressed for some time, and from whence I had intended to ride to Bushire on the Persian Gulf *via* Ispahan, etc But the prospect of spending two weeks at Baku was not inviting, so I determined to proceed to Constantinople, as I was rather pressed for time, and having therefore telegraphed to the British Minister at Teheran about my letters, I left Baku, and proceeded to Tiflis, which I reached at 6 P.M. the next evening, and I looked with interest upon the great fashionable city, with its splendid hotels, and places of public entertainment, so different from the small Circassian town I had known it in 1859, when there were no hotels, no railroad, not even a post-road to the Black Sea.

Travelling all night I arrived the next day at Batoum, and the afternoon following I got a passage on board of a little French steamer, called the 'Mingrelia,' laden with hides and petroleum, in which I was the only passenger. On Sunday the 12th, we anchored off Trebizonde, and took in more cargo, and at Samsoon, on the 13th, we anchored alongside of another steamer, on which were Mr. and Mrs. Littledale on their way East. Hearing there was an English traveller from

China and Central Asia on board the 'Mingrelia,' they put two and two together, and came to the conclusion it must be me. So they came on board to see, and we had a long talk: I being in a position to tell them much about the state of the country over which they propose to travel, as I had just come over it. Ramzan also, who now that we are in a civilized country, is of no use to me, I handed over to them, and they were delighted to get hold of such a good man to be head of their caravan.

It was rather odd seeing him quietly remove his luggage, which consisted only of his bedding, from one steamer to another, and return to travel all through Central Asia again, and over the Chinese Frontier with the Littledales, with as little concern as if he were only going from London to Brighton for the day, instead of on an arduous journey of nine months into China and Tibet.

I gave the Littledales a few useful things, including my big Poshtin, lined with lambs-wool, and so we parted, I wishing them God-speed on their journey, they congratulating me that I had brought mine to a termination.

Two days after this I reached Constantinople, not sorry that my wanderings had come to an end.

APPENDIX.

TABLE OF
PARATIVE HEIGHTS OF PASSES
WITH THE
SUMMIT OF MONT BLANC.

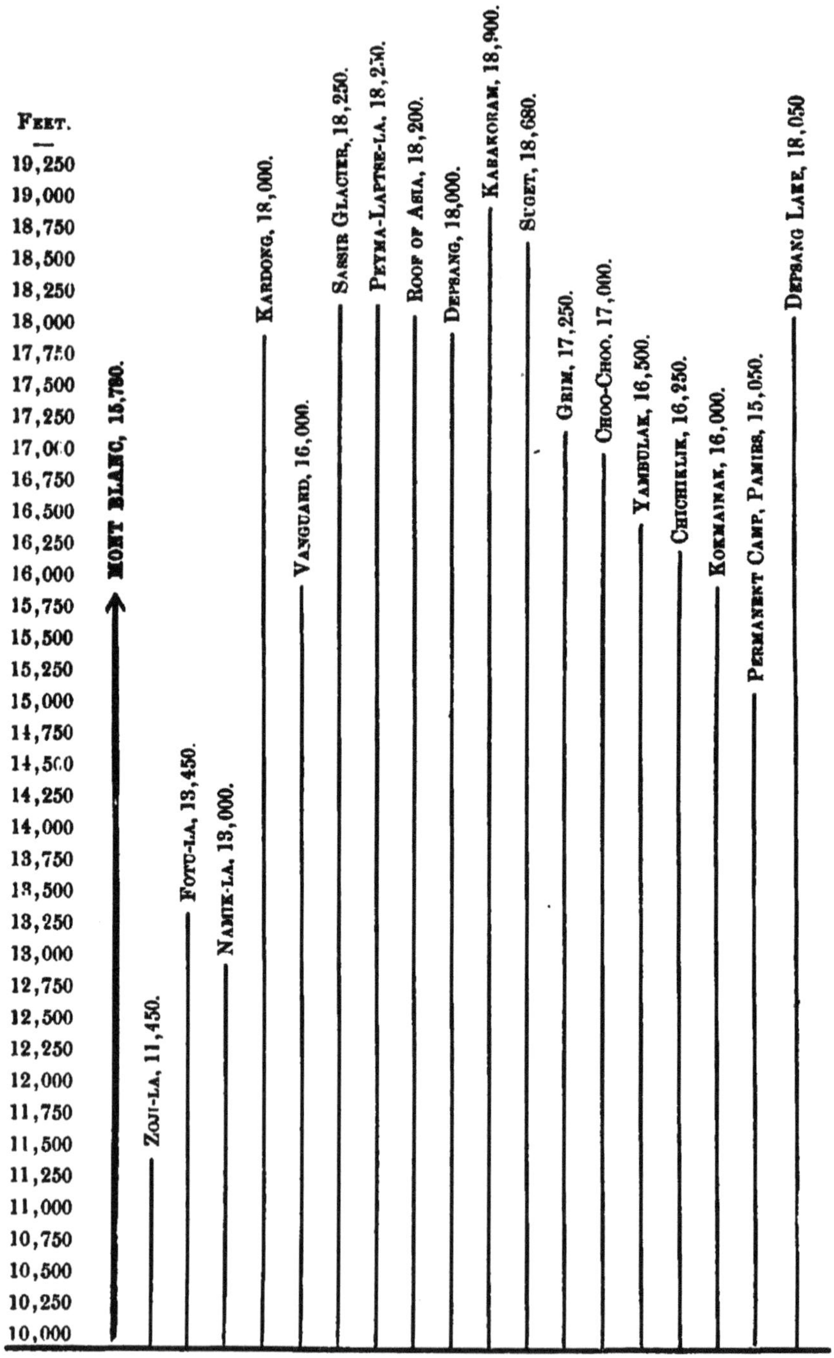
FEET.
19,250
19,000
18,750
18,500
18,250
18,000
17,750
17,500
17,250
17,000
16,750
16,500
16,250
16,000
15,750
15,500
15,250
15,000
14,750
14,500
14,250
14,000
13,750
13,500
13,250
13,000
12,750
12,500
12,250
12,000
11,750
11,500
11,250
11,000
10,750
10,500
10,250
10,000
MONT BLANC, 15,780.
ZOJI-LA, 11,450.
FOTU-LA, 13,450.
NAMIK-LA, 13,000.
KARDONG, 18,000.
VANGUARD, 16,000.
SASSIR GLACIER, 18,250.
PEYMA-LAPTSE-LA, 18,250.
ROOF OF ASIA, 18,200.
DEPSANG, 18,000.
KARAKORAM, 18,900.
SUGET, 18,680.
GRIM, 17,250.
CHOO-CHOO, 17,000.
YAMBULAK, 16,500.
CHICHIKLIK, 16,250.
KOKMAINAK, 16,000.
PERMANENT CAMP, PAMIRS, 15,050.
DEPSANG LAKE, 18,050

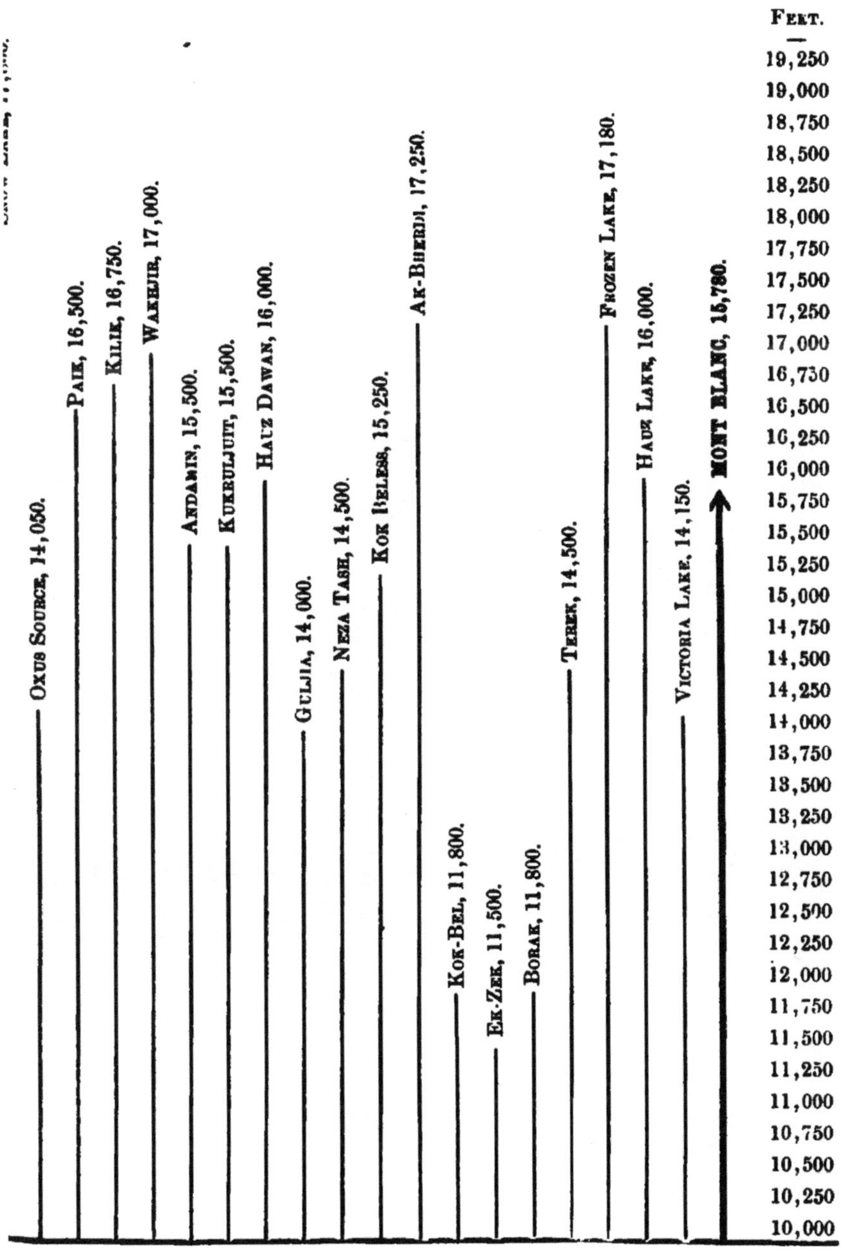

Oxus Source, 14,050.
Paik, 16,500.
Kilik, 16,750.
Wakhjir, 17,000.
Andamin, 15,500.
Kukbuljuit, 15,500.
Hauz Dawan, 16,000.
Guljia, 14,000.
Neza Tash, 14,500.
Kok Beless, 15,250.
Ak-Bherdi, 17,250.
Kok-Bel, 11,800.
Ek-Zek, 11,500.
Borak, 11,800.
Terek, 14,500.
Frozen Lake, 17,180.
Hauz Lake, 16,000.
Victoria Lake, 14,150.
MONT BLANC, 15,780.
Feet.
19,250
19,000
18,750
18,500
18,250
18,000
17,750
17,500
17,250
17,000
16,730
16,500
16,250
16,000
15,750
15,500
15,250
15,000
14,750
14,500
14,250
14,000
13,750
13,500
13,250
13,000
12,750
12,500
12,250
12,000
11,750
11,500
11,250
11,000
10,750
10,500
10,250
10,000

INDEX.

A.

B.

E.

F.

G.

H.

I.

J.

T.

LONDON: PRINTED BY WILLIAM CLOWES AND SONS, LIMITED, STAMFORD STREET AND CHARING CROSS.

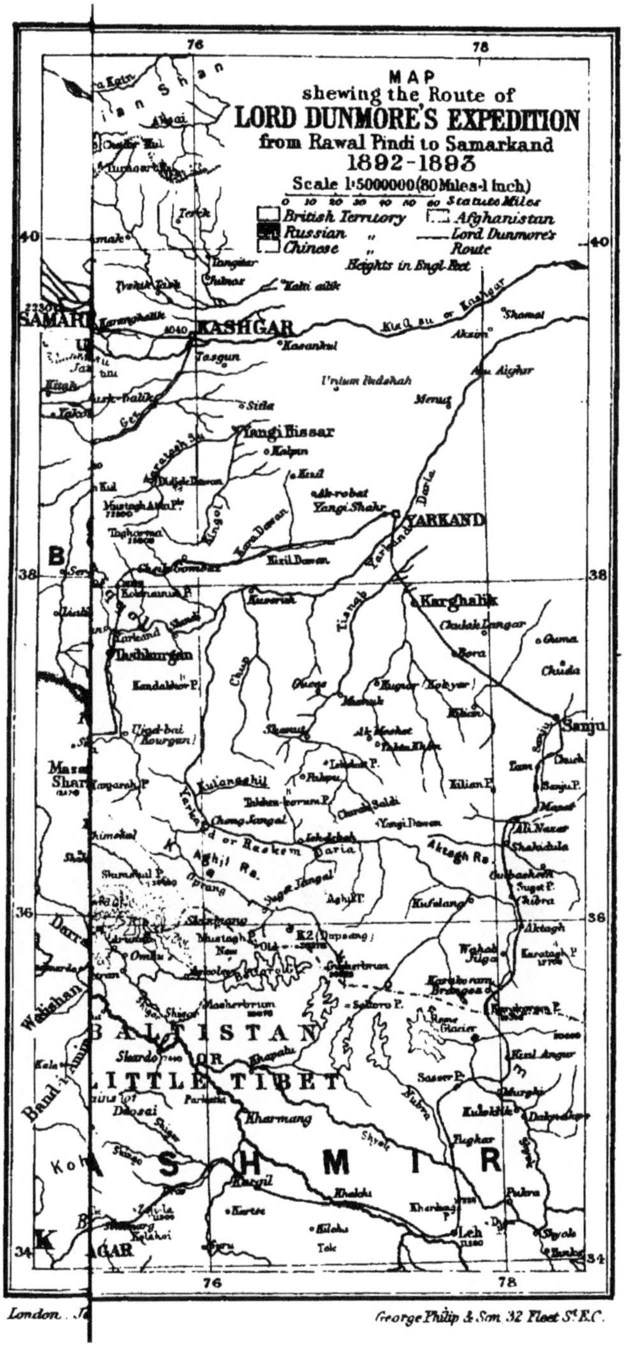

London . J

George Philip & Son 32 Fleet St. E.C.

www.ingramcontent.com/pod-product-compliance
Ingram Content Group UK Ltd.
Pitfield, Milton Keynes, MK11 3LW, UK
UKHW021441140125
4106UKWH00042B/574

9 781018 083780